For Bruce

You're still the one.

Contents

Acknowledgments

First I'd like to thank the team at Microsoft Press that turned my writing into a book. Without Jack Beaudry, the technical editor, I never would have gotten any sleep. His meticulous reviews saved me time and saved readers from much frustration. Kathleen Atkins, the project editor, kept everything running smoothly and improved my text considerably. Credit is also due to Danielle Bird, acquisitons editor; Rebecca McKay (Becka), manuscript editor; Cheryl Penner and Rebecca Wendling (Becky), copy editors; Gina Cassill, compositor; and Michael Kloepfer, electronic artist.

I also want to thank my colleagues at Microsoft who listened sympathetically to my complaints about deadlines and beta software. Editors Roger Haight and Meredith Waring made me a better writer. Mike Pope reminded me to put the reader ahead of being clever. Megan Shult and Ann Morris, my managers, were supportive even when writing consumed all my after-hours energy. Much of what I learned about .NET came from the material written by my team members Jina Chan, Seth Grossman, Steve Hoag, Steve Stein, and Matt Stoecker. And thank you to Diana Rain, my office mate.

I'd also like to thank Ruth McBride, my longtime manager, and my instructors at Seattle University. I appreciate their patience with my often experimental approaches to their assignments over the years.

I also have to mention the friends that still call to check on me, even though I haven't called them in months. Jennifer Wirt, Lisa Wiken, Molly Potteiger, and Julie Brinkley have been true friends.

This book would never have been written without the support of my husband, Bruce. He completely ran my life for the seven months I was writing this book. I worked and wrote; he did everything else. My friends are still laughing about how he RSVPs for me. Lastly, I thank my sons for just being there and for being proud of me.

Introduction

Microsoft Visual Basic developers have long clamored for complete object-oriented language support. Microsoft Visual Basic .NET supports all the features of an object-oriented language. In addition, the entire Microsoft .NET Framework, which includes the development support for Microsoft Windows applications, Web applications, Web services, graphics, and data access, is designed according to object-oriented principles. Developers who have a firm grasp of object-oriented principles will be the strongest .NET developers.

Also new to developers is C#, a C-based language that gives developers a language choice for developing with the .NET Framework. Some C, Java, and C++ development will move to C# to take advantage of .NET's features. Visual Basic programmers looking to learn a C language might also move to C#. Visual Basic .NET and C# both support object-oriented development with the .NET Framework. No matter what language you choose for development, being able to read code in either language will double your access to Microsoft Visual Studio documentation, .NET books, magazine articles, and other developer resources.

System Requirements

You'll need the following hardware and software to complete the exercises in this book:

- Microsoft Visual Studio .NET Professional edition. The Visual Studio .NET software isn't included with this book. You must purchase it separately and install it before you can complete the exercises in this book.

■ A computer capable of running Microsoft Visual Studio .NET. The following hardware configuration is recommended by the Microsoft Visual Studio .NET Web site, at *http://msdn.microsoft.com/vstudio/nextgen/*

Computer/Processor

PC with a Pentium II–class processor, 450 megahertz (MHz); Pentium III–class processor, 600 MHz recommended

Operating System

Microsoft Windows 2000, Server or Professional
Microsoft Windows XP Home or Professional
Microsoft Windows NT 4.0 Server

Memory

Windows 2000 Professional, 96 megabytes (MB) of RAM; 128 MB recommended
Windows 2000 Server, 192 MB of RAM; 256 MB recommended
Windows XP Professional, 128 MB of RAM; 160 Recommended

Hard Disk

500 MB on System Drive and 3.0 gigabyte (GB) on installation drive

Drive

CD-ROM drive

Display

VGA or higher–resolution monitor

Input Device

Microsoft Mouse or compatible pointing device

Finding Your Best Starting Point

This book is designed to teach you the fundamentals of object-oriented programming. You can use this book if you have a basic knowledge of Visual Basic 6, Visual Basic .NET, Visual C#, or another Windows programming language. The exercises in this book assume you can already perform the following tasks:

- Create a new Windows Application project, build it, and run it.
- Add Windows Forms controls to a Windows Form.
- Create a method to respond to the Click event of a Button control.
- Create a simple method (called a *Sub* or *Function* in Visual Basic .NET).
- Declare and use variables.

For an introduction to Visual Basic .NET, read *Microsoft Visual Basic .NET Step by Step* by Michael Halvorson (Microsoft Press, 2002). For an introduction to Visual C# , read *Microsoft Visual C# .NET Step by Step* by John Sharp and Jon Jagger (Microsoft Press, 2002).

Use the following table to find your best starting point in this book.

If you are	Follow these steps
New	
To object-oriented programming	Install the practice files as described in the following section, "Installing and Using the Practice Files."
	Work through the chapters sequentially for a complete introduction to object-oriented programming. Chapters 1 through 7, 9, and 11 concentrate on the mechanics of object-oriented programming, while the other chapters cover the concepts in more depth.
Migrating	
From Visual Basic 6	Install the practice files as described in "Installing and Using the Practice Files" on the next page.
	Work through the chapters sequentially for a complete introduction to object-oriented programming with Visual Basic .NET. Chapters 1 through 7, 9, and 11 concentrate on the mechanics of object-oriented programming, while the other chapters cover the concepts in more depth.

(continued)

continued

If you are	Follow these steps
Switching	
From another object-oriented programming language.	Install the practice files as described in "Installing and Using the Practice Files." Complete Chapter 1 to learn the basic syntax of properties and methods. Read the Quick Reference sections at the end of the chapters for information about specific class constructs.
Referencing	
The book after working through the exercises	Use the index or the Table of Contents to find information about particular subjects. Read the Quick Reference at the end of each chapter to find a brief review of the syntax and techniques presented in the chapter.

Installing and Using the Practice Files

The companion CD inside the back cover of this book contains the practice files that you'll use as you perform the exercises in the book. For example, when you're learning to create class events, you'll use a bitmap file named Train.bmp. By using the practice files, you won't waste time creating objects that aren't relevant to the exercise. Instead, you can concentrate on learning object-oriented programming with Visual Basic .NET and Visual C# .NET. The files and the step-by-step instructions in the lessons also let you learn by doing, which is an easy and effective way to acquire and remember new skills.

important

Before you break the seal on the *OOP with Microsoft Visual Basic .NET and Microsoft Visual C# Step by Step* companion CD package, be sure that this book matches your version of the software. This book is designed for use with Microsoft Visual Studio .NET Professional Edition for the Windows operating systems. To find out what software you're running, you can check the product package or you can start the software, and then click About Microsoft Development Environment in the Help menu at the top of the screen.

Install the practice files

Follow these steps to install the practice files on your computer's hard disk so that you can use them with the exercises in this book.

1   Remove the companion CD from the package inside the back cover of this book and insert the CD in your CD-ROM drive.

2   Double-click the My Computer icon on the Desktop.

> ## tip
> On some computers, the startup program might run automatically when you close the CD-ROM drive. In this case, skip steps 2 through 5 and follow the instructions on the screen.

3   Double-click the icon for your CD-ROM drive.

4   Double-click StartCD.exe

5   Click Install Sample Code.

The setup program window appears with the recommended options preselected for you. For best results in using the practice files with this book, accept these preselected settings.

6   When the files have been installed, remove the CD from your CD-ROM drive and replace it in the package inside the back cover of the book.

A folder called OOPVBCS has been created on your hard disk, and the practice files have been placed in that folder.

Using the Practice Files

Each lesson in this book explains when and how to use any practice files for that lesson. The practice files contain the complete source listings for all the applications created in this book, as well as any resources, such as bitmaps and databases, that you'll need to complete the exercises. For those of you who like to know all the details, here's a list of the Visual Basic and Visual C# projects on the practice disk:

Project	Description
Chapter 1	
ReadBooks	This simple program demonstrates the basics of creating, instantiating, and using a class.
Chapter 2	
ReadMoreBooks	This program expands on the ReadBooks program and adds constructors.
Chapter 3	
CodeAnalysis CodeAnalysis2	These two applications demonstrate different approaches to using class properties, and the interaction of class properties and the DataGrid control.
Chapter 4	
DeckOfCards	This application explores class methods by using dynamic creation of Windows Forms controls and drag-and-drop operations.
Chapter 5	
TheBank	This simple application demonstrates the basics of class inheritance.
ARoundButton	This small project shows how easy it is to derive from a Windows Forms control and redefine its drawing.
Chapter 6	
ABetterBank	This adaptation of Chapter 5's TheBank application uses an abstract class as a base class.
ABetterLibrary	This improvement on Chapter 1's ReadBooks application uses a strongly typed collection.
Variations	This application contains code snippets demonstrating variations on inheritance.
Chapter 7	
TrainGame	This application introduces delegates, events, and user-drawn controls in the context of a simple game.
ThrowSystemException	This small program throws a system exception and recovers by using exception handling.
PersonList	This application creates and throws a custom application exception.

Project	Description
Chapter 8	
GamesLibrary Memory	The GamesLibrary project creates a component library containing objects used to develop the simple Memory card game.
Chapter 9	
MoveIt	This application covers the basics of creating and implementing an interface.
Points	The Points project contains objects that implement the IComparable, IFormattable, and IEnumerable interfaces.
Chapter 10	
PatternMaker	Moving beyond the basics of inheritance, the PatternMaker program makes extensive use of inheritance and polymorphism.
Chapter 11	
BetterCard	This improvement on the Card class from Chapter 4 uses static methods to eliminate the project's dependency on file locations.
SortablePoint	The SortablePoint application from Chapter 10 is made more flexible through static properties.
Singleton	Static fields are used to implement the Singleton design pattern.
Chapter 12	
VectorAlgebra	The mathematical concept of vectors is used to demonstrate the definition and use of operator overloading in Visual C#.
Chapter 13	
Serialize	The Serialize application demonstrates the use of binary and XML serialization of data.
DataSetExercise	This very simple ADO.NET application reads data from an Access database.
Chapter 14	
PatternMaker	This example uses the PatternMaker exercise from Chapter 10 to demonstrate the way to make design changes after the initial development of an application.

Uninstall the practice files

If you are using the Windows XP Professional operating system, follow these steps to remove the practice files from your computer. If you are using a different version of Windows, refer to your Windows Help documentation for removing programs.

1   Click Start, and then click Control Panel.

2   In Control Panel, click Add Or Remove Programs.

3   In the Add Or Remove Programs window, click OOP Visual Basic And C# .NET Code in the Currently Installed Programs list.

4   Click Change/Remove. The Confirm File Deletion dialog appears.

5   Click Yes to delete the practice files.

6   Click Close to close the Add Or Remove Programs window.

7   Close Control Panel.

Conventions and Features in this Book

This book uses conventions designed to make the information more readable and easier to follow. The book also includes features that contribute to a deeper understanding of the material.

Conventions

- Each exercise is a series of tasks. Each task is presented as a series of numbered steps. If a task has only one step, the step is indicated by a round bullet.

- Notes labeled "tip" provide more information for completing a step successfully.

- Notes labeled "important" alert you to information you need to check before continuing.

- The book uses typographic styles to help organize the information presented. The following table describes the styles used.

Style	Used for	Example

Code	Code that you type in	` ' Visual Basic`
		`Public Class Book`
		`End Class`
		`// Visual C#`
		`public class Book {`
		`}`

Italics	Method argument or parameter	*aBook*
	Event Procedure	*showPage_Click*
	Field	*m_shelf*
	Fully Qualified Name	*SomeBook.Text*
	Keyword	*Public, public, If, if*
	Method	*GetPage*
	Property value	*listOfBooks*
Roman	Boolean values	True, true, False, false
	Class name	Book, Library, Train
	Control type	ListBox, TextBox
	Data type	String, string, Integer, int
	Event	Click
	Form	Form1
	Namespace	ReadBooks
	Parameter type	String, string, Integer, int
	Property	Name

Other Features

Shaded sidebars throughout the book provide more in-depth information about the exercise. The sidebars might contain debugging tips, design tips, or topics you might want to explore further.

Each chapter ends with a Quick Reference section. The Quick Reference provides a brief review of the syntax and techniques presented in the chapter.

Corrections, Comments, and Help

Every effort has been made to ensure the accuracy of this book and the contents of the practice files on the companion CD. Microsoft Press provides corrections and additional content for its books through the World Wide Web at

http://www.microsoft.com/mspress/support/

If you have problems, comments, or ideas regarding this book or the companion CD, please send them to Microsoft Press.

Send e-mail to

mspinput@microsoft.com

Or send postal mail to

Microsoft Press
Attn: Step by Step Series Editor
One Microsoft Way
Redmond, WA 98052-6399

Please note that support for the Visual Studio .NET software product itself is not offered through the preceding address. For help using Visual Studio .NET, visit *http://support.microsoft.com*.

Visit the Microsoft Press World Wide Web Site

You are also invited to visit the Microsoft Press World Wide Web site at

http://www.microsoft.com/mspress/

You'll find descriptions for the complete line of Microsoft Press books, information about ordering titles, notice of special features and events, additional content for Microsoft Press books, and much more.

You can also find out the latest in Visual Studio .NET software developments and news from Microsoft Corporation at

http://msdn.microsoft.com/vstudio/nextgen/

Check it out!

1

Writing Your First Object-Oriented Program

In this chapter, you'll learn how to

✔ *Decide which classes to implement in your program.*

✔ *Create a class with fields, properties, and methods.*

✔ *Use a class in an application.*

✔ *Use Microsoft Visual Studio .NET tools to create a class definition.*

ESTIMATED TIME
2 hr. 30 min.

Classes are the building blocks of object-oriented programs. Object-oriented program design is driven by the objects in the problem you need to solve. If your goal is to automate class registration, you might create classes for the instructor, student, and class schedule objects. Objects also have properties that describe them and their behavior. These are implemented as properties and methods of a class. Just as an instructor has a name, so does the Instructor class have a Name property. To assign a student to a class, you'd need to find an open section in the schedule. So your ClassSchedule class might implement a *FindOpenSection* method. The method would likely check the variable, called a *field*, in the class in which you've stored information about sections.

In this chapter, you'll learn how to identify the objects in your problem domain and their properties and behaviors (methods). Using this analysis, you'll design and implement the classes using property and method programming constructs. You'll then declare and initialize the variables of the classes you've coded. Finally, you'll implement the solution to your problem by calling the properties and methods of the class variables.

Reading Books: Your First Object-Oriented Program

Your task in this chapter is to implement a program that displays large text files in page-size pieces. Typically, your task begins with a specification, perhaps complete, perhaps not. The specification for Chapter 1 follows:

You have downloaded on your computer the text of several books. You want to be able to select a book and read one particular page at a time. You also want to be able to set the length of a page. You've already decided which user interface you want to use; it's shown here:

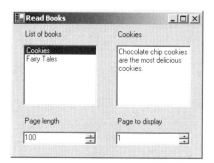

As you look at the user interface, you can see that you need to add some controls to a Windows form: a ListBox, a RichTextBox, two NumericUpDown controls, and some labels. How will you store the texts of the books? How will you fill the list? How will you retrieve the correct page of the book that you want to read? You can use object-oriented programming to answer these questions.

Designing the Classes

Before you can implement your classes, you must decide which classes you need. First you look for the objects in the problem. Having found the objects, you then look for properties, which are characteristics or qualities that belong to the object, and methods, which are behaviors of the object.

You can choose from many ways to design the classes in an application. The approach presented here begins with a textual analysis of the problem. The nouns are selected as candidates for classes, while verbs become candidates for the methods. In the course of the analysis, you'll eliminate many of the nouns as candidates, and you might discover classes that aren't among the nouns in the specification. After you determine the objects, properties, and methods that belong to your classes, you can then write the class specification that you'll use in the implementation.

Find the classes

1   Read the problem statement, and find all the nouns.

You have downloaded on your **computer** the **text** of several **books**. You want to be able to select a **book** and read one particular **page** at a **time**. You also want to be able to set the **length** of a **page**.

2   Eliminate candidates. Reasons to eliminate a candidate include

    ■   The class based on the noun would have only properties or only methods.

    ■   The class based on the noun wouldn't be relevant to the problem.

    ■   The class based on the noun wouldn't represent one object.

You can eliminate the irrelevant candidates: *computer* and *time*. *Length* (of a page) is merely an integer value and wouldn't generate enough behavior to qualify as a class. The same is true of *text* in this example—the only thing to be done with it is to display a piece of it, a *page*. By the same reasoning, *page* is also not a class. That leaves *book* and *books*. *Books* is just the plural of *book*, so you are left only with *book* as a potential class. But you aren't finished yet.

3   Search for missing candidates. Consider this specification, "The dealer deals four cards to each player." There's no mention of a deck of cards, although *deck* is a likely class in that problem.

Remember eliminating *books*? Another class does, in fact, represent the properties and behavior of a group of books. You can call this class Library. The library concept is different from the book concept. A book has a title and text and can be read. A library contains many books, which can be checked out and returned.

Left with the Book and Library classes, you can now search for properties and methods.

Find the methods and properties

1   Read the problem statement, and find all the verbs. You can leave out the helping verbs, such as *is*, *was*, and *have*. As in the case of the nouns, textual analysis of verbs is just the starting point for finding the methods.

You have **downloaded** on your computer the text of several books. You **want** to be able to **select** a book and **read** one particular page at a time. You also **want** to be able to **set** the length of a page.

2   Consider each verb. Is it a method, or does it indicate a method? Is it relevant to the problem?

Downloaded and *want* are clearly irrelevant to the problem. *Select* is an operation of the Library class. In a real library, this action would correspond to finding a book on the shelf and checking it out. So the Library has a *CheckOut* method. There's also a hidden property here because a book needs a title. *Read* is an operation of the Book class. This method allows you to read one particular page, so it can be named *GetPage*. The verb *set* indicates that a property needs to be changed, and that property is the length of a page, PageLength.

3   The same nouns that you eliminated as classes might in fact be properties of those classes.

Text, length (of a page), and *page* were eliminated as classes. A book does need text, so Text becomes a property of Book. You discovered that PageLength is a property in considering the verb *set*. *Page* represents one section of the text and represents the result of the *GetPage* operation, so it isn't a property.

4   Look for missing properties and methods.

If you're going to check books out of the library, you need a way to add books to the library and return the checked-out books. A *CheckIn* method will handle this.

Testing the Class Design

Reread the problem, and determine whether your classes, with their properties and methods, provide the functionality necessary to solve the problem.

You have downloaded on your computer the text of several books.

Do you have a way of storing and organizing several books? Yes, you can create one Book for each book and one Library to store them all.

You want to be able to select a book and read one particular page at a time.

Can you select one book and read one page? Yes, books can be selected by their titles, and the *GetPage* method retrieves one page.

You also want to be able to set the length of a page.

Can you set the length of a page? Yes, the Book class has a PageLength property.

The results are shown in the following table. The methods are shown as they might be declared in Visual Basic.

Class	Properties	Methods
Book	Integer PageLength	`GetPage (pageNumber As Integer) As String`
	String Text	
	String Title	
Library		`CheckIn (aBook As Book)`
		`CheckOut (title As String) As Book`

Creating the Book Class

The following exercise covers the basics of class implementation using the Book class as an example. To implement the Library class, you'll use some of the development tools provided by the Microsoft Visual Studio .NET integrated development environment (IDE).

Create the book class

1   In the IDE, click the File menu, point to New, and then click Project. The New Project dialog box opens.

2   Select Visual Basic Projects or Visual C# Projects in the Project Types tree, click Windows Application in the Templates list.

3   Enter *ReadBooks* in the Name box, and click OK.

4   Display the Solution Explorer by selecting Solution Explorer on the View menu. Click the ReadBooks project in the Solution Explorer.

5   On the Project menu, click Add Class. The Add New Item dialog box appears, as shown here:

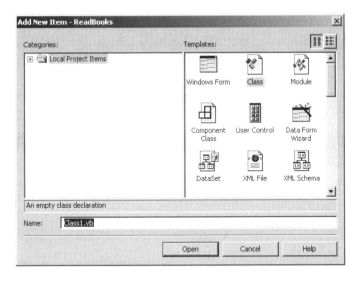

6   Enter either Book.vb or Book.cs in the Name box, depending on the language you are using. Note that the class name begins with a capital letter and is singular.

7   Click Open. The IDE adds a file to your project. The file includes the basic definition of a class, as shown in the following two screen shots.

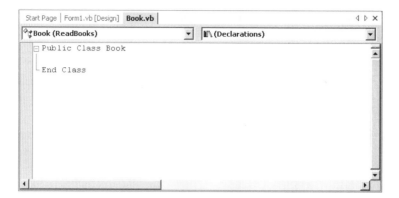

The Visual Basic class contains the minimum for a class declaration. Here's the syntax for declaring a class in Visual Basic:

```
Class ClassName
End Class
```

In this case, the class is named Book. The IDE adds the Public modifier that's shown to indicate that the class can be used throughout the project.

The Visual C# class contains the class declaration as well as a constructor. Here's the syntax for declaring a class in C#:

```
class ClassName {
}
```

A *constructor* contains code to initialize the fields of a class and perform other class initialization fun`ctions. In C#, it has the same name as the class. A constructor isn't required. I'll talk more about constructors in Chapter 2, "Creating Class Instances with Constructors."

Add the *Text* and *PageLength* fields

A *field* is a variable declared in a class block. Fields can be any .NET data type, such as Integer or Boolean; .NET class, such as TextBox or ListBox; or any class that you have created.

1 Locate the beginning of the class definition.

In Visual Basic, the class definition begins immediately after the line that shows the class name. In Visual C#, the class definition begins after the opening curly brace of the class.

2 Add the following code inside the class to create *Text* and *PageLength* fields.

```
' Visual Basic
Public Text As String = ""
Public PageLength As Integer = 10

// Visual C#
public string Text = "";
public int PageLength = 10;
```

tip

By convention, the initial letters of names of public members (fields, properties, methods, and events) of a class are capitalized (*Textfield*) or are intercapitalized (*PageLength* field).

According to the code, you have specified initial values for the fields: the empty string for *Text* and 10 for *PageLength*. A basic tenet of object-oriented programming is that an object should maintain a consistent state. That means that the state of the object (the values of its fields) should represent a usable state. If you didn't initialize the fields, values would default to " " for the *Text* field and 0 for the *PageLength* field. If those were acceptable values for a book, you could leave them uninitialized. But because compilers and their default values change, you can prevent maintenance problems by initializing the fields.

Your client code (the code that uses a Book object) is able to read and write to any field declared with the public keyword (*Public* in Visual Basic and *public* in Visual C#). Providing direct access to the class data is a violation of the object-oriented principle of *information hiding,* which stipulates that the client has no knowledge of the underlying data structure of an object. In the next section, you'll learn how to allow the client code to get and set the Title of the Book without giving away details about the implementation.

Add the Title property

A property is a programming construct that allows your code to get and set a value. Typically, the code in the property constructor will get and set the value of a private field in the class. In client code, a public field and a property are used in the same way—for example, *SomeBook.Text* and *SomeBook.Title.*

1   Add the following code to the Book class after the *Text* and *PageLength* declarations.

```
Private m_title As String      ' Visual Basic

private string m_title;        // Visual C#
```

This code creates a private field in the Book class. Client code doesn't have access to this property.

tip
Private fields of a class are declared using the *m_* prefix to identify them as member data. Private field names aren't capitalized.

2   Add the following code to the Book class, after the *m_title* declaration.

```
' Visual Basic
Public Property Title() As String
    Get
        Return m_title
    End Get
    Set(ByVal value As String)
        m_title = value
    End Set
End Property

// Visual C#
public string Title {
    get {
        return m_title;
    }
```

```
    set {
        m_title = value;
    }
}
```

These syntax blocks define class *properties*. The Title property appears in the
IntelliSense drop-down list just like any other property, such as the familiar
TextBox.Text or *Form.Backcolor*. The property block allows you to control access
to the property. You can add validation code to the Set block to ensure that only
reasonable values are assigned to the underlying *m_title* field.

note

Please notice an important difference between fields and properties. A place is
reserved in memory for fields. They contain the actual data of the class. Properties provide access to the data but are not data themselves.

In this book, I use the word *set* to mean changing a property. I use the word *get*
to mean retrieving the value of a property. The Get and Set blocks of a property
can be called *getters* and *setters*, or *accessors*.

The property block is more flexible than you've seen here. Properties can be
public or private, read/write, read-only, or write-only. In Visual Basic, the property
statements can even take a parameter. By the way, I cover properties in detail in
Chapter 2, but I need to talk about them at least a little bit in this chapter.

A Little Bit About Properties

We can use the word *properties*, in a general object-oriented sense, to mean
the descriptive information about an object. We can also use *properties* to
mean the particular syntactic construct provided by Visual Basic and C#.
The particular meaning of the word can be determined by context. Use
properties to validate class data and hide class implementation. You have
to make a strong case for using public fields in a class. The addition of a
property to a class to control access to the underlying data requires mini-
mal effort. The benefit of this practice is that you can easily add validation
or change the implementation if you need to without affecting clients already
using your objects.

Add the *GetPage* method

● Add the *GetPage* method to the class definition after the field declarations.

```vbnet
' Visual Basic
Public Function GetPage(ByVal pageNumber As Integer) As String
    Dim start As Integer = (pageNumber - 1) * PageLength
    If (start < Text.Length) And (start >= 0) Then
        If (start + PageLength) < Text.Length Then
            Return Text.Substring(start, PageLength)
        Else
            Return Text.Substring(start, Text.Length - start)
        End If
    Else
        Return ""
    End If
End Function
```

```csharp
// Visual C#
public string GetPage(int pageNumber) {
    int start = (pageNumber - 1) * PageLength;
    if ((start < Text.Length) && (start >= 0)) {
        if ((start + PageLength) < Text.Length) {
            return Text.Substring(start, PageLength);
        }
        else {
            return Text.Substring(start, Text.Length - start);
        }
    }
    else {
        return "";
    }
}
```

In Chapter 3, "Fields and Properties," you'll see how we can replace the *GetPage* method with a construct known as an indexer in Visual C# or with a default *Item* method in Visual Basic.

The complete class definitions for our project are shown here:

```vbnet
' Visual Basic
Public Class Book

    Public Text As String = ""
    Public PageLength As Integer = 10
    Private m_title As String

    Public Property Title() As String
        Get
            Return m_title
        End Get
```

```vbnet
            Set(ByVal Value As String)
                m_title = Value
            End Set
        End Property

        Public Function GetPage(ByVal pageNumber As Integer) As String
            Dim start As Integer = (pageNumber - 1) * PageLength
            If (start < Text.Length) And (start >= 0) Then
                If (start + PageLength) < Text.Length Then
                    Return Text.Substring(start, PageLength)
                Else
                    Return Text.Substring(start, Text.Length - start)
                End If
            Else
                Return ""
            End If
        End Function
    End Class
```

```csharp
// Visual C#
using System;

namespace ReadBooks
{
    /// <summary>
    /// Summary description for Book.
    /// </summary>
    public class Book {
        public string Text = "";
        public int PageLength = 10;
        private string m_title;


        public Book() {
            //
            // TODO: Add constructor logic here
            //
        }


        public string Title
        {
            get {
                return m_title;
            }
            set {
                m_title = value;
            }
        }
```

(continued)

```
public string GetPage(int pageNumber) {
    int start = (pageNumber - 1) * PageLength;
    if ((start < Text.Length) && (start >= 0)) {
        if ((start + PageLength) < Text.Length) {
            return Text.Substring(start, PageLength);
        }
        else {
            return Text.Substring(start,
                    Text.Length - start);
        }
    }
    else {
        return "";
    }
}
}
```

Fields, properties, methods, and constructors can appear in any order in a class definition. Good organization benefits future readers of your code. Here's a common organization and, in fact, the one I used in this book:

- Field declarations
- Constructors
- Properties
- Methods

Using the Book Class in an Application

You've just finished implementing the Book class. The class definition is just a template for an object. To put data in the fields and properties, you have to create an instance of the class in memory; this action is known as *instantiation*. When you create an instance, a section of memory is set aside to hold the fields of the object. If you create another instance of the class, another section of memory is set aside for its fields.

You aren't going to implement the full solution yet. First you need to write some code to test your class. You'll create two instances of the Book class in the ReadBooks project, and you'll display the fourth page of each book. (These will be *very* short books.) You'll create a cookbook and a book of fairy tales, so you'll need to create two separate instances of the Book class. Instead of creating a fancy interface, you'll write just enough code to see whether your class is working as you expected.

Test Drivers

A short program to test a class is called a *driver*. It's a good idea to exercise your class a bit with a driver before adding the class to a larger program. Use the driver to test your class without the interference of other code in the program.

Create an instance of Book

1 In the Solution Explorer, double-click Form1 to open it in the Windows form designer. If Form1 is opened in the code editor, select View, Designer.

2 Drag a button from the Toolbox onto Form1. If the Toolbox isn't visible, select View, Toolbox.

3 Right-click the button, and click Properties on the shortcut menu. In the Properties window, set the Name property of the button to *showPage* and set the Text property to *Show Page*.

The button on the Windows form is created from the Button class. Name and Text are properties of the Button class. So we can talk about getting and setting these properties. Form1 is a class as well, and the button you just created is a field of the Form1 class.

4 Double-click the button to create the Click event method.

5 Add the following code in boldface to the Click event to create a book of fairy tales.

```
' Visual Basic
Private Sub showPage_Click(ByVal sender As System.Object, _
ByVal e As System.EventArgs) Handles showPage.Click
    Dim fairyTales As Book
    fairyTales = New Book()
End Sub
```

```
// Visual C#
private void showPage_Click(object sender, System.EventArgs e) {
    Book fairyTales;
    fairyTales = new Book();
}
```

6 Add the following code to set the Text, PageLength, and Title properties immediately after the code you entered in step 5:

```
' Visual Basic
fairyTales.Text = "Once upon a time there was a bear."
```

(continued)

```
fairyTales.PageLength = 8
fairyTales.Title = "Fairy Tales"

// Visual C#
fairyTales.Text = "Once upon a time there was a bear.";
fairyTales.PageLength = 8;
fairyTales.Title = "Fairy Tales";
```

When the instance of Book is created, its fields contain the values specified in the class definition. The *Text* field is an empty string, the page length is 10, and the title is blank. Notice that it makes no difference in the client code whether you use a field or a property.

7 Add the following code after the *fairyTales* code to create another instance of the Book class. (This instance will be a recipe book.)

```
' Visual Basic
Dim cookies As Book = New Book()
cookies.Text = "Chocolate chip cookies are the most delicious cookies."
cookies.PageLength = 8
cookies.Title = "Cookie Recipes"

// Visual C#
Book cookies = new Book();
cookies.Text = "Chocolate chip cookies are the most delicious cookies.";
cookies.PageLength = 8;
cookies.Title = "Cookie Recipes";
```

In this case, you used a different syntax for declaring and initializing a variable of the Book class. Visual Basic and Visual C# allow declaration and initialization in the same statement. Declaring and initializing in the same statement has the following advantages:

- Programmers are less likely to forget to initialize the variable.
- When a class defines a constructor with parameters, the fields can be initialized at the same time. (You'll create constructors with parameters in Chapter 3.)

Use an instance of the Book class

1 Add the following code after the cookies code to display some of the text of the two books. In later chapters, you'll learn other ways to return the text of a particular page in the book.

```
' Visual Basic
Dim page As Integer = 3
Dim report As String
report = "Page " & page.ToString() & ControlChars.CrLf _
    & fairyTales.Title & ": " & fairyTales.GetPage(page) _
    & ControlChars.CrLf _
```

```
        & "Cookies: " & cookies.GetPage(page)
MessageBox.Show(report)
report = "Titles: " + fairyTales.Title & " and " & cookies.Title
MessageBox.Show(report)

// Visual C#
int page = 3;
string report;
report = "Page " + page.ToString() + "\n"
    + fairyTales.Title + ": " + fairyTales.GetPage(page) + "\n"
    + cookies.Title + ": " + cookies.GetPage(page);
MessageBox.Show(report);
report = "Titles: " + fairyTales.Title + " and " + cookies.Title;
MessageBox.Show(report);
```

This bit of code demonstrates that there are two separate instances of the Book class. We can refer to these instances using the variables *fairyTales* and *cookies*. The object-oriented concept that permits each instance to be referred to separately is known as *identity*. You'll see in later chapters that the identity principle doesn't mean that you have to create a variable for each instance. Creating so many variables is unwieldy if you need hundreds of instances of a class. Identity does mean that you *can* refer to each instance separately when you need to.

Notice that when you created an instance of Book, the fields of *fairyTales* were changed and the *GetPage* method was called. Later on we retrieved the value of the Title property. The value of Title was unchanged after the *GetPage* method was called. The fact that the value was unchanged demonstrates the concept of object *state*, the idea that the fields retain their values between method calls. Compare the way the *GetPage* method works with a method that has variable declarations. After the *GetPage* method ends, the variables go out of scope and their values are lost to the application.

2   Press F5 to run the code. Click the Show Page button. The results are shown here:

Click OK, and the book titles are displayed in a message box as shown here:

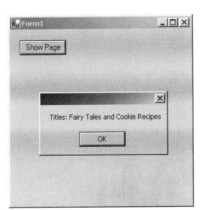

Click OK, and then close the application.

You've now created a class, Book, and two instances of it. Your code sent a message to the Book class through the *GetPage* method to ask for the third page of the text. In the next sections, you'll implement another class, Library. This time, however, you'll let some of the IDE tools do some of the syntactic work for you.

Using the Class View

The IDE provides a Class View that displays a tree view of the class structure of the project, namespaces, and classes. The Class View can share the same window as the Solution Explorer. On the View menu, click Class View to open the Class View. The expanded Class View is shown below for Visual Basic and Visual C#, respectively.

The highest-level node represents the project, ReadBooks. The next level of nodes represents the namespaces in the project. A project can contain several namespaces; in this case, there's only one. The project namespace contains two classes: the class that we created, Book, and the class for the Windows form, Form1. The Book class contains two public fields, *PageLength* and *Text*, represented by blue blocks, and one private field, *m_title*, represented by a blue block with a lock. The class contains one property, Title, represented by a graphical hand holding a letter. The class contains a method, *GetPage*, with one integer parameter that returns a string. The method is represented by a purple block.

In the case of Visual C#, the tree indicates the base classes and interfaces (which I'll cover in Chapters 5 and 9). If we were to expand the Bases And Interfaces node, we'd find that Book has Object as its base class. All classes in Visual Basic and Visual C# implicitly have Object as a base class. Base classes are covered in Chapter 5, "Using Inheritance to Create Specialized Classes."

Creating the Library Class

By means of the Class View, C# provides additional tools for creating class definitions. We'll use these tools to create the Library class. This class will have two methods: *CheckIn,* which adds an instance of Book to the Library class, and *CheckOut,* which removes a particular book from the Library class and returns a reference to that book.

The following wizards are available only in Visual C#. The code for Visual Basic is shown at the end of the section so that it can be added to the Visual Basic project.

Create the Library class

1   In the Class View, right-click the Visual C# project ReadBooks, point to Add, and then click Add Class on the shortcut menu.

2   The C# Class Wizard appears as shown here:

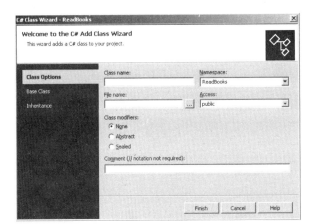

3   Enter *Library* in the Class Name box, select ReadBooks in the Namespace list and *public* in the Access list, click the None Class Modifiers option, and then click Finish.

4   The fields and tabs of the wizard are described in the following table.

Field or tab	Description
Class Name	The name of the new class. In this case, Library.
Namespace	The namespace controls the packaging of the types in the assembly and the qualified names used to refer to the class.
File Name	By default, this is the name of the class.
Access	This controls the ability to create references in other parts of the application and in other applications.
Class Modifiers	The abstract and sealed classes control use of the class in inheritance relationships. These will be discussed in Chapter 6, "Designing Base Classes and Abstract Classes."
Comment	Use this field to add a comment to the class.
Base Class tab	Allows you to choose a base class for your class. Classes from your project, from the .NET Framework, and other assemblies are available in drop-down lists.
Inheritance tab	Allows you to pick the interfaces you want to implement in your class.

Add a field to the Library class

To store the collection of books, you'll add an instance of the SortedList class to your project. The SortedList class is a data structure class provided by the .NET

Framework. It can store data in the same way that you might use an array. The SortedList class has two additional features: you can look up a particular piece of data based on a string key, and you can add or remove data as you like.

1   Add the following statement to the top of the Library.cs file.

```
using System.Collections;
```

Adding this statement allows you to use the SortedCollection class without having to use the fully qualified name, *System.Collections.SortedList.*

2   In the Class View, right-click the Library class and point to Add.

The IDE provides wizards for adding fields, properties, methods, and indexers, as shown here:

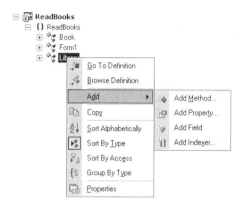

3   Click Add Field.

4   The C# Add Field Wizard appears, as you see here:

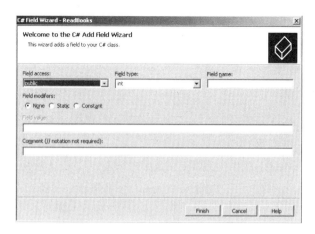

5   Click private in the Field Access list, enter *SortedList* in the Field Type box, and enter *m_shelf* in the Field Name box. Leave None for the Field Modifiers option. I'll talk about the Static modifier in Chapter 11, "Creating Static Members," and I'll cover the Const modifier in Chapter 7, "Responding to Changes with Events and Exceptions."

6   Click Finish.

7   Modify the declaration of *m_shelf* in the Library class to instantiate it. SortedList is a class, so it must be instantiated just as you instantiated the Book class.

```
private SortedList m_shelf = new SortedList();
```

Add the methods to the Library class

At the beginning of this chapter, you designed the Library class with a *CheckIn* method. In the last section, "Add a field to the Library class," you created a SortedList class for the instances of Book. The Library's *CheckIn* method calls the SortedList's *Add* method to store the instances of Book.

Add the *CheckIn* method to the Library class

1   In the Class View, right-click the Library class, point to Add, and click Add Method. The C# Add Method Wizard appears as shown here:

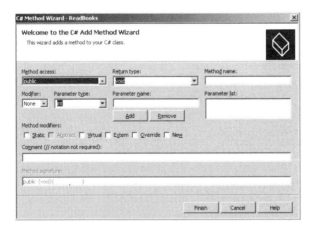

2   Enter *CheckIn* in the Method Name box.

You want the method to be public, and you don't want to return any value from the method. The method will have one parameter, *newBook*.

3   Enter *Book* in the Parameter Type box, enter *newBook* in the Parameter Name box, and click Add to add *newBook* to the Parameter List.

You can see the Method signature being created as you specify the information in the wizard's fields.

4 Click Finish to add the method to the Library class.

5 Modify the resulting method block to add the book to *m_shelf*, using the book's title as the key value. We'll use the same value to retrieve the book from the shelf in the *CheckOut* method.

```
public void CheckIn(Book newBook) {
    m_shelf.Add(newBook.Title, newBook);
}
```

Add the *CheckOut* method to the Library class

1 Run the Add Method Wizard by right-clicking Library in the Class View, pointing to Add, and clicking Add Method.

2 Enter *Book* in the Return Type box; enter *CheckOut* in the Method Name box, create one string type parameter named *title*, and click Finish.

3 Modify the code as shown in the following snippet so that the book is removed from SortedList and returned from the method.

```
public Book CheckOut(string title) {
    Book theBook;
    theBook = (Book)m_shelf[title];
    m_shelf.Remove(title);
    return theBook;
}
```

The *(Book)* notation in the second statement of the *CheckOut* method is known as a *cast*. The .NET Framework collection classes are extremely powerful because they'll hold any instance of any class that has the Object class as its base class. Because all classes you'll use in Visual Basic or Visual C# have Object as a base class, you can add an instance of any class you create to SortedList. The flipside of this is that anything you take out of SortedList is considered to be an Object. The cast *(Book)* lets the compiler know that you're taking out a Book instance so that you can use the Book properties and methods.

4 You've completed the code for the Library class. The complete listing for the class, in both Visual Basic and Visual C#, is shown here:

```
// Visual C#
using System;
using System.Collections;

namespace ReadBooks {
    /// <summary>
    ///
    /// </summary>
```

(continued)

```csharp
public class Library {
    private SortedList m_shelf = new SortedList();
    public Library() {
    }

    public void CheckIn(Book newBook) {
        m_shelf.Add(newBook.Title, newBook);
    }

    public Book CheckOut(string title) {
        Book theBook;
        theBook = (Book)m_shelf[title];
        m_shelf.Remove(title);
        return theBook;
    }
}
}
```

```vbnet
' Visual Basic
Imports System.Collections
Public Class Library
    Private m_shelf as New SortedList()

    Public Sub CheckIn(ByVal newBook As Book)
        m_shelf.Add(newBook.Title, newBook)
    End Sub

    Public Function CheckOut(ByVal title As String) As Book
        Dim theBook as Book
        theBook = CType(m_shelf(title), Book)
        m_shelf.Remove(title)
        Return theBook
    End Function
End Class
```

Creating the ReadBooks Program

Now it's time to create, code, and test the complete application shown in the problem statement.

Create the user interface

1   Delete the Show Page button from Form1.

2   Drag a ListBox control onto Form1. Set the Name property to *listOfBooks*.

3   Drag a NumericUpDown control onto Form1. Set the Name property to *pageLength* and the Minimum property to 1.

4   Drag another NumericUpDown control onto Form1. Set the Name property to *pageToDisplay* and the Minimum property to 1.

5   Drag a RichTextBox control onto Form1. Set the Name property to *page*, the Multiline property to True, and the Text property to blank.

6   Drag a Label control onto Form1 so that it's above the RichTextBox control. Set the Name property to *titleLabel* and the Text property to blank.

7   Add three more Label controls onto Form1. Use them to label the ListBox control and the two NumericUpDown controls. Reposition and resize the controls as shown in the complete user interface here:

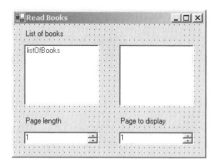

Add code to the application

1   In the Solution Explorer, right-click Form1 and click View Code on the shortcut menu.

     Form1 is a class, just as Book and Library are classes. All of the controls added to the form are fields of the form. If you expand the section labeled Windows Form Designer Generated Code, you can find the control declarations.

2   Add a *Library* field to the Form1 class. Add this declaration before the generated code section.

```
Private m_library As Library      ' Visual Basic

private Library m_library;        // Visual C#
```

3   If you're using Visual Basic, in the code editor, select Form1 (Base Class Events) from the Class Name list box, and then select *Load* from the Method Name list box. If you're using Visual C#, in the form designer, double-click on the form. Add the following code to the Load event method:

```
' Visual Basic
Private Sub Form1_Load(ByVal sender As Object, _
ByVal e As System.EventArgs) Handles MyBase.Load
```

(continued)

```
    m_library = New Library()
    Dim cookies As New Book()
    cookies.Text =
    _"Chocolate chip cookies are the most delicious cookies."
    cookies.PageLength = 8
    cookies.Title = "Cookies"

    Dim fairyTales As New Book()
    fairyTales.Text = "Once upon a time there was a bear."
    fairyTales.PageLength = 8
    fairyTales.Title = "Fairy Tales"

    m_library.CheckIn(cookies)
    m_library.CheckIn(fairyTales)

    listOfBooks.Items.Add(cookies.Title)
    listOfBooks.Items.Add(fairyTales.Title)
End Sub

// Visual C#
private void Form1_Load(object sender, System.EventArgs e) {
    m_library = new Library();
    Book cookies = new Book();
    cookies.Text =
        "Chocolate chip cookies are the most delicious cookies.";
    cookies.PageLength = 8;
    cookies.Title = "Cookies";

    Book fairyTales = new Book();
    fairyTales.Text = "Once upon a time there was a bear.";
    fairyTales.PageLength = 8;
    fairyTales.Title = "Fairy Tales";

    m_library.CheckIn(cookies);
    m_library.CheckIn(fairyTales);

    listOfBooks.Items.Add(cookies.Title);
    listOfBooks.Items.Add(fairyTales.Title);
}
```

The Load event of Form1 is inherited from the *System.Windows.Forms.Form* Load event. New classes are created from existing classes using inheritance. I'll talk about inheritance in Chapter 5.

4   If you're using Visual Basic, in the code editor, select *listOfBooks* from the Class Name list box of the code editor. Select *SelectedIndexChanged* from the Method Name list box. If you're using Visual C#, in the form designer, double-click the *listOfBooks* ListBox control. The *SelectedIndexChanged* method is created in the code editor.

5   Add the following code to the list box's *SelectedIndexChanged* event method:

```
' Visual Basic
Private Sub listOfBooks_SelectedIndexChanged(ByVal sender _
As System.Object, ByVal e As System.EventArgs) _
Handles listOfBooks.SelectedIndexChanged
    Dim title As String = listOfBooks.SelectedItem.ToString()
    Dim theBook As Book = m_library.CheckOut(title)
    theBook.PageLength = pageLength.Value
    titleLabel.Text = theBook.Title
    page.Text = theBook.GetPage(pageToDisplay.Value)
    m_library.CheckIn(theBook)
End Sub
```

```
// Visual C#
private void listOfBooks_SelectedIndexChanged(
object sender, System.EventArgs e) {
    string title = listOfBooks.SelectedItem.ToString();
    Book theBook = m_library.CheckOut(title);
    theBook.PageLength = (int)pageLength.Value;
    titleLabel.Text = theBook.Title;
    page.Text = theBook.GetPage((int)pageToDisplay.Value);
    m_library.CheckIn(theBook);
}
```

6   This code removes the book from the library (because it's not in the library anymore) and displays the first page of the (very short) book in the rich text box. For this example, we simply check the book back into the library so we can continue testing.

7   Run the program and select one of the books.

8   One page of the book is displayed in the text box, as shown here:

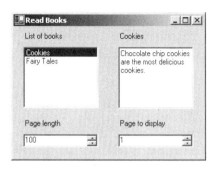

Quick Reference

To	Do this

Add a class to a project	On the Project menu, click Add Class.
	Or
	In Visual C#, right-click the project name in the Class View, point to Add, then click Add Class on the shortcut menu.
	The Visual Basic syntax is
	<pre>Class SomeClassName
	End Class</pre>The Visual C# syntax is
	<pre>class SomeClassName {
	}</pre>

Add a field to a class	Declare a variable in the class block. Or In Visual C#, right-click the class name in the Class View, point to Add, and then click Add Field on the shortcut menu.
Add a method to a class	Type the method into the class block. Or In Visual C#, right-click the class name in the Class View, point to Add, and then click Add Method on the shortcut menu.

Add a property	Type the property block in the class block.
	Or
	In Visual C#, right-click the class name in the Class View, then click Add, and then click Add Field on the shortcut menu.
	The Visual Basic syntax for an Integer property is
	<pre>Public Property Title() As String
	    Get
	        ' Return a field value here
	    End Get
	    Set(ByVal Value As String)
	        ' Set a field value here
	    End Set
	End Property</pre>

To	Do this
	The Visual C# syntax for an int property is
| | ```
public string Title {
    get {
        // return a field value here
    }
    set {
        // set a field value here
    }
}
``` |
| Create an instance of a class | Initialize the variable using the *new* keyword. In Visual Basic |
| | ```
Dim aBook as New Book()
``` |
| | In Visual C# |
| | ```
Book aBook = new Book();
``` |
| Set a class property | Instantiate the class, and then set the property. In Visual Basic |
| | ```
Dim aBook As New Book()
  aBook.Title = "Recipes"
``` |
| | In Visual C# |
| | ```
Book aBook = new Book();
  aBook.Title = "Recipes";
``` |
| Call a method of a class | Instantiate the class, and then call the method. In Visual Basic |
| | ```
Dim aBook As New Book()
  Dim onePage As String
  onePage = aBook.GetPage(4)
``` |
| | In Visual C# |
| | ```
Book aBook = new Book();
  string onePage = aBook.GetPage(4)
``` |
```

2

Creating Class Instances with Constructors

In this chapter, you'll learn how to

✔ *Create a class constructor.*

✔ *Create multiple constructors for one class.*

✔ *Initialize a class instance using a constructor.*

✔ *Implement the* ToString *method for a class.*

✔ *Instantiate an array of class instances.*

✔ *Use an array of class instances as the data source of a ListBox control.*

**ESTIMATED TIME
1.5 hrs.**

In the previous chapter, you created a Book class that included Text and Title properties. Creating a new instance of the class required three lines of code, one to declare and instantiate the class, one to set the Text property, and one to set the Title property. In this chapter, you'll create a class constructor that allows you to execute all three steps at once: declaration, instantiation, and initialization of the fields.

Constructors

A *constructor* is block of code that executes when you use the *new* keyword (*New* or *new*) to create an instance of a class. Constructors have the following powers:

▪ A constructor can take parameters that allow you to initialize the fields when the object is created.

■ A constructor can determine the validity of the parameters passed to it when the class is created.

■ A class can have multiple constructors, each taking a different set of parameters.

■ A constructor can call another constructor to do some of its work.

The syntax for defining constructors varies slightly between Visual Basic and Visual C#. In Visual Basic, a constructor without parameters is declared this way:

```
Public Sub New()
End Sub
```

In Visual C#, the same constructor is declared using the class name:

```
public Book() {
}
```

In both cases shown, the constructor is declared with the *public* keyword (*Public* or *public*). You must have a public constructor to use the *new* keyword to create a class instance.

You can also declare a constructor using the *private* keyword (*Private* or *private*). If you define only one constructor in your class, and it's private, the client code won't be able to create any class instances. If you define no constructors in your class, the compiler generates the public, parameterless, empty constructors shown in the preceding code snippets, so you should ensure that the fields of the class are properly initialized where they are declared.

Reading Books: Another Implementation

In the previous chapter, you set the Text and Title properties after you initialized the class. In this chapter, you'll create two different constructors for initializing the class fields. The first, a default constructor, creates an instance exactly the way one was created in Chapter 1. The second constructor initializes the Title and Text properties. Also, instead of creating a Library class, you'll store the books in a simple array. You'll use the array as the data source of the ListBox control.

Creating Constructors in the Book Class

This exercise builds on the exercise in Chapter 1. You create a new project but bring in the form and Book class you created in Chapter 1. You then modify the Book class by adding two constructors and a *ToString* method.

Create the project

To create this project, follow this procedure:

Create a new Microsoft Windows application project, naming it ReadMoreBooks.

1   In the Solution Explorer, right-click Form1, and click Delete on the shortcut menu. Click OK to confirm the deletion.

2   In the Solution Explorer, right-click ReadMoreBooks, point to Add, and then click Add Existing Item on the shortcut menu.

3   In the Add Existing Item dialog box, navigate to the Form1.vb or Form1.cs file from Chapter 1, click it, and click Open. A new copy of Form1 is added to the ReadMoreBooks project.

4   In the Solution Explorer, right-click ReadMoreBooks, point to Add, and then click Add Existing Item on the shortcut menu.

5   In the Add Existing Item dialog box, navigate to the Book file from Chapter 1, click it, and then click Open. A new copy of the Book class is added to the ReadMoreBooks project.

Convert the text from a field to a property

By creating a constructor, you will be able to determine whether the *Text* field or *Title* field of your Book class is blank. To further extend the validity of the text, convert it to a property. (You won't see many public fields in the remainder of this book.)

1   In the Solution Explorer, double-click Book.vb or Book.cs, depending on the language you're using, to open the file in the code editor.

2   Modify the *Text* field so that it's a private field. Remember that by convention private fields have the *m_* prefix.

```
Private m_text As String = ""          ' Visual Basic

private string m_text = "";            // Visual C#
```

3   Add a Text property definition to the class.

```
' Visual Basic
Public Property Text() As String
    Get
        Return m_text
    End Get
    Set(ByVal Value As String)
        m_text = Value
    End Set
End Property

// Visual C#
public string Text {
    get { return m_text; }
    set { m_text = value; }
}
```

Formatting C# Code

C# uses the semicolon to delimit statements, which gives you more control over formatting your code than Visual Basic offers. In the case of the preceding C# code, a more compact format for a property definition is shown. Never sacrifice readability for compactness.

Add a constructor without parameters

1   If you're using Visual C#, you should rename the namespace for Book.cs and Form1.cs to ReadMoreBooks. This step will keep all your class declarations in the same project namespace. It will make declaring class variables easier. Change the namespace declaration at the top of the file so that it looks like this:

```
// Visual C# only
// Change in Book.cs and Form1.cs
namespace ReadMoreBooks
```

2   If needed, in Visual Basic, click Book (ReadMoreBooks) in the Class Name list. In Visual C#, click ReadMoreBooks.Book in the Class Name list.

3   In the Method Name drop-down list, click New if you're using Visual Basic. Click Book if you're using Visual C#. The following code is added to the Book class:

```
Public Sub New()        ' Visual Basic
End Sub

public Book()           // Visual C#
{
    //
    // TODO: Add constructor logic here
    //
}
```

Your next task is to create a constructor that has parameters. You can create multiple constructors in one class, as long as they can be distinguished by their parameter lists.

Create a constructor with parameters

When creating constructors with parameters, remember that any code in a constructor is executed after the field initializations. You can therefore override any initializations of the fields.

1 Add the following code after the field declarations to declare a constructor with two parameters: *title* and *text*. Don't modify the exising constructor created in the preceding section. You're creating a second constructor.

```
' Visual Basic
Public Sub New(ByVal title As String, ByVal text As String)
End Sub
```

```
// Visual C#
public Book(string title, string text) {
}
```

2 Add the following code to your new constructor to ensure that neither the title nor the text is blank. If either is blank, raise an exception. An exception stops execution of the program and prevents the class from being instantiated.

```
' Visual Basic
If (title <> "") And (text <> "") And _
(Not IsNothing(title)) And (Not IsNothing(text)) Then
    m_title = title
    m_text = text
Else
    Throw New Exception("Title or text is an empty string.")
End If
```

```
// Visual C#
if ((title != "") && (text != "") && (title != null) && (text != null)) {
    m_title = title;
    m_text = text;
}
else {
    throw new System.Exception("Title or text is an empty string.");
}
```

If you deleted the parameterless constructor that you created in the section "Add a constructor without parameters," the client code would be forced to use this new constructor, which means that no instances could be created unless the text and title were known.

Add a *ToString* method

In Chapter 1, you used the *Title* field as the string to display the list box in the ReadBooks project. In this chapter, since you're using an array to store the Book instances, you can take advantage of the fact that you can use an array as a data source for a list box. If you have defined a *ToString* method for the class of objects you want to display, the list box uses the *ToString* method to display each of the objects in the array.

- Add this method to the Book class:

```
' Visual Basic
Public Overrides Function ToString() As String
    Return m_title
End Function

// Visual C#
public override string ToString() {
    return m_title;
}
```

In the .NET Framework, it's nearly impossible to miss seeing that all classes derive from the *System.Object* class. The *override* keyword (*Overrides* in Visual Basic, *override* in Visual C#) in the method declaration indicates that the *ToString* method in the Book class should be used instead of the *ToString* method defined in the *System.Object* class. The method defined in *System.Object* would simply print the name of the class, *ReadMoreBooks.Book*.

The changes in the Book class are complete.

Handling Data Validation Errors in a Constructor

You can choose from several ways to handle the situation in which either the *title* or *text* parameter is an empty string:

- You could throw an exception, as is done in this chapter. In this case, no new instance of the Book class is created. Program execution stops on the line of code containing the *new* keyword. You can use a *try* block (*Try* or *try*) to respond to and possibly recover from the error condition.

- You could replace the field with an empty string. If you supplied a constructor to enforce nonempty strings in the text and title fields, you wouldn't use this tactic. If you supplied a constructor as a convenience for setting properties in the initialization step, replacing the field with an empty string would be a reasonable decision.

If you choose to replace the field with an empty string, be sure to make developers aware that any instance of Book could contain an empty string for the title or text.

Using the Constructors

Now you'll replace the multiple lines of code with one call to the constructor. You will also replace the Library class with an array and exploit the data binding properties of the .NET Framework by using the array as a data source.

Delete the code to be replaced

1 In the Solution Explorer, right-click Form1 and click View Code on the shortcut menu to open it in the code editor.

2 Delete the *showPage_Click* method.

3 Delete the declaration of the Library field from the Form1 class. You'll replace it with an array of Book instances.

```
' Delete this line in the Visual Basic project.
Private m_library As Library

// Delete this line in the Visual C# project.
private Library m_library;
```

4 Delete the code from the *Form1_Load* event.

5 Delete the code from the *listOfBooks_SelectedIndexChanged* method. You're left with the interface.

Now add code to re-create the behavior of Chapter 1.

Create an instance of Book using the constructor

You must add code to the *Form1_Load* method so that the form can create the array of Book instances and bind the array to the ListBox control.

1 Create an instance of the fairy tales Book class using the constructor that has two parameters. Add this code to the *Form1_Load* method:

```
' Visual Basic
Dim fairyTales As Book = _
    New Book("Fairy Tales", "Once upon a time there was a bear.")

// Visual C#
Book fairyTales = new
    Book("Fairy Tales", "Once upon a time there was a bear.");
```

Notice that when you type *new* or *New*, depending on the language you're using, IntelliSense indicates that you have two constructors defined, as shown in the next graphic. When you have more than one constructor, the constructor are said to be *overloaded*.

```
Private Sub Form1_Load(ByVal sender As Object, ByVal e As S
    Dim fairyTales As Book = _
        New Book("Fairy Tales", "Once upon a time there was
        ▲1 of 2▼ New (title As String, text As String)

End Sub
```

2   Create an instance of the Book class for the Cookies book using the constructor that has two parameters:

```
' Visual Basic
Dim cookies As Book = New Book("Cookies", _
    "Chocolate chip cookies are the most delicious cookies.")

// Visual C#
Book cookies = new Book("Cookies",
    "Chocolate chip cookies are the most delicious cookies.");
```

Create an array of Book instances

1   Add the following code after the Book declarations to create an array:

```
' Visual Basic
Dim m_library() As Book = New Book() {fairyTales, cookies}

// Visual C#
Book[] m_library = new Book[] {fairyTales, cookies};
```

2   Add the following code after the array declaration to use the array as the data source for the ListBox control:

```
listOfBooks.DataSource = m_library      ' Visual Basic

listOfBooks.DataSource = m_library;    // Visual C#
```

The complete method is shown in the following code:

```
' Visual Basic
Private Sub Form1_Load(ByVal sender As Object, _
ByVal e As System.EventArgs) Handles MyBase.Load
    Dim fairyTales As Book = _
        New Book("Fairy Tales", "Once upon a time there was a bear.")
    Dim cookies As Book = New Book("Cookies", _
        "Chocolate chip cookies are the most delicious cookies.")
    Dim m_library() As Book = New Book() {fairyTales, cookies}
    listOfBooks.DataSource = m_library
End Sub

// Visual C#
private void Form1_Load(object sender, System.EventArgs e) {
    Book fairyTales = new
        Book("Fairy Tales", "Once upon a time there was a bear.");
    Book cookies = new Book("Cookies",
        "Chocolate chip cookies are the most delicious cookies.");
    Book[] m_library = new Book[] {fairyTales, cookies};
    listOfBooks.DataSource = m_library;
}
```

Respond to selections in the ListBox control

What you see in the ListBox control when you run the application is the title of each book. Because the data source of the ListBox is an array of Book instances, each item in the list represents one instance of the Book class. Now add code to retrieve that instance and display the selected page.

1 Add the following code to the SelectedIndexChanged event handler of the ListBox control, which is named *listOfBooks*:

```
' Visual Basic
Dim theBook As Book = CType(listOfBooks.SelectedItem, Book)

// Visual C#
Book theBook = (Book)(listOfBooks.SelectedItem);
```

As you saw in Chapter 1, the objects in the ListBox control are treated like *System.Object* instances. The *CType* method doesn't change the instance at all, it just changes the runtime's view of it. The C# syntax is slightly different but has the same effect. Instead of being treated like a *System.Object*, the book instance will now be treated like a Book.

2 Below the *CType* statement, add the following code to display one page of the text:

```
' Visual Basic
titleLabel.Text = theBook.Title
theBook.PageLength = Decimal.ToInt32(pageLength.Value)
page.Text = theBook.GetPage(Decimal.ToInt32(pageToDisplay.Value))

// Visual C#
titleLabel.Text = theBook.Title;
theBook.PageLength = Decimal.ToInt32(pageLength.Value);
page.Text = theBook.GetPage(Decimal.ToInt32(pageToDisplay.Value));
```

Because *pageLength.Value* is a string property of the *pageLength* control, you can't directly assign it's value to *theBook.PageLength*, an integer property. The method *Decimal.ToInt32* converts *pageLength.Value*, a string, to an integer.

3 Run and test the program. It has the same behavior as the application in Chapter 1.

These two exercises demonstrate some of the options you have as you design objects and applications. In Chapter 1, you designed the classes Book and Library to model the problem. In this chapter, you designed only a Book class, and then relied on the capabilities of .NET Windows controls to implement the behavior of the Library. The ListBox control, together with the array, provided the Library behavior.

Declaring and Initializing Arrays

You can choose from several ways to declare and initialize an array of class instances. The syntax you used in the previous section was (in Visual Basic) the following:

```
Dim m_library() As Book = New Book() {fairyTales, cookies}
```

Here's another way to declare the same array:

```
Dim books() As Book = _
    {New Book("Title1", "Text1"), New Book("Title2", "Text2")}
```

And another:

```
Dim m_library() As Book = {fairyTales, cookies}
```

And yet another way:

```
Dim books(2) As Book
books(0) = New Book("Title1", "Text1")
books(1) = New Book("Title2", "Text2")
books(2) = New Book("Title3", "Text3")
```

Reference and Value Types

To understand what is going on in these last three code snippets, you need to understand the concepts of *reference types* and *value types* in Visual Basic and Visual C#. Any variable you declare in the chapters in this book will be either a reference type or a value type.

Visual Basic, C#, and Types

In Visual Basic, all variables are either reference type or value type. C# has a third type, the *pointer* type. You can use a pointer type variable, similar to a C++ pointer, only in an *unsafe* code block. This book doesn't cover unsafe coding.

A reference type variable is created any time you declare a variable as

- A class (for example, Book)
- An interface (Interfaces will be discussed in Chapter 9.)
- An array (for example, *Dim numbers() as Integer*)
- A string

- An object (for example, *Dim x As Object*)
- A delegate (Delegates will be discussed in Chapter 7.)

A value type variable is created any time you declare a variable as

- An integral type (for example, *Integer* or *int*)
- A floating type (for example, *Double* or *double*)
- A Boolean (for example, *Boolean* or *bool*)
- An enumeration (for example, *System*)
- A structure (for example, *DateTime*)

When you declare either a value type or a reference type variable, the location in memory is allocated to the variable. In the case of the value type, that location contains the value of the variable. In the case of a reference type, the memory allocated contains the location of an instance of the class in memory. Thus, reference declarations allocate only enough memory to point to an instance of a Book.

```
Dim aBook as Book;      ' Visual Basic

Book aBook;             // Visual C#
```

When an instance of a class is created through the *new* operator (*New* in Visual Basic and *new* in C#), memory is allocated for the fields declared in the class. These expressions cause the allocation of memory for the *Text*, *PageLength*, and *Title* fields for the Book class. The *new* operator returns the address of the location of the fields in memory.

```
New Book("theTitle", "theText")     ' Visual Basic

new Book("theTitle", "theText")     // Visual C#
```

These statements, then, create the instance of the Book class and set the *aBook* variable to the location of the new instance.

```
aBook = New Book("theTitle", "theText")     ' Visual Basic

aBook = new Book("theTitle", "theText")     // Visual C#
```

So, in the first set of statements, what is the value of *aBook* before it's set as in the last set of statements? By definition, the value of a reference type before it's initialized is *Nothing* in Visual Basic or *null* in C#. The following code snippet reports *True*:

```
' Visual Basic
Dim aBook as Book
```

(continued)

```
MessageBox.Show((aBook Is Nothing).ToString())

// Visual C#
Book aBook;
MessageBox.Show((aBook == null).ToString());
```

Visual Basic provides a keyword, *Is*, for testing the value of reference types. C# uses the equality operator ==. Visual Basic also provides the *IsNothing* method to test the value of the reference. It returns the Boolean value *True* if the reference is *Nothing*. This code snippet is equivalent to the preceding one:

```
Dim aBook As Book
MessageBox.Show(IsNothing(aBook).ToString())
```

If you try to use the properties or methods of a reference when it's *Nothing*, an error occurs because there's no instance data to operate on. You will come to recognize this error as *System.NullReferenceException*. To make a program more robust, you should test whether the reference is *null* or *Nothing*. You should be especially careful to make this test if the reference has been passed to the method as a parameter. In this case, your code has less control over the state of the variable before it's passed to the method.

The concept of reference types also affects copying, equality testing, and garbage collection. Copying is discussed in Chapter 10, equality testing in Chapter 12, and Chapter 8 discusses garbage collection.

Understanding Array Declarations

The first three examples in the section "Declaring and Initializing Arrays" use variations of the syntax

```
Dim m_library() As Book = {fairyTales, cookies}
```

In this case, the braces, {}, are defined so that they produce an array of values. You can replace *fairyTales* with *New Book*("Fairy Tales", "Once upon a time") because the *New* expression returns a reference to a class instance.

This example is slightly different from the rest:

```
Dim books(2) As Book
books(0) = New Book("Title1", "Text1")
books(1) = New Book("Title2", "Text2")
books(2) = New Book("Title3", "Text3")
```

The first statement doesn't create any instances of the Book class. It merely creates an *array of references* to Book instances. In the second through fourth lines, the instances of Book are created and assigned to the references.

Quick Reference

To	Do this

Create a constructor without parameters	In the code editor, select the class name in the Class Name drop-down list, and select New (for Visual Basic) or the class name (for Visual C#) in the Method Name drop-down list. Or
	
	Add this code for Visual Basic:
	
	`Public Sub New()`
	`End Sub`
	
	Add this code for C#:
	
	`public Book() {`
	`}`

Create a constructor with parameters	Create a constructor without parameters. Add parameters exactly as you would for a class method.

Create an array of instance references	Add this code for Visual Basic:
	`Dim books() As Book`
	
	Add this code for C#:
	
	`Book[] books;`

Create and initialize an array of instances	Add this code for Visual Basic:
	`Dim books() As Book = _`
	`{ New Book(), New Book()}`
	
	Add this code for C#:
	
	`Book[] books =`
	`{ new Book(), new Book()};`

Test a reference for *Nothing* or *null*	Add this code for Visual Basic:
	`Dim aBook As Book`
	
	`If IsNothing(aBook) Then`
	`' Add code here for a`
	`' null reference`
	`End If`
	
	Add this code for C#:
	
	`Book aBook;`
	`if (aBook == null) {`
	`// Add code here for a`
	`// null reference`
	`}`

3

Creating Fields and Properties

In this chapter, you'll learn how to

- ✔ *Create a read-only property.*
- ✔ *Create a property that takes a parameter.*
- ✔ *Create documentation comments for Visual C# properties.*
- ✔ *Use an array of class instances as a data source in a DataGrid control.*
- ✔ *Create an indexer property in Visual C#.*
- ✔ *Create a default property in Visual Basic.*
- ✔ *Create and use an ArrayList object.*

ESTIMATED
TIME
2 hr. 30 min.

As I've mentioned, properties tell you about the objects to which they belong. When you move a Button control around on a form, the Location property tells you where that button is. After you load a bitmap into a PictureBox control, the Size property tells you how large the image is. You can see an interplay between the properties and behaviors of an object. Moving a button (a behavior) changes the location (a property). Loading a bitmap (a behavior) into a control changes the size (a property) of the control. You'll see this pattern repeatedly in object-oriented design.

In the preceding chapters, you created a class with two fields (*PageLength* and *Text*) and a property (Title). You saw how fields are used to implement properties. In this chapter, you'll extend your use of properties, using fields as private class members to implement the properties. You'll create a read-only property. Using Visual Basic, you'll create a property that takes a parameter, which will make it behave, in some ways, like a function. You'll create and initialize an array of class instances and then use that array as a data source in a data grid.

Visual Studio .NET will even recognize the properties in the class defintion and convert those to column headings. You'll then redesign your application to take advantage of Visual Basic's default property or Visual C# indexer to implement a class that represents a group of objects.

Design Considerations for Properties

When designing and implementing properties, the following considerations apply:

- Properties can be read-write, read-only, or write-only. A read-write property can be retrieved and set by client code. A read-only property can only be retrieved and a write-only property can only be set. Write-only properties are rare. Developers tend to use write-only properties to send data to hardware devices so that the value sent to the device can't be retrieved later.

- Use a read-only property when the property is completely determined by other properties. For example, in a Rectangle class, the Length and Width properties can be read-write, but the Area property would be read-only.

- Reading the value of a property should have no side effects; no other instance data should change simply because it retrieved a property value. For example, a developer wouldn't expect the Width property of a Rectangle object to change just because the Area property was retrieved.

- Design properties so that they can be changed independently and in any order. If properties are dependent, use a method to set them. For example, if you need to set the LastName property of a Person object before you set the FirstName property, use a *SetFirstAndLast* function instead of two properties.

- A *getter* (the read part of a property definition) and *setter* (the write part of a property definition) of a property are conceptually simple methods that return or set values. The Length property of a rectangle object could be replaced easily with *GetLength* and *SetLength* methods. The advantage of using a property is the syntax. *Rectangle.Length = 15* is obviously more elegant than *Rectangle.SetLength(15)*.

Code Analysis: A Host of Properties

In this chapter, you'll implement a program to analyze your code so that you can convince your manager that you're getting work done and, at the same time, using object-oriented designs.

A project is made of several source files (files with code). For each source file, you will

- Count the lines of code, skipping blank lines and comments.
- Count the number of classes defined.
- Maintain a list of the names of the classes defined. (Source files can contain more than one class definition.)

The user interface will consist of

- A Button control with Text property set to *Browse*, which allows a user to select a source file.
- A DataGrid control, with each row representing one source file. The columns should be lines of code, filename, number of classes, and the file path.
- A Button control with the Text property set to *Display*. When this button is clicked, the list of classes from the selected source file in the DataGrid control is displayed.

The C# version reads C# source files. The Visual Basic version reads Visual Basic source files. The completed application is shown in the following screen shot.

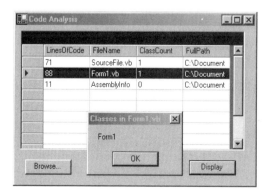

Designing the SourceFile Class

The class implemented in this chapter has been designed with these .NET capabilities in mind:

- The DataGrid control can use an array as a data source.
- If the type of the array is a class, the DataGrid control uses the public properties of the class as the columns.

To take advantage of these properties, you need to create a SourceFile class with LinesOfCode, FileName, ClassCount, and FullPath properties. The data source for the DataGrid control will then be an array of SourceFile instances.

Because a SourceFile instance can make sense only if it's based on an existing file, you need to create a constructor that takes one string parameter, the filename.

The LinesOfCode, FileName, ClassCount, and FullPath properties are all dependent on the name of the source file. It isn't reasonable for the client to be able to change these properties. So you'll make these properties read-only.

That leaves only the list of class names for you to make. Again, this should be a read-only list. Conveniently, Visual Basic allows you to define a property that takes a parameter. You use this capability to return one class name, based on an index. C# doesn't have a parameterized property, so you must implement a method to return a class name. Later in this chapter, you'll see how C# provides an indexer construct to serve the same purpose.

The SourceFile class provides the following public members:

- **Filename**   A read-only string property that returns just the name of the source file.

- **FullPath**   A read-only string property that returns the full path of the source file.

- **LinesOfCode**   A read-only integer property that returns the number lines in the source file that aren't blank and aren't comments.

- **ClassCount**   A read-only integer property that returns the number of classes defined in the source file.

- **Classes**   A read-only string property that returns the name of one class defined in the source file. This property is implemented in Visual Basic only.

- *GetClass*   This method returns a string and takes one integer parameter. It returns the name of one class defined in the source file. This is implemented in C# only.

- **Constructor**   The class defines only one constructor that takes one string parameter, the full path of the source file. You won't be defining a parameterless constructor, so a SourceFile instance can't be created unless the full path is known.

important

In general, you don't want your design to depend on the user interface. Rather, you want your class design to reflect the problem you are trying to solve. Then add the properties and methods you need to support the user interface. In Chapter 9, "Providing Services Using Interfaces," you'll learn how to use an *interface* to provide a view on your class design that exposes only those parts of the model that the user interface needs. An *interface* is similar to a class and defines a set of properties and methods that a class must implement.

Create the user interface

1   Create a new project, and name it CodeAnalysis.

2   Set the Text property of Form1 to *Code Analysis*.

3   Drag a DataGrid control onto Form1, and set the Name property to *listOfFiles*.

4   Drag a Button control onto Form1. Set its Name property to *browse* and its Text property to *Browse*.

5   Drag a Button control onto Form1. Set its Name property to *display* and its Text property to *Display*.

6   Drag an OpenFileDialog control onto Form1. It will be displayed in the component tray. Set its Name property to *openSourceFile*.

     The complete form is shown in the following screen shot. Now create the SourceFile class so that you can add code to Form1.

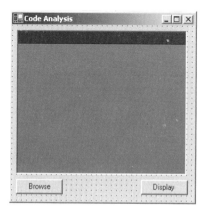

Creating the SourceFile Class

The SourceFile class represents one file in a project. This class contains the LinesOfCode, FileName, ClassCount, and FullPath properties, the parameterized Classes property (in Visual Basic) or *GetClass* method (in Visual C#), and the constructor. A SourceFile class is instantiated in the application for each source file analyzed.

Create the read-only properties

1　On the Project menu, click Add Class. The Add New Item dialog box appears.

2　Type *SourceFile.vb* or *SourceFile.cs* in the Name box, depending on the language you're using, and click Open.

3　Add the following fields to the class definition:

```
' Visual Basic
Private m_fullPath As String
Private m_linesOfCode As Integer
Private m_classNames() As String
Private m_classCount As Integer


// Visual C#
private string m_fullPath;
private int m_linesOfCode;
private string[] m_classNames;
private int m_classCount;
```

The *m_fullPath* field contains the full path of the source file.

4　Add the FullPath property by inserting the code below into your class:

```
' Visual Basic
Public ReadOnly Property FullPath() As String
    Get
        Return m_fullPath
    End Get
End Property

// Visual C#
/// <summary>
/// Returns the full path of the source file.
/// </summary>
public string FullPath {
    get { return m_fullPath; }
}
```

To create a read-only property in Visual Basic, you add the ReadOnly modifier and define only a Get block. To create a read-only property in C#, you define only a Get block. No modifier is added. Note that statement completion in Visual Basic creates the Get and Set blocks as needed, depending on the presence or absence of the ReadOnly modifier.

C# Property Wizard

In Visual C#, the C# Property Wizard can create most of the property block for you. To use the wizard, right-click the class name in Class View, and click Add from the shortcut menu. Then click Add Property, and complete the steps in the wizard. For an example, see Chapter1.

The special comment in Visual C#, /// <summary>, is used to add descriptive information when the property signature is displayed in IntelliSense.

XML Documentation Support in Visual C#

The <summary> tag is one of several documentation tags supported by the C# language and the .NET Framework. Tags can be used to document other code elements, such as parameters, exceptions, and return values. To create an XML documentation file from your C# source file, right-click the project in Solution Explorer, and click Properties on the shortcut menu. In the Project Property Pages dialog box, expand Configuration Properties in the list, and then click Build. Enter a filename for the XML Documentation File property, and click OK. You might get compiler warnings if you enter a documentation filename and don't document all the code elements.

5   Add the FileName property:

```
' Visual Basic
Public ReadOnly Property FileName() As String
    Get
        Dim lastSlash As Integer
        lastSlash = m_fullPath.LastIndexOf("\")
        Return m_fullPath.Substring(lastSlash + 1)
    End Get
End Property
```

(continued)

```csharp
// Visual C#
/// <summary>
/// Returns the filename, without the path of the source file.
/// </summary>
public string FileName {
    get {
        int lastSlash = m_fullPath.LastIndexOf("\\");
        return m_fullPath.Substring(lastSlash + 1);
    }
}
```

The FileName property returns only the filename of the full path. It searches for the last backslash in the filename and returns the rest of the string.

6   Add the ClassCount property:

```vb
' Visual Basic
Public ReadOnly Property ClassCount() As Integer
    Get
        Return m_classCount
    End Get
End Property
```

```csharp
// Visual C#
/// <summary>
/// The total number of classes defined in the source file.
/// </summary>
public int ClassCount {
    get { return m_classCount; }
}
```

7   Add the LinesOfCode property:

```vb
' Visual Basic
Public ReadOnly Property LinesOfCode() As Integer
    Get
        Return m_linesOfCode
    End Get
End Property
```

```csharp
// Visual C#
/// <summary>
/// Lines of code in the source file, excluding blank and comment lines.
/// </summary>
public int LinesOfCode {
    get { return m_linesOfCode; }
}
```

Your next step depends on the language you're using. If you're using Visual Basic, you can create the Classes property, which takes an integer parameter to select one of the class names. If you're using Visual C#, you need to create the *GetClass* method.

Create the Classes property (Visual Basic only)

● Add the Classes property:

```
' Visual Basic
Public ReadOnly Property Classes(ByVal index As Integer) As String
    Get
        If index < m_classCount Then
            Return m_classNames(index)
        Else
            Throw New System.IndexOutOfRangeException( _
                "There are only " & m_classCount & " classes defined.")
        End If
    End Get
End Property
```

The syntax for this property is the same as for any other property, with the addition of the *index* parameter.

If you wanted this property to be read-write, you would remove the *ReadOnly* modifier and add a Set block as shown in the next code snippet. Notice that the Set block has two local variables, *index* and *value*, instead of just one, *index*.

```
' Visual Basic
' Remove the ReadOnly property modifier, and add this Set block.
Set(ByVal Value As String)
    If index < m_classCount Then
        m_classNames(index) = Value
    Else
        Throw New System.IndexOutOfRangeException( _
            "There are only " & m_classCount & " classes defined.")
    End If
End Set
```

Create the *GetClass* method (Visual C# only)

● Add the *GetClass* method:

```
// Visual C#
/// <summary>
/// Returns one of the names of the classes defined in the
/// source file, based on an index.
/// </summary>
/// <param name="index">A zero-based index</param>
```

(continued)

```
/// <returns>A class name</returns>
public string GetClass(int index) {
    if (index < m_classCount) {
        return m_classNames[index];
    }
    else {
        throw new System.IndexOutOfRangeException("There are only "
            + m_classCount + " classes defined.");
    }
}
```

This code also shows more of the documentation tags available for C# code.

With the properties and methods complete, you can now move on to creating the constructor.

Create the constructor

Most of the work of the SourceFile class is accomplished here. The class constructor sets the data fields.

1   In the Class Name drop-down list, click SourceFile if it isn't already selected.

2   In the Method Name drop-down list, click New if you're working with a Visual Basic project, or click SourceFile if you're working with a Visual C# project. This action adds a parameterless constructor to the class. (For Visual C#, the constructor was created when you added the class through the Add New Item dialog box.)

3   Add a string parameter, *fullPath*, to the constructor as shown.

```
' Visual Basic
Public Sub New(ByVal fullPath As String)
End Sub

// Visual C#
public SourceFile(string fullPath)
{
    //
    // TODO: Add constructor logic here
    //
}
```

4   Add code for the constructor, as shown here:

```
' Visual Basic
Public Sub New(ByVal fullPath As String)
    m_classCount = 0
    m_linesOfCode = 0
    m_fullPath = fullPath
    m_classNames = New String(10) {}
```

```vb
    Try
        Dim reader As New System.IO.StreamReader(m_fullPath)
        Dim nameStart As Integer
        Dim oneline As String
        oneline = reader.ReadLine()
        While (Not (oneline Is Nothing))
            oneline = oneline.Trim()
            ' Don't count blank lines and comment lines.
            If ((oneline <> "") And (Not oneline.StartsWith("'"))) Then
                m_linesOfCode += 1
            End If

            If (oneline.StartsWith("Public Class")) Then
                nameStart = oneline.IndexOf("Class") + 6
                Dim names() As String
                Dim separators() As Char = {ControlChars.Tab, " "c}
                names = oneline.Substring( _
                    nameStart).Trim().Split(separators)
                Dim className As String = names(0).Trim()
                m_classNames(m_classCount) = className
                m_classCount += 1
            End If
            oneline = reader.ReadLine()
        End While
        reader.Close()
    Catch ex As System.Exception
        Throw New System.Exception( _
            "Problems parsing source file: " + ex.Message)
    End Try
End Sub

// Visual C#
public SourceFile(string fullPath)
{
    m_linesOfCode = 0;
    m_classNames = new string[10];
    m_classCount = 0;
    m_fullPath = fullPath;

    try {
        System.IO.StreamReader reader = new
            System.IO.StreamReader(m_fullPath);
        int nameStart;
        string oneline;
        while ((oneline = reader.ReadLine()) != null) {
            oneline = oneline.Trim();
            // Don't count blank or comment lines.
            if ((oneline != "") && (!oneline.StartsWith("\\"))) {
```

(continued)

```
                m_linesOfCode++;
            }

            if (oneline.StartsWith("public class")) {
                nameStart = oneline.IndexOf("class") + 6;
                char[] separators = { ' ', '\t', '{'};
                string[] names =
                    oneline.Substring(nameStart).Trim().Split(separators);
                string className = names[0].Trim();
                m_classNames[m_classCount++] = className;
            }
        }
        reader.Close();
    }
    catch (System.Exception ex) {
        throw new System.Exception("Problems parsing source file: "
        + ex.Message);
    }
}
```

The first thing the constructor does is initialize all the instance data. The syntax for the array initialization creates an array of references that are all *Nothing* or *null*.

The *While* loop reads one line from the file, using a StreamReader object. The *StreamReader.ReadLine* method returns *Nothing* or *null* at the end of the file. In C#, the assignment statement, *oneline = reader.ReadLine()*, returns the value of *oneline*, which can be tested directly in the *while* statement. In Visual Basic, the similar syntax would be interpreted as an equality test of *oneline* and *reader.ReadLine()*. So the test for *null* in the *While* statement isn't possible in Visual Basic.

Each line is tested to determine whether it starts with *Public Class* or *public class*, depending on language. This process is a simple way to find class declarations, but it's not exhaustive because other modifiers might precede the class keyword. To find the class name, the code looks for the next word after the word *class*, using the *Split* method. The line

```
names = oneline.Substring(nameStart).Trim().Split(separators)
```

is an example of chaining method calls. Each method returns a string, so you can then call a string method on the result. How many methods you chain in one statement depends on the readability of the code.

With the properties, methods, and constructors defined, the SourceFile class is complete. You can now add the client code to Form1.

Adding Code to the User Interface

The *Form1_Load* event is used to initialize the controls on the form. The Browse button allows the user to select one file for analysis. The Display button displays the classes contained in a selected source file.

Program the *Form1_Load* method

1   Add an array for the SourceFile instances as a field of the Form1 class.

```
' Visual Basic
Private Const MaxFiles As Integer = 10
Private m_sourceFiles(MaxFiles) As SourceFile
Private m_files As Integer = 0

// Visual C#
private const int MaxFiles = 10;
private SourceFile[] m_sourceFiles = new SourceFile[MaxFiles];
private int m_files = 0;
```

This particular syntax for declaring an array creates an array of 10 references to SourceFile instances and sets each instance to *Nothing* or *null*, depending on the language.

2   In the form designer, double-click Form1 and then add this code to the *Form1_Load* event to set the data source of the DataGrid.

```
' Visual Basic
Private Sub Form1_Load(ByVal sender As Object, _
ByVal e As System.EventArgs) Handles MyBase.Load
    listOfFiles.DataSource = m_sourceFiles
End Sub

// Visual C#
private void Form1_Load(object sender, System.EventArgs e) {
    listOfFiles.DataSource = m_sourceFiles;
}
```

When the application starts, 10 blank rows will be displayed in the DataGrid. Now you'll add code to the Click event method for the Browse button to replace those rows with data.

Program the Browse button

The Browse button prompts the user to specify a source file and adds a row to the DataGrid control with the results of the file analysis.

1   In the form designer, double-click the Browse button to create the *browse_Click* method.

2   Add the following code to the *browse_Click* method:

```vb
' Visual Basic
Private Sub browse_Click(ByVal sender As System.Object, _
ByVal e As System.EventArgs) Handles browse.Click
    Try
        openSourceFile.Filter = "Visual Basic files (*.vb)|*.vb"
        Dim result As System.Windows.Forms.DialogResult
        result = openSourceFile.ShowDialog()
        If (result = DialogResult.OK) Then
            Dim aFile As New SourceFile(openSourceFile.FileName)
            m_sourceFiles(m_files) = aFile
            m_files += 1
            If (m_files = m_sourceFiles.Length) Then
                m_files = m_sourceFiles.Length - 1
            End If
        End If
        listOfFiles.Refresh()
    Catch ex As System.Exception
        MessageBox.Show(ex.Message)
    End Try
End Sub
```

```csharp
// Visual C#
private void browse_Click(object sender, System.EventArgs e) {
    try {
        openSourceFile.Filter = "Visual C# files (*.cs)|*.cs";
        System.Windows.Forms.DialogResult result;
        result = openSourceFile.ShowDialog();
        if (result == System.Windows.Forms.DialogResult.OK) {
            SourceFile aFile = new SourceFile(openSourceFile.FileName);
            m_sourceFiles[m_files++] = aFile;
            if (m_files == m_sourceFiles.Length) {
                m_files = m_sourceFiles.Length - 1;
            }
        }
        listOfFiles.Refresh();
    }
    catch (System.Exception ex) {
        MessageBox.Show(ex.Message);
    }
}
```

The *browse_Click* method sets the Filter property of the OpenFileDialog control, which can also be done in the Properties window of the form designer. The Filter property limits the selection of files to only the appropriate source files. Because the array is used as a fixed-length array (arrays in C# can't be resized during execution), a test keeps the *m_files* field within the range of the length of the array. To understand the use of the indexes in the method, remember that arrays are zero-based.

With some analyzed files listed in the DataGrid control, the user can then select a row to retrieve the classes defined in a particular source file. To implement that functionality, add code to the Click event method of the Display button.

Program the Display button

The Display button uses the Classes property of the SourceFile class to display the list of classes defined in the source file.

1 In the form designer, double-click the Display button to create the *display_Click* method.

2 Add the following code to the *display_Click* method:

```
Private Sub display_Click(ByVal sender As System.Object, _
ByVal e As System.EventArgs) Handles display.Click
    Dim row As Integer = listOfFiles.CurrentCell.RowNumber
    If row < m_files Then
        Dim theFile As SourceFile = m_sourceFiles(row)
        Dim message As String = ""
        Dim index As Integer
        For index = 0 To theFile.ClassCount - 1
            message &= theFile.Classes(index) & ControlChars.CrLf
        Next
        MessageBox.Show(message, "Classes in " & theFile.FileName)
    Else
        MessageBox.Show("Please select a row with data.")
    End If
End Sub


// Visual C#
private void display_Click(object sender, System.EventArgs e) {
    int row = listOfFiles.CurrentCell.RowNumber;
    if (row < m_files) {
        SourceFile theFile = m_sourceFiles[row];
        string message = "";
        for (int index = 0; index < theFile.ClassCount; index++) {
            message += theFile.GetClass(index) + "\n";
        }
        MessageBox.Show(message, "Classes in " + theFile.FileName);
    }
    else {
        MessageBox.Show("Please select a row with data.");
    }
}
```

There's a one-to-one correspondence between the rows in the DataGrid control and the elements in the *m_sourceFiles* array. You can therefore use the value of *listOfFile.CurrentCell.RowNumber* to retrieve the selected file from the array. Because the DataGrid control displays all 10 elements of the array, even if the element is *Nothing* or *null*, you need to add a test to determine whether the user has picked an unused row.

IntelliSense displays the property documentation created for the properties in the class, as shown in the following screen shot.

```
private void display_Click(object sender, System.EventArgs e) {
    int row = listOfFiles.CurrentCell.RowNumber;
    if (row < m_files) {
        SourceFile theFile = m_sourceFiles[row];
        string message = "";
        for (int index = 0; index < theFile.ClassCount; index++) {
            message += theFile.GetClass(index) + [property] int SourceFile.ClassCount
        }                                       The total number of classes defined in the source file.
        MessageBox.Show(message, "Classes in " + theFile.FileName);
    }
}
```

The application is complete and ready for testing.

Test the program

1   Test the program by analyzing the source files from Chapters 1 and 2.

2   You can test the program further by adding more than one class definition to a source file. Remember that the application detects only classes that are declared *Public Class* (in Visual Basic) or *public class* (in C#).

3   Make testing easier by turning on the line numbering in the code editor. On the Tools menu, click Options. Expand the Text Editor folder in the list, and expand the language you're using. Click General in the language folder, select the Line Numbers check box, and click OK to close the dialog box. Remember to subtract blank lines and comments from the total.

Code Analysis: Using Indexers and Default Properties

In your first implementation of CodeAnalysis, the objects were based on each source file. Suppose you wanted to list the classes in the DataGrid control, rather than listing the files. Or perhaps you wanted to accumulate the classes and lines of code over an application rather than by file. In this case, you can take advantage of Visual Basic's default property syntax and C# indexer syntax to create a class that represents a collection of objects. You'll create a class, Classes, that represents all the classes in all the files you parse. Instead of instancing an array of SourceFile objects, you'll need only to create one instance of Classes. The default indexer or property will return one instance of AClass, a class that represents one class in a source file.

Creating the AClass Class

The AClass class represents one class found in a source file. The Classes class will contain many instances of AClass.

Create the project, and add AClass

1   Create a new project, and name it CodeAnalysis2.

2   On the Project menu, click Add Class. The Add New Item dialog box appears.

3   In the Name box, type *AClass.vb* or *AClass.cs*, depending on the language you are using, and then click Open.

Next add properties for the name of the class and the name of the source file to which the class belongs. Because the only way you can get AClass instances is from parsing a source file, these properties are read-only.

Add the Name and FileName properties

1   Add the following field and property declaration for the Name property:

```
' Visual Basic
Private m_name As String
Public ReadOnly Property Name() As String
    Get
        Return m_name
    End Get
End Property
```

```
// Visual C#
string m_name;
public string Name {
    get { return m_name; }
}
```

2   Add the following field and property declaration for the FileName property.

```
' Visual Basic
Private m_filename As String
Public ReadOnly Property FileName() As String
    Get
        Return m_filename
    End Get
End Property
```

```
// Visual C#
string m_filename;
public string FileName {
    get { return m_filename; }
}
```

Create the constructor

1 If you're using Visual C#, delete the default parameterless constructor. The client code is able to create an instance of AClass only if the class name and source file are known.

2 Add the following constructor:

```
' Visual Basic
Public Sub New(ByVal name As String, ByVal filename As String)
    m_name = name
    m_filename = filename
End Sub

// Visual C#
public AClass(string name, string filename) {
    m_name = name;
    m_filename = filename;
}
```

Now that you have a class to represent one class in a source file, you can implement a class that organizes a group of AClass instances.

Create the Classes class

1 On the Project menu, click Add Class. The Add New Item dialog box appears.

2 In the Name box, type *Classes.vb* or *Classes.cs*, depending on the language you are using, and then click Open.

Instead of a constructor that creates one instance of a SourceFile class for each source file, you'll create a *ReadFromFile* method that adds instances of AClass to an ArrayList object.

Add fields to track the lines of code and store the classes

1 Create a field to track the total lines of code. This field represents the number of lines of code read across all source files.

```
' Visual Basic
Private m_linesOfCode As Integer = 0

// Visual C#
private int m_linesOfCode = 0;
```

2 Create a field to hold the AClass instances.

```
' Visual Basic
Private m_classNames As New System.Collections.ArrayList()
```

```
// Visual C#
private System.Collections.ArrayList m_classNames =
    new System.Collections.ArrayList();
```

An ArrayList is a data structure class available from the .NET Framework that allows you to create an array that grows dynamically. You can add new objects to the collection without having to resize the ArrayList structure, which you wouldn't be able to do in C# with an array. You'll still be able to retrieve objects from the ArrayList class using an index.

Add the *ReadFromFile* method

● Add the following code for the *ReadFromFile* method. The code differs slightly from the previous implementation in the constructor. Instead of adding one more string to an array for the class names, you're adding one more AClass object to an ArrayList object.

```
' Visual Basic
Public Sub ReadFromFile(ByVal fullPath As String)
    Try
        Dim reader As New System.IO.StreamReader(fullPath)
        Dim nameStart As Integer
        Dim oneline As String
        oneline = reader.ReadLine()
        While (Not (oneline Is Nothing))
            oneline = oneline.Trim()
            If ((oneline <> "") And (Not oneline.StartsWith("'"))) Then
                m_linesOfCode += 1
            End If
            If (oneline.StartsWith("Public Class")) Then
                nameStart = oneline.IndexOf("Class") + 6
                Dim names() As String
                Dim separators() As Char = {ControlChars.Tab, " "c}
                names = oneline.Substring( _
                    nameStart).Trim().Split(separators)
                Dim className As String = names(0).Trim()
                m_classNames.Add(New AClass(className, fullPath))
            End If
            oneline = reader.ReadLine()
        End While
        reader.Close()
    Catch ex As System.Exception
        Throw New System.Exception( _
            "Problems parsing source file: " + ex.Message)
    End Try
End Sub
```

(continued)

```csharp
// Visual C#
public void ReadFromFile(string fullPath) {
    try {
        System.IO.StreamReader reader = new
            System.IO.StreamReader(fullPath);
        int nameStart;
        string oneline;
        while ((oneline = reader.ReadLine()) != null) {
            oneline = oneline.Trim();
            // Don't count blank or comment lines.
            if ((oneline != "") && (!oneline.StartsWith("\\"))) {
                m_linesOfCode++;
            }

            if (oneline.StartsWith("public class")) {
                nameStart = oneline.IndexOf("class") + 6;
                char[] separators = { ' ', '\t', '{'};
                string[] names =
                    oneline.Substring(nameStart).Trim().Split(separators);
                string className = names[0].Trim();
                m_classNames.Add(new AClass(className,fullPath));
            }
        }
        reader.Close();
    }
    catch (System.Exception ex) {
        throw new System.Exception(
            "Problems parsing source file: " + ex.Message);
    }
}
```

Add the Indexer or Default property

1   If you're using Visual Basic, add the following default ReadOnly property:

```vbnet
' Visual Basic
Default Public ReadOnly Property Classes(ByVal index As Integer) As AClass
    Get
        If (index >= 0) And (index < m_classNames.Count) Then
            Return CType(m_classNames(index), AClass)
        Else
            Throw New System.IndexOutOfRangeException( _
            "Index must be between 0 and " & _
            m_classNames.Count.ToString() & ".")
        End If
    End Get
    'Set(ByVal Value As AClass)
    '    If (index >= 0) And (index < m_classNames.Count) Then
    '        m_classNames(index) = Value
    '    Else
```

```
'           Throw New System.IndexOutOfRangeException( _
'               "Index must be between 0 and " & _
'               m_classNames.Count.ToString() & ".")
'       End If
'   'End Set
End Property
```

To create a default property in Visual Basic, add the *Default* keyword to the property declaration. Default properties in Visual Basic must have at least one parameter. You can have more than one parameter, and those parameters can be of any type. Only one property in a class can have the *Default* keyword.

When a property is a default property, you use it by following the instance name with the index in parentheses. You don't need to include the property name. Note that your code is responsible for checking that the index value from the client code is valid.

This property is read-only. The setter method is shown in comments as an example of implementing a property setter.

2 If you're using Visual C#, add the following indexer:

```
// Visual C#
public AClass this[int indexer] {
    get {
        if ((indexer >= 0) && (indexer < m_classNames.Count))
            return (AClass)m_classNames[indexer];
        else
            throw new System.Exception("Index must be between 0 and "
            + m_classNames.Count.ToString() + ".");
    }
    //set {
    //    m_classNames[indexer] = value;
    //}
}
```

The C# indexer doesn't have a name. Instead, you specify it by using the *this* keyword. If you're using Visual Basic, you can access the default property with or without the property name, but there's no property name for a C# indexer. You can access the indexed value only by indexing the instance name.

The C# indexer requires no special keyword for a read-only indexer. You obtain the meaning in context. The setter method is shown in comments in the code listing to demonstrate how a setter would be implemented. As in the Visual Basic example, your code is responsible for checking the validity of the indexer value.

Add the LinesOfCode and Count properties

1   Add this code for the LinesOfCode property:

```
' Visual Basic
Public ReadOnly Property LinesOfCode() As Integer
    Get
        Return m_linesOfCode
    End Get
End Property
```

```
// Visual C#
public int LinesOfCode {
    get { return m_linesOfCode; }
}
```

2   Add this code for the Count property. When you implemented the SourceFile class, you named this property ClassCount. In this case, a reader already knows you are working with a group of classes. The word *Class* would be redundant: *Classes.ClassCount*. So, you use Count: *Classes.Count*.

```
' Visual Basic
Public ReadOnly Property Count() As Integer
    Get
        Return m_classNames.Count
    End Get
End Property
```

```
' Visual Basic
public int Count {
    get { return m_classNames.Count; }
}
```

The classes are complete.

Creating the User Interface

You'll need to add some controls to the form for testing the classes.

Place the controls on the form

1   Drag a DataGrid control onto Form1 and set the Name property to *listOfFiles*.

2   Drag a Button control onto Form1. Set its Name property to *browse* and its *Text* property to *Browse*. You'll use this button to browse for a source file that you want to analyze.

3   Drag a Label control onto Form1. Set its Name property to *linesOfCode* and its Text property to *Lines of code*. You'll use this label to display the cumulative lines of code in all the files you analyze.

4 Drag an OpenFileDialog control onto Form1. It will be displayed in the component tray. Set its Name property to *openSourceFile*. Here's the complete user interface:

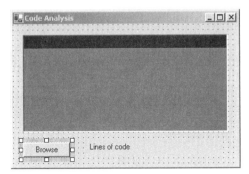

Write the *DisplayClasses* method

1 In the Solution Explorer window, right-click Form1 and click View Code on the shortcut menu.

2 Add this declaration of one instance of the Classes class:

```
' Visual Basic
Private m_classes As New Classes()
```

```
// Visual C#
private Classes m_classes = new Classes();
```

You need only one instance of the Classes class because it contains multiple instance of the AClass class. Also note that no instances of AClass are created by the code in the form. The instances of AClass are created only by means of the *ReadFromFile* method of Classes.

3 Add the following method to the Form1 class. Note that this is a private method of the Form1 class. You can call this method only by code within the Form1 class. It's a helper function for displaying the classes.

```
' Visual Basic
Private Sub DisplayClasses()
    Dim classes(m_classes.Count) As AClass
    Dim i As Integer
    For i = 0 To m_classes.Count - 1
        ' Using the default property
        classes(i) = m_classes(i)
    Next
    listOfFiles.DataSource = classes
    linesOfCode.Text = _
```

(continued)

```
            "Lines of code:    " & m_classes.LinesOfCode.ToString()
End Sub

// Visual C#
private void DisplayClasses() {
    AClass[] classes = new AClass[m_classes.Count];
    for (int i = 0; i < m_classes.Count; i++ ) {
        // Using the indexer
        classes[i] = m_classes[i];
    }
    this.listOfFiles.DataSource = classes;
    linesOfCode.Text =
        "Lines of code: " + m_classes.LinesOfCode.ToString();
}
```

In this example, the AClass instances of *m_Classes* are placed in an array that's used as the data source for the DataGrid control. As in the first implementation, the public properties of AClass are used as the column headings.

Note the use of the default property and indexer. You don't need to use the name of the property. Simply typing in the indexing character, *(* in Visual Basic or *[* in Visual C#, prompts IntelliSense to display the default property or indexer signature.

tip

When you're using an indexer, it needs to make sense. In the .NET Framework, you typically find indexers on properties whose names are plurals, such as the Rows property of a table, which is a collection of Row objects. It wouldn't make sense to use an indexer on a Dog class that returned a Leg object!

Program the Browse button

1   In the form designer, double-click the Browse button to create the Click event method in the code editor. Add the following code to the Click event method.

```
' Visual Basic
Private Sub browse_Click(ByVal sender As System.Object, _
ByVal e As System.EventArgs) Handles browse.Click

End Sub

// Visual C#
private void browse_Click(object sender, System.EventArgs e) {
}
```

2 Add this code to the Click event method to prompt the user for a file and parse it into the *m_classes* object.

```
' Visual Basic
Try
    openSourceFile.Filter = "Visual Basic files (*.vb)|*.vb"
    Dim result As System.Windows.Forms.DialogResult
    ' If user selected a file, create a SourceFile from it.
    result = openSourceFile.ShowDialog()
    If (result = DialogResult.OK) Then
        m_classes.ReadFromFile(openSourceFile.FileName)
    End If
    DisplayClasses()
Catch ex As System.Exception
    MessageBox.Show(ex.Message)
End Try
```

```
// Visual C#
try {
    openSourceFile.Filter = "Visual C# files (*.cs)|*.cs";
    System.Windows.Forms.DialogResult result;
    result = openSourceFile.ShowDialog();
    if (result == System.Windows.Forms.DialogResult.OK) {
        m_classes.ReadFromFile(openSourceFile.FileName);
    }
    DisplayClasses();
}
catch (System.Exception ex) {
    MessageBox.Show(ex.Message);
}
```

Test the program

1 Press F5 to run the program.

2 Click Browse, and in the Open dialog box navigate to the source files for the project. Select a source file, and click Open.

3 Add some empty classes to the source file to further test the application. An example is shown here.

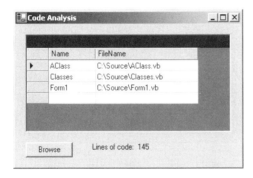

Quick Reference

To	Do this
Create a read-write property	In Visual Basic, the syntax is

```
Public Property Name() As String
    Get
        ' Return a value here.
    End Get
    Set(ByVal Value As String)
        ' Set a value here.
    End Set
End Property
```

In C#, the syntax is

```
public string Name {
    get {
        // Return a value here.
    }
    set {
        // Set a value here.
    }
}
```

Or

Use the C# Property Wizard.

| Create a read-only property | In Visual Basic, the syntax is |

```
Public ReadOnly Property Name() As String
    Get
        ' Return a value here.
    End Get
End Property
```

In C#, the syntax is

```
public string Name {
    get {
        // Return a value here.
    }
}
```

Or

Use the C# Property Wizard.

| Create a write-only property | In Visual Basic, the syntax is |

```
Public WriteOnly Property Name() As String
    Set(ByVal Value As String)
        ' Set a value here.
    End Set
End Property
```

To	Do this
	In C#, the syntax is

	<pre>public string Name {
	    set {
	        // Set a value here.
	    }
	}</pre>

	Or
	Use the C# Property Wizard.
Create a property that takes a parameter (Visual Basic only)	In Visual Basic, the syntax is

	<pre>Public Property Classes(ByVal index As Integer)
	    Get
	        ' Return a value, based on index
	    End Get
	    Set(ByVal Value)
	        ' Set a value, based on index
	    End Set
	End Property</pre>

Create documentation comments for Visual C# properties	Add this comment immediately before the property declaration:

	<pre>/// <summary>
	/// Returns the full path of the source file.
	/// </summary>
	public string FullPath {
	    get { return m_fullPath; }
	}</pre>

Use an array of class instances as a data source in a DataGrid control	Create an array of class instances, and then set the *DataSource* property of the DataGrid to the array. In Visual Basic

	<pre>Private m_sourceFiles(MaxFiles) _
	    As SourceFile
	listOfFiles.DataSource = m_sourceFiles</pre>

	In Visual C#

	<pre>private SourceFile[] m_sourceFiles =
	    new SourceFile[MaxFiles];
	listOfFiles.DataSource = m_sourceFiles;</pre>

Create a C# indexer	The syntax is

	<pre>public AClass this[int indexer] {
	    get {
	        // Return a value here.
	    }
	    set {
	        // Set a value here.
	    }
	}</pre>

(continued)

To	Do this
Create a Visual Basic default property	The syntax is

```
Default Public ReadOnly Property Classes_
    (ByVal index As Integer) As AClass
    Get
        ' Return a value here.
    End Get
    Set(ByVal Value As AClass)
        ' Set a value here.
    End Set
End Property
```

4

Working with Methods

In this chapter, you'll learn how to

- ✔ *Create a private method.*
- ✔ *Create an overloaded method.*
- ✔ *Add a control to a form at run time.*
- ✔ *Use the Randomize and ArrayList classes.*
- ✔ *Perform drag-and-drop operations.*

**ESTIMATED
TIME
3 hr.**

In previous chapters, the classes you created were heavy on properties, and most of the work of the class was done in the constructor to initialize the properties. In this chapter, you'll explore a range of behaviors that objects can display. You'll create a class that has a private method, which is used by the class but not available to client code. You'll create an overloaded method, which is a method that can take more than one set of arguments. Finally, in testing the classes you develop, you'll add a control to a form at run time, rather than in the form designer.

A Deck of Cards

In this chapter, you'll build three classes to represent the actions of manipulating a deck of playing cards, and you'll build an application to test these classes. This deck of cards has no particular application but will provide properties and methods that any of several card games might use. Because you don't have a specific application to target, you'll implement a set of methods extensive enough to be useful. At the same time, you must be careful not to add methods that aren't really part of the abstraction of the class.

The first class, Card, represents one playing card. This class has only two properties, Suit (Hearts, Clubs, Spades, or Diamonds) and Value (Ace, King, Queen, and so on). This class also has a constructor.

The second class is Hand, representing the cards held by one player in a game. You'll want to be able to deal cards to a hand, find and remove pairs of cards in a hand, add cards to a hand, or remove cards from a hand.

The third class, Deck, represents a deck of cards. The methods and properties of this class mimic the ways that you use a deck of cards in a game. You might want to start with the standard 52-card deck or with a deck limited to certain suits or values. For most card games, you will shuffle the deck. You might want to remove one card or add an extra card. In most games, you'll also want to deal the cards to players. The classes are shown in the following table.

Class	Properties	Methods
Card	Suit	Constructor
	Value	
Hand	Count	Constructor
		Indexer
		Add
		FindAndRemovePairs
		Contains
		Remove
Deck	Count	Constructor
		Shuffle
		Deal
		Draw

Considerations in Designing Reusable Classes

When you design reusable classes, certain concepts are important to keep in mind. Some of these are object-oriented concepts, while some are general programming concepts.

Containment   You won't know what kind of object is hosting the class. Your Deck class could be a field in a Game class, a Microsoft Windows Form class, or a custom control. Therefore, you want to be careful not to make any assumptions about the context of the Deck class. Although you'll develop the Deck class in the context of a Windows application, the Deck class won't contain any references to a form.

You might want to add behavior that's dependent on the client code. For example, you might want to add code that draws the card. You could add a method that takes an argument to specify a form to draw on. However, you could also add a method that takes a .NET Framework Graphics object. This would allow you to write code to draw the card on any object that can create a Graphics object, and your object would be usable across a wider client base.

Abstraction   Be clear about your abstraction; a class should do one thing well. It's tempting to add a lot of support functions when you're designing a reusable class. Yet every method, property, and event that you add to the interface limits your choices in implementation, making it more difficult for the class to do one job well. A clear abstraction is easier for developers to use correctly because the properties and methods make sense and the behavior is predictable.

Interface   Provide a complete interface but don't go overboard. Implement the interface well enough so that the next developer can extend it. For example, the Hand class you implement in this chapter has a method to remove pairs. You could also add a method to remove runs of cards—for example, the Jack, Queen, and King of Hearts. However, you could instead create a new class, based on the Hand class. Because the Hand class exposes all the cards through an indexer and provides a *Remove* method, you can implement the method to remove the run of cards in the new extended class.

Client code   Well-designed classes streamline the client code. Much of the looping and decision structures are contained in the class methods rather than in the client code. The method calls are marked by an absence of arguments because the class encapsulates the information needed to execute the method.

In this chapter, you'll create a Deck class that has a parameterless constructor to create the standard 52-card deck. The Deck class will have a *deal* method that takes an array of Hand instances to which to deal the cards. Dealing cards to two hands is straightforward and even reads like a problem: get a deck, shuffle it, find a couple of players, and deal the cards to the players.

```
' Visual Basic
Dim aDeck As New Deck()
aDeck.Shuffle()
hand1 = New Hand()
hand2 = New Hand()
aDeck.Deal(New Hand() {hand1, hand2})

// Visual C#
Deck aDeck = new Deck();
aDeck.Shuffle();
hand1 = new Hand();
hand2 = new Hand();
aDeck.Deal(new Hand[] {hand1, hand2});
```

Creating the Card Class

The first class to implement is the Card class, because the Hand and Deck classes can't exist without the Card class. You'll run into fewer compilation errors by implementing the Card class first.

Create the class

1   Create a new project and name it *DeckOfCards*.

2   On the Project menu, click Add Class. The Add New Item dialog box appears.

3   Name the file Card.vb or Card.cs, depending on the language you're using.

The suit and value of the card will be based on enumerations.

Create the enumerations

1   Add the following code for the Suit enumeration. If you're using Visual Basic, add the code to Card.vb before the Card class block. This enumeration is declared outside the Card class. If you're using Visual C#, add this code before the Card class block and within the DeckOfCards namespace block. If you define the Suit enumeration within the Card class, the Suit property will collide with the Suit enumeration.

```
' Visual Basic
Public Enum Suit
    Hearts
    Diamonds
```

```
        Clubs
        Spades
End Enum

// Visual C#
public enum Suit {
    Hearts,
    Diamonds,
    Spades,
    Clubs,
}
```

2   Add the following code after the Suit enumeration for the FaceValue enumeration:

```
' Visual Basic
    Public Enum FaceValue
            Ace
            One
            Two
            Three
            Four
            Five
            Six
            Seven
            Eight
            Nine
            Ten
            Jack
            Queen
            King
    End Enum

// Visual C#
public enum FaceValue {
    Ace, Two, Three, Four, Five, Six, Seven,
    Eight, Nine, Ten, Jack, Queen, King
}
```

Create the fields and properties

1   Add the following code for the Suit property:

```
' Visual Basic
Private m_suit As Suit
Public Property Suit() As Suit
    Get
        Return m_suit
    End Get
```

(continued)

```
        Set(ByVal Value As Suit)
            m_suit = Value
        End Set
End Property

// Visual C#
private Suit m_suit;
public Suit Suit {
    get { return m_suit; }
    set { m_suit = value; }
}
```

2   Add the following code for the FaceValue property:

```
' Visual Basic
Private m_faceValue As FaceValue
Public Property FaceValue() As FaceValue
    Get
        Return m_faceValue
    End Get
    Set(ByVal Value As FaceValue)
        m_faceValue = Value
    End Set
End Property

// Visual C#
private FaceValue m_faceValue;
public FaceValue FaceValue {
    get { return m_faceValue; }
    set { m_faceValue = value; }
}
```

Create the constructor

●   Add the following code for the constructor:

```
' Visual Basic
Public Sub New(ByVal newSuit As Suit, ByVal newValue As FaceValue)
    m_suit = newSuit
    m_faceValue = newValue
End Sub

// Visual C#
public Card(Suit newSuit, FaceValue newValue) {
    m_suit = newSuit;
    m_faceValue = newValue;
}
```

That completes the Card class. The Card class itself isn't terribly interesting, but what you can do with a group of cards is. You can work with a whole deck, shuffling, sorting, and dealing. You can also work with a small collection of cards (a hand), adding and removing cards and finding and removing pairs.

Creating the Hand Class

Because the Deck class uses the Hand class, you'll create the Hand class next. That way, you'll won't run into compilation errors by using the Hand class before it's been defined.

Create the class and constructors

1   On the Project menu, click Add Class. The Add New Item dialog box appears.

2   Name the file Hand.vb or Hand.cs, depending on the language you're using.

3   Add the following constructors for the Hand class. A new hand could start out without cards or with an array of cards. The cards are contained in an ArrayList object. (The parameterless constructor for C# is created with the source file.)

```
' Visual Basic
Private m_cards As New System.Collections.ArrayList()

Public Sub New()
End Sub

Public Sub New(ByVal cards() As Card)
    m_cards.AddRange(cards)
End Sub

// Visual C#
private System.Collections.ArrayList m_cards =
    new System.Collections.ArrayList();
public Hand() {
}

public Hand(Card[] cards) {
    m_cards.AddRange(cards);
}
```

Create the fields and properties

1   Add the following code to return the count of the cards in the hand. The value must be passed out of the class through a property because *m_cards* is a private member of the Hand class.

```
' Visual Basic
Public ReadOnly Property Count() As Integer
```

(continued)

```
    Get
        Return m_cards.Count
    End Get
End Property

// Visual C#
public int Count {
    get { return m_cards.Count; }
}
```

2   Add the following code to create a default property or indexer for the class:

```
' Visual Basic
Default Public ReadOnly Property Cards(ByVal indexer As Integer) As Card
    Get
        Return CType(m_cards(indexer), Card)
    End Get
End Property

// Visual C#
public Card this[int indexer] {
    get { return (Card)m_cards[indexer]; }
}
```

This code gives you a way to examine each card in the hand, in case you wanted to create a user interface, for example. Using an indexer allows you to iterate through the private collection of cards using an integer index. You have probably also iterated through collections using the *For Each* or *foreach* control structure. Because the *m_cards* ArrayList is private in the class, it isn't available for iteration in the client code. In Chapter 9, you see how the Hand class could also support the *For Each* and *foreach* control structures.

The value returned by *m_cards(indexer)* is a *System.Object* object. You must cast this object to the Card type to have access to the Suit and FaceValue properties.

Casting from a Collection Class

ArrayList is another of the collection types provided by the .NET Framework. These collections are powerful because they can contain any type of object. The disadvantage of using collections is that they aren't type-safe; one collection could be holding several different types of objects. When you cast the object that you retrieve from the collection, you're counting on it being of a particular type. In Chapter 6, you see how you can specialize the ArrayList class (or other collection class) using inheritance to guarantee that only one type of object is added and removed from it.

3   Add this method to add cards to the hand:

```vb
' Visual Basic
Public Sub Add(newCard As Card)
    m_cards.Add(newCard)
End Sub
```

```csharp
// Visual C#
public void Add(Card newCard) {
    m_cards.Add(newCard);
}
```

Create the overloaded methods *Contains* and *Remove*

1   Add this *Contains* method to determine whether a particular instance of Card is contained in the Hand:

```vb
' Visual Basic
Public Function Contains(ByVal cardToFind As Card) As Boolean
    Return m_cards.Contains(cardToFind)
End Function
```

```csharp
// Visual C#
public bool Contains(Card cardToFind) {
    return m_cards.Contains(cardToFind);
}
```

2   Add this second *Contains* method to determine whether a card of a given suit and value exists in the Hand:

```vb
' Visual Basic
Public Function Contains(ByVal suitToFind As Suit, _
ByVal valueToFind As FaceValue) As Boolean
    Dim found As Boolean = False
    Dim aCard As Card
    Dim i As Integer
    For i = 0 To m_cards.Count - 1
        aCard = CType(m_cards(i), Card)
        If ((aCard.Suit = suitToFind) And _
        (aCard.FaceValue = valueToFind)) Then
            found = True
        End If
    Next
    Return found
End Function
```

```csharp
// Visual C#
public bool Contains(Suit suitToFind, FaceValue valueToFind) {
    bool found = false;
```

(continued)

Working with Methods

4

```
        Card aCard;
        for (int i = 0; i < m_cards.Count; i++) {
            aCard = (Card)m_cards[i];
            if ((aCard.Suit == suitToFind) &&
            (aCard.FaceValue == valueToFind)) {
                found = true;
            }
        }
        return found;
    }
```

These two methods both search the hand for a particular card. In the first method, the algorithm looks for a particular instance of Card. Thus it has only one parameter, which is of type Card. The *ArrayList.Contains* method determines whether a reference to that instance is contained in the collection. The second method asks where a card with a particular suit and value is in the deck. This method answers the question, "Is there a ten of diamonds in your hand?" You don't particularly care which instance represents the ten of diamonds—you just want to know if there is one.

The *Contains* method is said to be *overloaded*, which means that you have two methods with the same name but different parameter lists. The compiler can determine which method to call by examing the argument list when the method is called. For the compiler to be able to select the correct overload, the methods must differ by more than the return type.

Using overloaded methods simplifies the class interface. Instead of *ContainsCard* and *ContainsSuitValue* methods, you need only one method, *Contains*.

3   Add these overloaded methods for the *Remove* method:

```
' Visual Basic
Public Sub Remove(ByVal cardToRemove As Card)
    If (m_cards.Contains(cardToRemove)) Then
        m_cards.Remove(cardToRemove)
    End If
End Sub

Public Sub Remove(ByVal suitToRemove As Suit, _
ByVal valueToRemove As FaceValue)
    Dim aCard As Card
    Dim i As Integer
    For i = 0 To m_cards.Count - 1
        aCard = CType(m_cards(i), Card)
        If ((aCard.Suit = suitToRemove) And _
        (aCard.FaceValue = valueToRemove)) Then
            m_cards.Remove(aCard)
            Exit For
        End If
```

```
        Next
    End Sub

    // Visual C#
    public void Remove(Suit suitToFind, FaceValue valueToFind) {
        Card aCard;
        for (int i = 0; i < m_cards.Count; i++) {
            aCard = (Card)m_cards[i];
            if ((aCard.Suit == suitToFind) &&
            (aCard.FaceValue == valueToFind)) {
                m_cards.Remove(aCard);
                break;
            }
        }
    }

    public void Remove(Card cardToRemove) {
        if (m_cards.Contains(cardToRemove)) {
            m_cards.Remove(cardToRemove);
        }
    }
```

Add the *RemovedPairs* method

● Add this method to eliminate all the pairs in a hand:

```
' Visual Basic
Public Sub RemovePairs()
    Dim findMatch, possibleMatch As Card
    Dim found As Boolean
    Dim noMatches As New System.Collections.ArrayList()
    Dim i As Integer

    While (m_cards.Count > 0)
        findMatch = CType(m_cards(0), Card)
        found = False
        For i = 1 To m_cards.Count - 1
            possibleMatch = CType(m_cards(i), Card)
            If (possibleMatch.FaceValue = findMatch.FaceValue) Then
                found = True
                m_cards.Remove(findMatch)
                m_cards.Remove(possibleMatch)
                Exit For
            End If
        Next
        If Not found Then
            noMatches.Add(findMatch)
            m_cards.Remove(findMatch)
```

(continued)

```
        End If
    End While
    m_cards = noMatches
End Sub

// Visual C#
public void RemovePairs() {
    Card findMatch, possibleMatch = null;
    bool found;
    System.Collections.ArrayList noMatches =
        new System.Collections.ArrayList();
    while (m_cards.Count > 0) {
        findMatch = (Card)m_cards[0];
        found = false;
        for (int i = 1; i < m_cards.Count; i++) {
            possibleMatch = (Card)m_cards[i];
            if (possibleMatch.FaceValue == findMatch.FaceValue) {
                found = true;
                m_cards.Remove(findMatch);
                m_cards.Remove(possibleMatch);
                break;
            }
        }
        if (! found) {
            noMatches.Add(findMatch);
            m_cards.Remove(findMatch);
        }
    }
    m_cards = noMatches;
}
```

The algorithm for the *RemovePairs* method can be described this way:

- Add an ArrayList class for the cards that don't have a match.
- Look at each card in the hand.
- Look in the rest of the hand for a match, based on *FaceValue*.
- If you find a match, remove both cards from the hand.
- If no match is found, remove the card from the hand and put it in the ArrayList for cards without a match.
- When all the cards have been examimed, the ArrayList for cards without a match is the resulting hand.
- Assign the *m_cards* field to the ArrayList for cards without a match. Because *m_cards* is a reference value, you can simply assign the reference to the new ArrayList.

Testing the Hand Class

Having completed the Card and Hand classes, you've implemented a fair amount of functionality. Before you go any further, it's a good idea to try out the new classes before integrating them with the rest of the program. You've probably done this before by creating a form, maybe adding a button or a label, and writing a short program to test the class. In Visual Basic and Visual C#, you can build some test code right into the class, using a *Shared Main* method in Visual Basic or a *static Main* method in Visual C#. Adding some test code to the class has some advantages:

- It doesn't intefere with the readability of the rest of your program. Because the code is in the class, it's not sitting in your application's main form.

- When you create classes in a *Main* method in your class definition, you have access to the private members of the class.

- It's always available. When you put an extra button on your user interface to do some testing, you then have to remove the button. When something changes and you want to retest, the button is gone and you have to add it again. With the test code in your class, it's available to run again whenever you need it.

- It's easy to rerun your test when you make changes to the class. When you have made these changes, you'll want to make sure that you didn't break something in the process. With a well-planned set of tests, you can quickly determine whether the old code is still working with the new code.

What should you test?

- Test each property and method.
- Test the constructor.
- Test any behavior that's based on a boundary. For example, test that your indexer method fails gracefully if the client code tries to retrieve a value that doesn't exist.
- Test any behavior that's based on a decision. If you have a method that does two different things depending on whether the third parameter is true or false, test the method with true and with false.

■ Test the parameters of your methods. If you're expecting a string parameter to have a particular format, make sure your method handles a well-formed string properly and that it rejects a string that isn't well formed.

Add the *Main* method

● Add this method to the Hand class:

```vbnet
Public Shared Sub Main()
    Console.WriteLine("Visual Basic Hand Test")
    Dim queenOfHearts As New Card(Suit.Hearts, FaceValue.Queen)
    Dim twoOfClubs As New Card(Suit.Clubs, FaceValue.Two)
    ' Test: Add(Card[])
    Dim aHand As New Hand(New Card() {queenOfHearts, twoOfClubs})
    ' Test: Contains(Card)        Expect: True
    Console.WriteLine( _
        "Hand contains queenOfHearts: {0}.", _
        aHand.Contains(queenOfHearts))
    ' Test: Contains(Suit, Value) Expect: True
    Console.WriteLine("Hand contains Queeen of Hearts: {0}.", _
        aHand.Contains(Suit.Hearts, FaceValue.Queen))
    ' Test: Contains(Card)        Expect: False
    Console.WriteLine("Hand contains new queenOfHearts: {0}.", _
        aHand.Contains(New Card(Suit.Hearts, FaceValue.Queen)))

    aHand.Remove(queenOfHearts)
    ' Test: Remove(Card)          Expect: False
    Console.WriteLine("Hand contains Queeen of Hearts: {0}.", _
        aHand.Contains(Suit.Hearts, FaceValue.Queen))

    Dim pair As New Hand()
    ' Test: Add(Suit, Value)
    pair.Add(New Card(Suit.Diamonds, FaceValue.Ace))
    pair.Add(New Card(Suit.Clubs, FaceValue.Ace))
    ' Test: Count Expect: 2 cards
    Console.WriteLine("Pair has {0} cards.", pair.Count)
    pair.RemovePairs()
    ' Test: Remove Pairs Expect: 0 cards
    Console.WriteLine("After RemovePairs, Pair has {0} cards.", pair.Count)
End Sub

// Visual C#
public static void Main() {
    Card queenOfHearts = new Card(Suit.Hearts, FaceValue.Queen);
    Card twoOfClubs = new Card(Suit.Clubs, FaceValue.Two);
```

```
// Test: Add(Card[])
Hand aHand = new Hand(new Card[] { queenOfHearts, twoOfClubs });
// Test: Contains(Card)        Expect: True
Console.WriteLine(
    "Hand contains queenOfHearts: {0}.",
    aHand.Contains(queenOfHearts));
// Test: Contains(Suit, Value) Expect: True
Console.WriteLine("Hand contains Queeen of Hearts: {0}.",
    aHand.Contains(Suit.Hearts, FaceValue.Queen));
// Test: Contains(Card)        Expect: False
Console.WriteLine("Hand contains new queenOfHearts: {0}.",
    aHand.Contains(new Card(Suit.Hearts,FaceValue.Queen)));

// Test: Remove(Card)          Expect: False
aHand.Remove(queenOfHearts);
Console.WriteLine("Hand contains Queeen of Hearts: {0}.",
    aHand.Contains(Suit.Hearts, FaceValue.Queen));

Hand pair = new Hand();
// Test: Add(Suit, Value)
pair.Add(new Card(Suit.Diamonds, FaceValue.Ace));
pair.Add(new Card(Suit.Clubs, FaceValue.Ace));
// Test: Count Expect: 2 cards
Console.WriteLine("Pair has {0} cards.", pair.Count);
pair.RemovePairs();
// Test: Remove Pairs Expect: 0 cards
Console.WriteLine("After RemovePairs, Pair has {0} cards.",
    pair.Count);
}
```

This method doesn't do anything complicated, but it does act in these ways:

- It uses the constructors for Card and Hand.
- It uses the Suit and FaceValue enumerations.
- It tests the *Add, Contains, Remove,* and *RemovePairs* methods of the Hand class.

The *Main* methods here are declared with the *Shared* or *static* modifier. These methods are class members that aren't associated with any particular instance of the class. Thus they can be called even before any instance of the class is created. When a program begins execution, no instances of any class exist. These shared and static methods can therefore be called as soon as the program starts up. In fact, each C# program is required to have such a start-up method. Visual Basic has options for starting programs. The *Shared* and *static* keywords will be discussed at length in Chapter 11, "Using Shared and Static Members."

The results of the tests are written to the Console object and appear in the Output window during execution of the program.

Change the project properties

1   In the Solution Explorer, right-click the project name and click Properties on the shortcut menu. The project's Property Pages dialog box appears, as you see here.

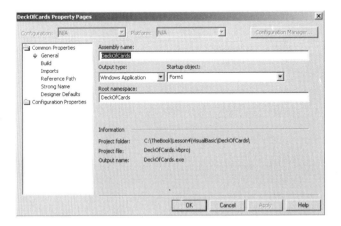

2   In the properties tree, expand the Common Properties folder if necessary and, click General.

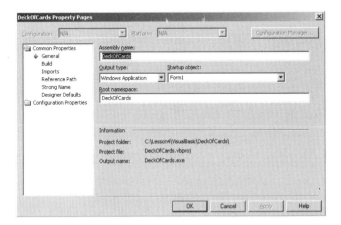

3   In the Startup Object list, click Hand and then click OK.

4   Press F5 to run the application. Here are the results:

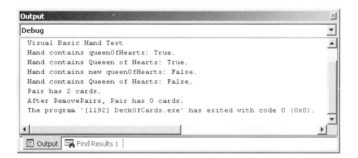

Creating the Deck Class

The methods of the Deck class correspond closely to the real-world uses of a deck of cards: shuffle, deal, and draw.

Create the class

1 On the Project menu, click Add Class. The Add New Item dialog box appears.

2 Name the file Deck.vb or Deck.cs, depending on the language you're using.

Create the fields and properties

1 Add the following code for the Count property. The Count property returns the number of cards in the deck. The cards are stored in an instance of the ArrayList class. This class accepts objects of any type and allows access to members by an index value. New members can be added to the ArrayList class without your having to resize the list. The value of the Count property is determined by the number of cards in the deck. Therefore, Count is a read-only property.

```
' Visual Basic
Private m_cards As New System.Collections.ArrayList()
Public ReadOnly Property Count() As Integer
    Get
        Return m_cards.Count
    End Get
End Property

// Visual C#
private System.Collections.ArrayList m_cards =
    new System.Collections.ArrayList();
public int Count {
    get { return m_cards.Count; }
}
```

2   Add the following default property or indexer to return a specific card from the ArrayList, based on an index:

```vb
' Visual Basic
Default Public ReadOnly Property Cards(ByVal indexer As Integer) As Card
    Get
        If ((indexer >= 0) And (indexer < m_cards.Count)) Then
            Return CType(m_cards(indexer), Card)
        Else
            Throw New ArgumentOutOfRangeException("Index out of range.")
        End If
    End Get
End Property
```

```csharp
// Visual C#
public Card this[int indexer] {
    get {
        if ((indexer >= 0) && (indexer < m_cards.Count)) {
            return((Card)m_cards[indexer]);
        }
        else {
            throw new ArgumentOutOfRangeException("Index out of range.");
        }
    }
}
```

Now that you have a container for your cards, you can implement the constructors. You'll implement two constructors: one that creates the standard 52-card deck and one that creates a custom deck.

Create the constructors

1   Add this private method to create a deck of cards:

```vb
' Visual Basic
Private Sub MakeDeck(ByVal suits() As Suit, ByVal values() As FaceValue)
    Dim aSuit, aValue As Integer
    Dim newValue As FaceValue
    Dim newSuit As Suit
    Dim newCard As Card

    For aSuit = 0 To suits.Length - 1
        For aValue = 0 To values.Length - 1
            newSuit = suits(aSuit)                  ' Select a suit.
            newValue = values(aValue)               ' Select a value.
            newCard = New Card(newSuit, newValue)   ' Create a card.
            m_cards.Add(newcard)                    ' Add the card.
            ' You can replace the four preceding lines with this:
```

```
          ' m_cards.Add(New Card(suits(aSuit), values(aValue)))
       Next
    Next
End Sub

// Visual C#
private void MakeDeck(Suit[] suits, FaceValue[] values) {
    for (int aSuit = 0; aSuit < suits.Length; aSuit++) {
        for (int aValue = 0; aValue < values.Length; aValue++) {
            m_cards.Add(new Card(suits[aSuit], values[aValue]));
        }
    }
}
```

This method pairs each suit listed in the suits array with each value in the values array. A card is created for each suit/value pair. The Visual Basic method is verbose and shows the following steps:

■ Select one of the suits.

■ Select one of the values.

■ Create a card with that suit and value.

■ Add the card to the ArrayList object.

2 Add the following constructor to create a 52-card deck:

```
' Visual Basic
Public Sub New()
    Dim suits() As Suit = {Suit.Clubs, Suit.Diamonds, Suit.Hearts, _
        Suit.Spades}
    Dim values() As FaceValue = {FaceValue.Ace, FaceValue.Two, _
        FaceValue.Three, FaceValue.Four, FaceValue.Five, _
        FaceValue.Six, FaceValue.Seven, FaceValue.Eight, _
        FaceValue.Nine, FaceValue.Ten, FaceValue.Jack, _
        FaceValue.Queen, FaceValue.King}
    Me.MakeDeck(suits, values)
End Sub

// Visual C#
public Deck()
{
    Suit[] suits = { Suit.Clubs, Suit.Diamonds, Suit.Hearts,
        Suit.Spades };
    FaceValue[] values = { FaceValue.Ace, FaceValue.Two,
    FaceValue.Three, FaceValue.Four, FaceValue.Five, FaceValue.Six,
    FaceValue.Seven, FaceValue.Eight, FaceValue.Nine, FaceValue.Ten,
    FaceValue.Jack, FaceValue.Queen, FaceValue.King};
    this.MakeDeck(suits, values);
}
```

3 Add the following constructor to allow creation of a custom deck. This method would allow the user to create a deck containing, for example, only face cards, only hearts and diamonds, or even only aces. This method is also useful for testing. It's much easier to test a program with 12 cards than to test a program with 52 cards.

```
' Visual Basic
Public Sub New(ByVal suits() As Suit, ByVal values() As FaceValue)
    Me.MakeDeck(suits, values)
End Sub
```

```
// Visual C#
public Deck(Suit[] suits, FaceValue[] values) {
    this.MakeDeck(suits, values);
}
```

Now that you have a way to fill the deck with cards, you can shuffle and deal the cards.

Create the methods

1 Add the following code for the *Shuffle* method. This method uses the .NET Framework *System.Random* class to shuffle the deck of cards. The algorithm is described in steps 2 through 7 of this procedure.

2 Create a new empty ArrayList object named *newdeck*.

3 Generate a random number between 0 and the last index of the *m_cards* ArrayList object.

4 Use that number as an index to remove one card from *m_cards*.

5 Add that card to the new ArrayList object.

6 Continue removing cards at random from *m_cards* and adding them to newdeck until *m_cards* is empty.

7 Assign the *m_cards* reference to newdeck, which now contains all the cards in a random order.

```
' Visual Basic
Public Sub Shuffle()
    Dim rGen As New System.Random()
    Dim newDeck As New System.Collections.ArrayList()
    While (m_cards.Count > 0)
        ' Choose one card at random to remove.
        Dim removeIndex As Integer = rGen.Next(0, m_cards.Count - 1)
```

```
        Dim removeObject As Object = m_cards(removeIndex)
        m_cards.RemoveAt(removeIndex)
        ' Add the removed card to the new deck.
        newDeck.Add(removeObject)
    End While

    ' replace the old deck with the new deck
    m_cards = newDeck
End Sub

// Visual C#
public void Shuffle() {
    System.Random rGen = new System.Random();
    System.Collections.ArrayList newDeck =
        new System.Collections.ArrayList();
    while (m_cards.Count > 0) {
        // Choose one card at random to remove.
        int toRemove = rGen.Next(0, m_cards.Count - 1);
        Card remove = (Card)m_cards[toRemove];
        m_cards.Remove(remove);
        // Add the removed card to the new deck.
        newDeck.Add(remove);
    }

    // Replace old deck with new deck.
    m_cards = newDeck;
}
```

8   Add the following code for the *Deal* method:

```
' Visual Basic
' The deck is empty after dealing the cards.
Public Sub Deal(ByVal hands() As Hand)
    Dim handIndex As Integer = 0
    While (m_cards.Count > 0)
        hands(handIndex).Add(CType(m_cards(0), Card))
        m_cards.RemoveAt(0)
        handIndex += 1
        If handIndex = hands.Length Then
            handIndex = 0
        End If
    End While
End Sub
```

(continued)

```
// Visual C#
// The deck is empty after dealing the cards.
public void Deal(Hand[] hands) {
    int handIndex = 0;
    while (m_cards.Count > 0) {
        hands[handIndex].Add((Card)m_cards[0]);
        m_cards.RemoveAt(0);
        handIndex = (handIndex == hands.Length - 1) ? 0 : handIndex+1;
    }
}
```

9   Add this code for the *Draw* method. This method removes the top card from the deck and returns it.

```
' Visual Basic
Public Function Draw() As Card
    Dim topCard As Card = Nothing
    If m_cards.Count > 0 Then
        topCard = CType(m_cards(0), Card)
        m_cards.RemoveAt(0)
    End If
    Return topCard
End Function
```

```
// Visual C#
public Card Draw() {
    Card topCard = null;
    if (m_cards.Count > 0) {
        topCard = (Card)m_cards[0];
        m_cards.RemoveAt(0);
    }
    return topCard;
}
```

The classes are complete. Now you can use the Card, Hand, and Deck classes to write a small application that looks something like a card game.

Writing the Test Application

Static and shared methods are fine for testing classes, but when you use Microsoft Visual Studio you can create some interesting user interfaces without much work. In this small application, you'll create a deck of cards, deal the cards to a couple of hands, and remove the pairs from the hand. You'll display the cards as controls that you can drag from one hand to another. By moving the cards from hand to hand and removing the pairs, you can eliminate all the cards from both hands.

The user interface is shown here:

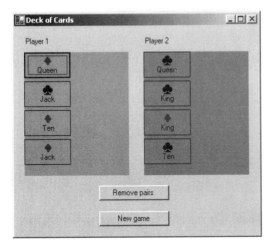

Create the user interface

1   Open Form1 in the designer.

2   Set the Text property of Form1 to *Deck of Cards*.

3   Drag two Panel controls onto Form1. Set the Name property of one to *panel1*. Set the Name of the other to *panel2*. The cards will be displayed as button controls on these panels.

4   Choose a value for the BackColor property for each panel.

5   Set the AutoScroll property of both panels to True. Scroll bars will be automatically added to the panels if there are buttons that can't been seen in the panel.

6   Set the AllowDrop property to True for both panel controls. With the AllowDrop property set to True, the user will be able to drag buttons around the form and drop them on the Panel controls.

7   Add a label above each panel. Set the Text property of one label to *Player 1* and the Text property of the other to *Player 2*. In the code, you'll create two instances of Hand, one for each player, and display the cards in the panel for each player.

8   Add a button to the form. Set the Name property to *removePairs* and the Text property to *Remove pairs*.

9   Add another button to the form. Set the Name property to *newGame* and the Text property to *New game*. Here's the completed user interface:

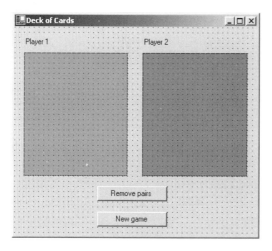

Add icons for the card suits

A directory full of icons is installed with Visual Studio .NET. You can use these icons in your programs by copying them to your project folder.

1   Locate the directory where Visual Studio is installed. Browse to the Common7\Graphics\icons\Misc folder and find the four icons for the card suits. For your convenience, the icons are also included in the \Chapter04 folder on this book's companion CD.

2   Copy the four icons to your project folder.

3   Right-click on Form1, and click View Code on the shortcut menu.

4   Add these fields to the Form1 class. The *m_icons* field will hold a key-indexed collection of Image instances. The hand fields will hold cards for the two players. The Button field will be used in the drag-and-drop operations.

```
' Visual Basic
Private m_icons As New System.Collections.SortedList()
Private m_hand1 As New Hand()
Private m_hand2 As New Hand()
Private m_pickedUp As Button

// Visual C#
private System.Collections.SortedList m_icons = new
    System.Collections.SortedList();
private Hand m_hand1 = new Hand();
```

```
private Hand m_hand2 = new Hand();
private Button m_pickedUp;
```

5   Return to the designer and double-click on the form to create the
Form1_Load event method in the code editor. Add the following code to
load the icon files into the SortedList object. By using the SortedList object,
you can retrieve the proper image using the Suit value of a Card object. You
need to replace the folder shown in the code with the folder for your project.

```
' Visual Basic
Private Sub Form1_Load(ByVal sender As System.Object, _
ByVal e As System.EventArgs) Handles MyBase.Load
    m_icons.Add(Suit.Clubs, Image.FromFile("projectPath\Clubs.ico"))
    m_icons.Add(Suit.Diamonds, Image.FromFile("projectPath\Diamonds.ico"))
    m_icons.Add(Suit.Hearts, Image.FromFile("projectPath\Hearts.ico"))
    m_icons.Add(Suit.Spades, Image.FromFile("projectPath\Spades.ico"))
End Sub
```

```
// Visual C#
private void Form1_Load(object sender, System.EventArgs e) {
    m_icons.Add(Suit.Clubs, Image.FromFile(@"projectPath\Clubs.ico"));
    m_icons.Add(Suit.Diamonds, Image.FromFile(@"projectPath\Diamonds.ico"));
    m_icons.Add(Suit.Hearts, Image.FromFile(@"projectPath\Hearts.ico"));
    m_icons.Add(Suit.Spades, Image.FromFile(@"projectPath\Spades.ico"));
}
```

6   Also add a call to the *SetUp* method, which you will create in the next section. The *SetUp* method creates a deck, deals the cards to the players, and
displays the cards. Add this line of code after the four *m_icons.Add* calls:

```
' Visual Basic
SetUp()
```

```
// Visual C#
SetUp();
```

Create a new deck and deal to the hands

1   Double-click on the New Game button to create the Click event method.
Add a call to the *SetUp* method, which you will create in the next step.

```
' Visual Basic
Private Sub newGame_Click(ByVal sender As System.Object, _
ByVal e As System.EventArgs) Handles newGame.Click
    SetUp()
End Sub
```

(continued)

```csharp
// Visual C#
private void newGame_Click(object sender, System.EventArgs e) {
    SetUp();
}
```

2   Add this code for the *SetUp* method to the Form1 class to create a deck, shuffle it, deal the cards to two hands, and then display the hands on the form. Next you'll write the *ShowHand* method to display the cards.

```vb
' Visual Basic
Private Sub SetUp()
    Dim suits() As Suit = New Suit() {Suit.Diamonds, Suit.Clubs}
    Dim values() As FaceValue = New FaceValue() {FaceValue.King, _
        FaceValue.Queen, FaceValue.Jack, FaceValue.Ten}
    Dim aDeck As New Deck(suits, values)
    aDeck.Shuffle()
    m_hand1 = New Hand()
    m_hand2 = New Hand()
    aDeck.Deal(New Hand() {m_hand1, m_hand2})
    ShowHand(panel1, m_hand1)
    ShowHand(panel2, m_hand2)
End Sub
```

```csharp
// Visual C#
private void SetUp() {
    Deck aDeck = new Deck(
        new Suit[] { Suit.Diamonds, Suit.Clubs },
        new FaceValue[] { FaceValue.King, FaceValue.Queen,
        FaceValue.Jack, FaceValue.Ten });
    aDeck.Shuffle();
    m_hand1 = new Hand();
    m_hand2 = new Hand();
    aDeck.Deal(new Hand[] { m_hand1, m_hand2 });
    ShowHand(panel1, m_hand1);
    ShowHand(panel2, m_hand2);
}
```

This method uses the Deck constructor that takes two parameters. This call creates only eight cards, which will make it easy for you to tell if the program is working correctly. The cards in the deck are dealt to the two hands, and the *ShowHand* method is called to display the cards in the panel.

Display the cards on the form

●   Add this code to display the cards in the hand on the form:

```vb
' Visual Basic
Private Sub ShowHand(ByVal aPanel As Panel, ByVal aHand As Hand)
    aPanel.Controls.Clear()
```

```
Dim aCard As Card
Dim aButton As Button
Dim i As Integer
For i = 0 To aHand.Count - 1
    aCard = aHand(i)

    ' Make the button and add it to the form.
    aButton = New Button()
    aPanel.Controls.Add(aButton)

    With aButton
        ' Modify the appearance of the button.
        .Image = CType(m_icons(aCard.Suit), Image)
        .Text = aCard.FaceValue.ToString()
        .TextAlign = ContentAlignment.BottomCenter
        .ImageAlign = ContentAlignment.TopCenter
        .FlatStyle = FlatStyle.Flat
        .Height = 40
        ' Locate the button on the panel.
        .Top = 45 * i
        ' Save the associated card.
        .Tag = aCard
    End With

    ' Add a MouseDown event to the new button.
    AddHandler aButton.MouseDown, AddressOf ButtonMouseDown
Next
End Sub

// Visual C#
private void ShowHand(Panel aPanel, Hand aHand) {
    aPanel.Controls.Clear();
    Card aCard;
    Button aButton;
    for (int i = 0; i < aHand.Count; i++) {
        aCard = aHand[i];

        // Make the button and add it to the form.
        aButton = new Button();
        aPanel.Controls.Add(aButton);

        //Modify the appearance.
        aButton.Image = (Image)m_icons[aCard.Suit];
        aButton.Text = aCard.FaceValue.ToString();
        aButton.TextAlign = ContentAlignment.BottomCenter;
        aButton.ImageAlign = ContentAlignment.TopCenter;
        aButton.FlatStyle = FlatStyle.Flat;
        aButton.Height = 40;
```

(continued)

```
        // Locate the button on the panel.
        aButton.Top = 45 * i;
        // Save the associated card.
        aButton.Tag = aCard;
        // Add a MouseDown event to the new button.
        aButton.MouseDown += new
            System.Windows.Forms.MouseEventHandler(ButtonMouseDown);
    }
}
```

These 30 lines of code do a lot of work, and an explanation is in order for this method:

1   If there are any controls on the panel, delete them.

2   Using the count and indexer properties of the Hand class, look at each Card instance.

3   Create a new Button object, and add it to the Controls collection of the panel. Any controls added to the panel's Controls collection will be displayed on the panel.

4   Set the Image property of the button from the *m_icons* SortedList object.

5   Set the Text property of the button to the FaceValue of the Card. Enumerated values have an implicitly defined *ToString* method that returns the symbolic name of the enumeration value. For example, *FaceValue.King.ToString()* returns "*King*".

6   Make the button tall enough to hold both the image and the text. Display the image at the top of the button (TopCenter) and the value at the bottom of the button (BottomCenter).

7   Because the buttons are 40 pixels high, display them 45 pixels apart. When there are enough buttons on the panel so that the value of the Top property of one button is larger than the size of the panel, scroll bars will appear.

8   Set the FlatStyle property of the button so that the button is displayed as a flat rectangle instead of a 3-dimensional button.

9   Use the Tag property to associate each button with its Card instance. In Chapter 8, you'll see a more object-oriented way to handle this association by creating a specialized control through inheritance.

10 Associate a method with the MouseDown event of the button. Because the button doesn't exist in the form designer, you can't just click it to create the MouseDown event method. No matter how many cards are created, one method will respond to all the MouseDown events. You'll use the MouseDown event to start the drag-drop functionality.

Add the MouseDown event method to start the drag

A minimum of three steps is required to implement drag-and-drop behaviors:

1   When the user selects a control to move, usually by a mouse click or MouseDown event, call the control's *DoDragDrop* method to start the drag. In this case, the user will be dragging the buttons that represent cards.

2   When the user drags the control over another control, the DragEnter event is raised. In this event, you set the Effect property of the DragEventArgs object to allow dragging. In this case, the user will drag the button controls over the Panel controls.

3   When the user releases the mouse button, the DragDrop event is raised. In this event, perform the result of the drag. In this case, the button will be moved to a different panel.

In the *ShowHand* method, the MouseDown event of each button was assigned to the *ButtonMouseDown* method. Now add this method, as shown here:

```
' Visual Basic
Private Sub ButtonMouseDown(ByVal sender As Object, _
ByVal e As System.Windows.Forms.MouseEventArgs)
    m_pickedUp = CType(sender, Button)
    m_pickedUp.DoDragDrop(sender, DragDropEffects.Move)
End Sub

// Visual C#
private void ButtonMouseDown(object sender,
System.Windows.Forms.MouseEventArgs e) {
    m_pickedUp = (Button)sender;
    ((Button)sender).DoDragDrop(sender,DragDropEffects.Move);
}
```

Enable dragging with the DragOver event

●   Add code to the DragOver events of both panel controls to allow the button being dragged, *m_pickedUp*, to be dropped on the panels:

```
' Visual Basic
Private Sub panel1_DragEnter(ByVal sender As Object, ByVal e _
As System.Windows.Forms.DragEventArgs) Handles panel1.DragEnter
    e.Effect = DragDropEffects.Move
End Sub

Private Sub panel2_DragEnter(ByVal sender As Object, ByVal e _
As System.Windows.Forms.DragEventArgs) Handles panel2.DragEnter
    e.Effect = DragDropEffects.Move
End Sub
```

(continued)

Working with Methods

4

```csharp
// Visual C#
private void panel1_DragEnter(object sender,
System.Windows.Forms.DragEventArgs e) {
    e.Effect = DragDropEffects.Move;
}

private void panel2_DragEnter(object sender,
System.Windows.Forms.DragEventArgs e) {
    e.Effect = DragDropEffects.Move;
}
```

Enable dropping using the DragDrop event

● Add code to the DragDrop events of the Panel controls to move the dragged control to the new panel. Before moving the button, the code checks that the button is being moved to a different panel.

```vb
' Visual Basic
Private Sub panel1_DragDrop(ByVal sender As Object, ByVal e _
As System.Windows.Forms.DragEventArgs) Handles panel1.DragDrop
    Dim theCard As Card = CType(m_pickedUp.Tag, Card)
    If (Not m_hand1.Contains(theCard)) Then
        m_hand1.Add(theCard)
        m_hand2.Remove(theCard)
    End If
    ShowHand(panel1, m_hand1)
    ShowHand(panel2, m_hand2)
    m_pickedUp = Nothing
End Sub

Private Sub panel2_DragDrop(ByVal sender As Object, ByVal e _
As System.Windows.Forms.DragEventArgs) Handles panel2.DragDrop
    Dim theCard As Card = CType(m_pickedUp.Tag, Card)
    If (Not m_hand2.Contains(theCard)) Then
        m_hand2.Add(theCard)
        m_hand1.Remove(theCard)
    End If
    ShowHand(panel1, m_hand1)
    ShowHand(panel2, m_hand2)
    m_pickedUp = Nothing
End Sub
```

```csharp
// Visual C#
private void panel1_DragDrop(object sender,
System.Windows.Forms.DragEventArgs e) {
    Card theCard = (Card)m_pickedUp.Tag;
    if (!m_hand1.Contains(theCard)) {
        m_hand1.Add(theCard);
        m_hand2.Remove(theCard);
    }
```

```
      ShowHand(panel2, m_hand2);
      ShowHand(panel1, m_hand1);
      m_pickedUp = null;
   }

   private void panel2_DragDrop(object sender,
   System.Windows.Forms.DragEventArgs e) {
      Card theCard = (Card) m_pickedUp.Tag;
      if (!m_hand2.Contains(theCard)) {
         m_hand2.Add(theCard);
         m_hand1.Remove(theCard);
      }
      ShowHand(panel2, m_hand2);
      ShowHand(panel1, m_hand1);
      m_pickedUp = null;
   }
```

All that remains now is to program the Remove Pairs button to remove the pairs from the hands and from the form.

Match the cards

● Add code to the Click event of the Remove Pairs button. This code simply calls the *RemovePairs* method for each Hand object and redisplays the Hand objects.

```
' Visual Basic
Private Sub removePairs_Click(ByVal sender As System.Object, ByVal e _
As System.EventArgs) Handles removePairs.Click
    m_hand1.RemovePairs()
    m_hand2.RemovePairs()
    ShowHand(panel2, m_hand2)
    ShowHand(panel1, m_hand1)
End Sub
```

```
// Visual C#
private void removePairs_Click(object sender, System.EventArgs e) {
    m_hand1.RemovePairs();
    m_hand2.RemovePairs();
    ShowHand(panel2, m_hand2);
    ShowHand(panel1, m_hand1);
}
```

Run the application

1 In the Solution Explorer window, right-click the project name and click Properties in the shortcut menu.

2 In the properties tree, expand the Common Properties folder if necessary and select General.

3   In the Startup Object list, click Form1, and click OK.

4   Press F5 to run the application. The following screen shot shows the results after the pairs have been matched. You can clear all the cards by dragging them all to one panel and clicking the Remove Pairs button.

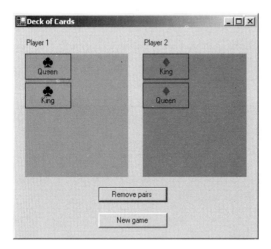

Quick Reference

To	Do this

Create a public method	Add the *Public* or *public* modifier to a class method.
	In Visual Basic
	`Public Sub SomeMethod()`
	`End Sub`
	In Visual C#
	`public void SomeMethod() {}`

Create a private method	Add the *Private* or *private* modifier to a class method.
	In Visual Basic
	`Private Sub SomeMethod()`
	`End Sub`
	In Visual C#
	`Private void SomeMethod() {}`

Create an overloaded method	Create methods with the same name but with different parameter lists. The methods must differ by more than return type.

To	Do this
	In Visual Basic
| | ```
Public Function Add(I as Integer) As Integer
End Function
Public Function Add(I as Integer, J as Integer) As Integer
End Function
``` |
| | In Visual C# |
| | ```
public int Add(int i) { }
public int Add(int i, int j) {}
``` |
| Create a *Main* method as a startup object | First create a *Main* method: |
| | In Visual Basic |
| | ```
Public Shared Sub Main()
End Sub
``` |
| | In Visual C# |
| | ```
public static void Main() {
}
``` |
	Open the project's Property Pages dialog box, and in the Startup Object list on the General page, click the class that contains the *Main* method.
Create a control at run time	Declare a new instance of the control and add it to the form's Controls collection:
	In Visual Basic
| | ```
Dim aButton As New Button()
Me.Controls.Add(aButton)
``` |
| | In Visual C# |
| | ```
Button aButton = new Button();
this.Controls.Add(aButton);
``` |
| Implement drag and drop | Respond to the MouseDown or Click event of the control to be dragged, and call the *DoDragDrop* method. |
| | Set the AllowDrop property to True for the control that will be dropped on to. Respond to the DragEnter and DragDrop events for this control. |

Working with Methods

4

5

Using Inheritance to Create Specialized Classes

ESTIMATED TIME
2 hr. 30 min.

In this chapter, you'll learn how to

✔ *Inherit from a class you develop.*

✔ *Use the Me and this keywords.*

✔ *Use the MyBase and base keywords.*

✔ *Create class fields using the Protected and protected keywords.*

✔ *Create Overridable and virtual methods.*

✔ *Create Overrides and override methods and properties.*

✔ *Create a Windows Forms control using inheritance.*

In the previous chapters, you created a new class for each object in your solution. Starting with an empty class, you added fields, properties, constructors, and methods to implement a fully functional class. Using inheritance, you can create a new class by adding to or otherwise modifying an existing class. In this chapter, you'll create that first class, BankAccount, and then use inheritance to create two specialized classes, SavingsAccount and CheckingAccount. Inheritance isn't limited to classes you create; you can inherit from many of the classes in the Microsoft .NET Framework.

Inheritance: An Overview

In previous chapters, you created classes that contained instances of other classes. These designs model a *has-a* relationship between an object and its properties. A Deck *has-a* Card; a Form *has-a* Button; a SourceFile *has-a* Class. The *has-a* relationship is central to object-oriented design. It allows you to build an application by combining already existing objects. The term used for the *has-a* relationship is *composition*.

Inheritance is the programming method used to implement the *is-a* relationship of object-oriented design. A Button *is-a* Control; a Dog *is-a* Mammal; a Savings-Account *is-a* BankAccount. If you've already written the code to model an account's owner, balance, withdrawal and deposit transactions, you'd like to be able to use that code again. You can do that using inheritance; it allows you to create new classes from existing classes.

You create new classes from the *base class*. You create the *derived class* by adding to or specializing the base class. You could also say that the derived class *inherits from* or *derives from* the base class. Another common terminology uses *superclass* for the base class and *subclass* for the derived class. This book uses the *base* and *derived* terms because these terms more closely match the keywords used in Visual Basic and C# to implement inheritance.

Polymorphism describes the behavior of classes that derive from a common base class. A savings account isn't the only type of bank account. There are also checking accounts, money market accounts, and mutual fund accounts. So Checking, Savings, MoneyMarket, and MutualFund all derive from BankAccount. Polymorphic behavior allows a developer to use a BankAccount variable to refer to any of the derived classes of BankAccount. Polymorphism allows each derived class to handle identical method names with different behavior. For example, both Savings and Checking provide a *Withdraw* method through inheritance, but the Checking class's *Withdraw* method deducts a small service charge along with each withdrawal.

This chapter concentrates on the mechanics of inheritance. Even with rudimentary techniques, you can develop sophisticated results by inheriting from .NET Framework classes. Later chapters develop other aspects of inheritance, such as base class design, polymorphism, and component development.

BankAccount: A Simple Example

The simple bank account provides the basis for this exercise in inheritance. You will implement a BankAccount class as a base class with the following members:

Member	Description
Owner	A string property that identifies the owner of the account.
ID	A read-only string property that identifies the account.
Balance	A read-only decimal property. The value of this property depends on the deposits and withdrawals made to the account.
Deposit	This method takes one parameter: the amount to deposit. It returns the balance after the deposit.
Withdraw	This method takes one parameter: the amount to withdraw. It returns the balance after the withdrawal.
Constructor	The constructor takes one parameter: the account owner's name (a string), to use for the ID property.

Create the base class, BankAccount

1   Create a new project and name it TheBank.

2   On the Project menu, click Add Class. The Add New Item dialog box appears.

3   Name the file BankAccount.vb or BankAccount.cs, depending on the language you're using.

Add the properties and constructor

The account ID is based on the owner's name. In the limited world of this exercise, each person can have only one account, and all names are unique. So the ID is the same as the owner's name.

1   Add this code for the read-only ID property:

```
' Visual Basic
Private m_owner As String
Public ReadOnly Property ID() As String
    Get
        Return m_owner
    End Get
End Property

// Visual C#
private string m_owner;
public string ID {
    get {
        return m_owner;
    }
}
```

The next property, Balance, will also be read-only. In the real world, you can't just tell the bank you have a certain amount of money. To change your balance, you have to make a deposit or a withdrawal. So it will be with this example: the Balance is read-only and can be changed only by means of the *Deposit* and *Withdraw* methods.

The balance is stored in a decimal field. The decimal data type (*System. Decimal*) is used to store numbers with a particular precision. Thus 2.37 is stored as 2.37, not something extremely close to 2.37, as might happen in using a *System.Double* variable. The advantage of using the *System.Decimal* data type is that rounding doesn't occur, so the *System.Decimal* type is appropriate for representing currency.

2   Add this code for the read-only Balance property:

```
' Visual Basic
Private m_balance As Decimal
Public ReadOnly Property Balance() As Decimal
    Get
        Return m_balance
    End Get
End Property

// Visual C#
private decimal m_balance;
public decimal Balance {
    get {
        return m_balance;
    }
}
```

3   Add the following code to the BankAccount class to create a constructor. All accounts need to have an owner, so the only constructor provided has one string parameter for the owner's name. In Visual C#, replace the default constructor with the one below.

```
' Visual Basic
Public Sub New(ByVal owner As String)
    m_owner = owner
    m_balance = 0D
End Sub

// Visual C#
public BankAccount(string owner) {
    m_owner = owner;
    m_balance = 0M;
}
```

Add the methods

1 Add the following code to the BankAccount class for the *Deposit* method. This method adds the indicated amount to the balance and returns the new balance.

```
' Visual Basic
Public Function Deposit(ByVal amount As Decimal) As Decimal
    m_balance += amount
    Return m_balance
End Function
```

```
// Visual C#
public decimal Deposit(decimal amount) {
    m_balance += amount;
    return m_balance;
}
```

2 Add the following code to the BankAccount class for the *Withdraw* method. This method subtracts the indicated amount from the balance and returns the new balance.

```
' Visual Basic
Public Function Withdraw(ByVal amount As Decimal) As Decimal
    m_balance -= amount
    Return m_balance
End Function
```

```
// Visual C#
public decimal Withdraw(decimal amount) {
    // since an assignment returns the assigned value,
    // only need one line
    return (m_balance -= amount);
}
```

Test the BankAccount interface

The base class, BankAccount, is now complete. Before moving on to the first derived class, SavingsAccount, take a look at the public interface of the BankAccount class.

1 Open Form1 in the designer.

2 Double-click on the form to create the *Form1_Load* method in the code editor.

3 Add the following code to the method, and note the members displayed in IntelliSense, shown in the subsequent graphic.

```
' Visual Basic
Private Sub Form1_Load(ByVal sender As System.Object, _
ByVal e As System.EventArgs) Handles MyBase.Load
    Dim account As BankAccount = New BankAccount("Robin")
    account.Deposit(25D)
    MessageBox.Show(String.Format("{0:C}", account.Balance))
End Sub

// Visual C#
private void Form1_Load(object sender, System.EventArgs e) {
    BankAccount account = new BankAccount("Robin");
    account.Deposit(25M);
    MessageBox.Show(String.Format("{0:C}", account.Balance));
}
```

String.Format

The *String.Format* method gives you a way to create strings based on variable values without using long string concatenation statements. The *String.Format* method has several overloads. In each case, the first parameter is a format statement, which is a string that's interspersed with formatting specifications. For example, *{0:C}* specifies that a value should be converted to a string using a currency format. The rest of the parameters of the method are used to replace the formatting specifications. Thus the following statements are equivalent and produce *You have $1.23 in the bank.*

```
String.Format("You have {0:C} in the bank.", balance)
"You have " + balance.ToString("C") + " in the bank."
```

The class members contain the public properties and methods of the BankAccount class: Balance, ID, *Deposit*, and *Withdraw*. The members list also contains those members inherited from the Object class: *GetType*, *Equals* (C# only), *GetHashCode* (C# only), and *ToString* (C# only). In the next section, you'll create a derived class from BankAccount, and it will contain the public interface of Object and BankAccount.

4   Press F5 to run the application. The result is shown in the following screen. You have created the completely functional base class, BankAccount.

Creating the SavingsAccount Derived Class

The first derived class you create will be the SavingsAccount class. In this example SavingsAccount is identical to BankAccount except in the following respects:

- A savings account offers interest. The SavingsAccount class will have an additional property, Interest.

- A savings account can accrue interest over time. The SavingsAccount class will have an additional method, *AddInterest*.

- One person can have both a savings account and a checking account, an expansion of your banking world. To distinguish between the two accounts, the ID property will indicate the type of account.

Create the SavingsAccount class

1   On the Project menu, click Add Class. The Add New Item dialog box appears.

2   Name the file SavingsAccount.vb or SavingsAccount.cs, depending on the language you're using.

3   Modify the class declaration to indicate that BankAccount is the base class as shown here:

```
' Visual Basic
Public Class SavingsAccount
    Inherits BankAccount
End Class

// Visual C#
public class SavingsAccount : TheBank.BankAccount {
    public SavingsAccount() {
    }
}
```

If you're using Visual Basic, the following message appears in the Task List:

"Cannot implicitly create a constructor for 'Class SavingsAccount' because its base class 'BankAccount' doesn't declare a public constructor that has no parameters. Either define a constructor on 'Class SavingsAccount' or a parameterless constructor on base 'Class BankAccount'."

If you're using Visual C#, the following message appears in the Task List:

No overload for method 'BankAccount' takes '0' arguments

As you create and modify base classes and derived classes, various messages appear in the Task List. These messages help you correctly implement the classes. Although inheritance lets you reuse much of the code in the base class, you will, of course, want to modify and add to the derived class. Getting the behavior you want in the derived classes requires a certain syntactical handshaking between the base class and derived classes. The messages that you receive as you work indicate that this handshaking isn't yet correctly implemented.

The C# Class Wizard

The C# Class Wizard allows you to specify a base class when you create a new class. In the wizard, click the Base Class tab and click a class in the Base Class list. If the class you want to derive from isn't part of your project, first find the namespace that contains the class in the Namespace list.

Leaving the constructor work aside for a moment, modify the ID property so that you form the ID by adding -S to the end of the owner's name. This process has three steps:

- By default, the class inherits the behavior of the base class. To override this behavior, you redefine the property in the derived class and add the override modifier to the property declaration.

- In the base class, you modify the property declaration by adding the *virtual* keyword to it.

- Because the *m_owner* field in BankAccount is defined as a private field, it isn't accessible in the SavingsAccount code. And because the *m_owner* field is the basis for the ID, the third step is to redefine the scope of the *m_owner* field in the base class.

The interaction between the virtual base class property and the overridden derived class property becomes apparent when the classes are used polymorphically.

Examine the development environment

Take a moment to examine the changes in the development environment now that you have declared a base class for SavingsAccount.

1   Expand the Class View window. The base class and its members are now included as you see in the following screens. Notice the *m_balance* and *m_owner* fields have a small lock on the icon, indicating that they're private fields. A public field wouldn't have a lock.

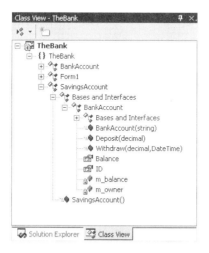

2   If you're using Visual Basic, open the source file for the SavingsAccount class in the code editor. Click the Class Name list. Two new entries appear, (Overrides) and (Base Class Events). Click (Overrides) in the list and then examine the entries in the Method Name list. It's empty. As you add overridable properties and methods to the BankAccount class, they appear in the Method Name list.

Override the ID property

1   Open the BankAccount class in the code editor and modify the declaration of the *m_owner* field so that it's protected:

```
' Visual Basic
Protected m_owner As String
```

```
// Visual C#
protected string m_owner;
```

Protected fields are available to derived classes. They're treated as private in client code. Private fields aren't available to derived classes or client code. Not all class fields need to be protected. If you examine the class in the Class View, the icon on the *m_owner* field has a key on it, indicating that the field is protected.

Modify the ID property by adding the *Overridable* or *virtual* keyword, as you see here:

```
' Visual Basic
Public Overridable ReadOnly Property ID() As String
    Get
        Return m_owner
    End Get
End Property
```

```
// Visual C#
virtual public string ID {
    get {
        return m_owner;
    }
}
```

2   Open the SavingsAccount source file in the code editor.

3   If you're using Visual Basic, click (Overrides) in the Class List, and then click ID in the Method Name list. The following empty property definition is added to the class:

```
' Visual Basic
Public Overrides ReadOnly Property ID() As String
    Get

    End Get
End Property
```

If you're using Visual C#, expand the Bases And Interfaces node of the SavingsAccount class in the Class View. Expand the BankAccount node and right-click the ID property. On the shortcut menu, point to Add and then click Override. The following empty property definition is added to the class:

```
// Visual C#
public override string ID {
    get {
        return null;
    }
}
```

4   Modify the property to return the ID. As you type in the code, notice the IntelliSense list as you type *Me.* or *this.* (including the period in either case). The list is shown in the screen that follows.

```
' Visual Basic
Public Overrides ReadOnly Property ID() As String
    Get
        Return Me.m_owner & "-S"
    End Get
End Property
```

```
// Visual C#
override public string ID {
    get {
        return this.m_owner + "-S";
    }
}
```

```
Public Class SavingsAccount
    Inherits BankAccount

    Public Overrides ReadOnly Property ID() As String
        Get
            Return Me.m_owner & "-S"
        End Get
    End Property

End Class
```

Balance
Deposit
GetType
ID
m_owner
Withdraw

This code introduces the keywords *Me* and *this*. The *Me* and *this* keywords refer to the class instance. In this case using *Me* or *this* is not required. You could simply type *m_owner*. You use a keyword in situations in which you might have variable name collisions. Perhaps you have the same field declared in the class and in the method. This keyword indicates which variable to use.

You also use the *Me* and *this* keywords if you need to pass a reference to the instance to another method. For example, suppose you had a method that took a Form as a parameter:

```
' Visual Basic
Public Sub MakeFormBlue(aForm As Form)
```

```
// Visual C#
public void MakeFormBlue(Form aForm)
```

You would make this call from within a form's code, like this:

```
' Visual Basic
MakeFormBlue(Me)
```

```
// Visual C#
MakeFormBlue(this);
```

Adding the Constructor

Constructors aren't inherited, so you must add them to the derived class. Also, whenever a constructor is defined, it includes an implicit call to the parameterless constructor that belongs to the base class. In the BankAccount class, you created only one public constructor, and that constructor had one parameter for the owner's name. Because that parameterless constructor doesn't exist in the base class, you need to make an explicit call to the constructor that does exist.

Add this constructor for the SavingsAccount class. If you're using Visual C#, you need to delete the constructor without parameters.

```
' Visual Basic
Public Sub New(ByVal owner As String)
    MyBase.New(owner)
End Sub
```

```
// Visual C#
public SavingsAccount(string owner) : base(owner) {
}
```

The error message about the constructor is now resolved.

This code introduces the *MyBase* and *base* keywords. *MyBase* and *base* refer to the base class of a class. In the case of the constructor, there's no sense in rewriting the code that you wrote in the base class, BankAccount. A call to the base class is sufficient. C# provides a syntax for calling base class members of the same name, *: base()*. Unlike the *Me* keyword, *MyBase* doesn't refer to any instance, so it can't be passed to methods that require an instance reference.

Add the Interest property and the *AddInterest* method

1 Add this code for the Interest property:

```vb
' Visual Basic
Private m_interest As Decimal = 0.01D
Public Property Interest() As Decimal
    Get
        Return m_interest
    End Get
    Set(ByVal Value As Decimal)
        m_interest = Value
    End Set
End Property
```

```csharp
// Visual C#
private decimal m_interest = 0.01M;
public decimal Interest {
    get {
        return m_interest;
    }
    set {
        m_interest = value;
    }
}
```

2 Add this code for the *AddInterest* method:

```vb
' Visual Basic
Public Function AddInterest() As Decimal
    Me.Deposit(m_interest * Me.Balance)
    Return Me.Balance
End Function
```

```csharp
// Visual C#
public decimal AddInterest() {
    this.Deposit(m_interest * this.Balance);
    return this.Balance;
}
```

Using Inheritance

5

The *m_balance* field is private to the base class, BankAccount, and the Balance property is read-only. Therefore the only way to add money to the account is, by design, through the *Deposit* method.

You have completed the implementation of the SavingsAccount class. You can now write some test code.

Test the SavingsAccount class

1 Open Form1 in the code editor.

2 Delete the code that you added to test the BankAccount class, so that the *Form1_Load* method is empty.

3 Add this code to test the SavingsAccount class:

```
' Visual Basic
Private Sub Form1_Load(ByVal sender As System.Object, _
ByVal e As System.EventArgs) Handles MyBase.Load
    Dim savings As SavingsAccount = New SavingsAccount("Your Name")
    savings.Deposit(150D)
    savings.Withdraw(50D)
    savings.Interest = 0.05D
    savings.AddInterest()
    MessageBox.Show( _
        String.Format("{0}: {1:C}", savings.ID, savings.Balance))
End Sub
```

```
// Visual C#
private void Form1_Load(object sender, System.EventArgs e) {
    SavingsAccount savings = new SavingsAccount("Your Name");
    savings.Deposit(150M);
    savings.Withdraw(50M);
    savings.Interest = 0.05M;
    savings.AddInterest();
    MessageBox.Show(
        String.Format("{0}: {1:C}", savings.ID, savings.Balance));
}
```

As you type in the code, notice the members of the class listed by IntelliSense. The list includes the members of the BankAccount class, plus the members of the SavingsAccount class, shown in the following screen. In C#, the members of the *System.Object* class also appear on the list.

```
Public Class Form1
    Inherits System.Windows.Forms.Form

Windows Form Designer generated code

    Private Sub Form1_Load(ByVal sender As System.Obj
        Dim savings As SavingsAccount = New SavingsA
        savings.Deposit(150D)
        savin  ◆ AddInterest
        savin  🖻 Balance        .05D
        savin  ◆ Deposit
        Messa  ◆ GetType        ): (1:C)", savings.ID, :
        S      🖻 ID
    End Sub      🖻 Interest
End Class       ◆ Withdraw
```

4   Press F5 to run the application. The result is shown here:

Your Name-S: $105.00

Creating the Derived Class CheckingAccount

The second derived class you create is the CheckingAccount class. CheckingAccount is identical to BankAccount except that every withdrawal from CheckingAccount incurs a $0.25 check charge. As in the SavingsAccount example, the ID property indicates the type of account.

Create the CheckingAccount class

1   On the Project menu, click Add Class. The Add New Item dialog box appears.

2   Name the file CheckingAccount.vb or CheckingAccount.cs, depending on the language you're using.

3   Modify the class declaration to indicate that BankAccount is the base class as you see here:

```
' Visual Basic
Public Class CheckingAccount
    Inherits BankAccount
End Class
```

(continued)

```
// Visual C#
public class CheckingAccount : TheBank.BankAccount {
    public CheckingAccount() {
    }
}
```

Add the constructor

● Add this code for the CheckingAccount constructor. If you're using Visual C#, you need to delete the constructor without parameters.

```
' Visual Basic
Public Sub New(ByVal owner As String)
    MyBase.New(owner)
End Sub
```

```
// Visual C#
public CheckingAccount(string owner) : base(owner) {
}
```

Override the *Withdraw* method

Overriding a method is similar to overriding a property. You add the *Overridable* keyword in Visual Basic or the *virtual* keyword in C# to the base class and redefine the method in the derived class by using the *override* keyword.

1   Open the source file for BankAccount in the code editor.

2   Modify the declaration of the *Withdraw* method to include the overridable keyword.

```
' Visual Basic
Public Overridable Function Withdraw(ByVal amount As Decimal) As Decimal
```

```
// Visual C#
virtual public decimal Withdraw(decimal amount)
```

3   Open the source file for CheckingAccount in the code editor.

4   Add this code for the *Withdraw* method:

```
' Visual Basic
Public Overrides Function Withdraw(ByVal amount As Decimal) As Decimal
    MyBase.Withdraw(amount)
    MyBase.Withdraw(0.25D)
    Return Me.Balance
End Function
```

```
// Visual C#
override public decimal Withdraw(decimal amount) {
    base.Withdraw(amount);
```

```
    base.Withdraw(0.25M);
    return this.Balance;
}
```

In this method, the *MyBase* or *base* keyword is required. Without the keyword, the CheckingAccount version of the *Withdraw* method would be called, which would in turn call the same *Withdraw* method, over and over again, until a stack overflow error occurred. You would have induced this error because each call to the *Withdraw* method takes up a little more memory from the stack, which is the memory available for the program. When the stack overflows, an error occurs.

Override the ID property

● Add this code to override the ID property:

```
' Visual Basic
Public Overrides ReadOnly Property ID() As String
    Get
        Return Me.m_owner & "-C"
    End Get
End Property

// Visual C#
override public string ID {
    get {
        return this.m_owner + "-C";
    }
}
```

Test the CheckingAccount class

1 Open Form1 in the code editor.

2 Delete the code that you added to test the SavingsAccount class, so that the *Form1_Load* method is empty.

3 Add the following code to test the CheckingAccount class:

```
' Visual Basic
Private Sub Form1_Load(ByVal sender As System.Object, _
ByVal e As System.EventArgs) Handles MyBase.Load
    Dim checking As CheckingAccount = New CheckingAccount("Your Name")
    checking.Deposit(50D)
    checking.Withdraw(5D)
    MessageBox.Show( _
        String.Format("{0}: {1:C}", checking.ID, checking.Balance))
End Sub
```

(continued)

```
// Visual C#
private void Form1_Load(object sender, System.EventArgs e) {
    CheckingAccount checking = new CheckingAccount("Your Name");
    checking.Deposit(50M);
    checking.Withdraw(5M);
    MessageBox.Show(
        String.Format("{0}: {1:C}", checking.ID, checking.Balance));
}
```

4   Press F5 to run the application. The result is shown here:

Using the Derived Classes Polymorphically

In the preceding sections, you demonstrated that inheritance allows you to reuse code from a base class. You defined a *Deposit* method in the base class, BankAccount. You used that method from an instance of SavingsAccount, even though you wrote no code for the *Deposit* method in the SavingsAccount class.

Not only does inheritance let you reuse code, but it also allows you to use classes polymorphically. This means that you can refer to an instance of the derived class as though it were an instance of the base class, as shown here:

```
' Visual Basic
Dim account as BankAccount
account = New CheckingAccount("Your Name")
account.Deposit(25D)
account.Withdraw(5D)
' Balance is 20.
```

```
// Visual C#
BankAccount account;
account = new CheckingAccount("Your Name");
account.Deposit(25M);
account.Withdraw(5M);
// Balance is 19.75.
```

Polymorphism also provides that when this code is executed, the runtime determines the actual type of the instance, BankAccount, SavingsAccount, or CheckingAccount. It then calls the *Withdraw* method defined for the actual type. There are ways to override this behavior, but in the code you've written the *Withdraw* method of the CheckingAccount object would be called in the preceding example.

In the next section, you'll see how you can use classes polymorphically.

Create the user interface

1 Open Form1 in the designer.

2 Set the Text property of Form1 to *The Bank*.

3 Drag a Label onto Form1 and set its Text property to *Account*.

4 Drag a ComboBox control onto Form1 next to the Label and set its Name property to *account*. Delete the Text property, so that it's blank.

5 Drag another Label onto Form1 and set its Text property to *Transaction*.

6 Drag a ComboBox control onto Form1 and set its Name property to *action*. Delete the text in the Text property's box so that it's blank.

7 In the Properties window, click the ellipsis button (...) next to the Items property of the action ComboBox. Use the String Collection Editor dialog box to enter two strings, *Deposit* and *Withdraw*.

8 Drag another Label onto Form1 and set its Text property to *Amount*.

9 Drag a TextBox onto Form1 and set its Name property to *amount*. Delete the Text property, so that it is blank.

10 Drag a Button onto Form1. Set its Name property to *submit* and its Text property to *Submit*. Here's the complete user interface:

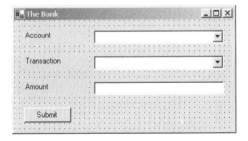

Create the accounts

1 Double-click Form1 to display the *Form1_Load* method in the code editor.

2 Delete the test code for the CheckingAccount class.

3 Add these fields to Form1:

```vb
' Visual Basic
Private checking As New CheckingAccount("Your Name")
Private savings As New SavingsAccount("Your Name")
```

```csharp
// Visual C#
private CheckingAccount checking = new CheckingAccount("Your Name");
private SavingsAccount savings = new SavingsAccount("Your Name");
```

4   Add this code to the *Form1_Load* method to initialize the accounts:

```
' Visual Basic
Private Sub Form1_Load(ByVal sender As System.Object, _
ByVal e As System.EventArgs) Handles MyBase.Load
    Me.account.Items.Add(checking)
    Me.account.Items.Add(savings)
    Me.account.SelectedIndex = 0
    Me.action.SelectedIndex = 0
    Me.amount.Text = "100"
End Sub
```

```
// Visual C#
private void Form1_Load(object sender, System.EventArgs e) {
    this.account.Items.Add(checking);
    this.account.Items.Add(savings);
    this.account.SelectedIndex = 0;
    this.action.SelectedIndex = 0;
    this.amount.Text = "100";
}
```

In the designer, you used the String Collection Editor dialog box to add strings to the ComboBox control. You can add any item to the ComboBox using the *Items.Add* method. At run time, the name of the class will be displayed in the ComboBox control, as shown in the following screen. If you have defined a *ToString* method for the class, the *ToString* method would be called and displayed in the ComboBox. For example, if you had defined a *ToString* method in the SavingsAccount object that returned the ID property, the ComboBox would display Your Name-S instead of TheBank.SavingsAccount.

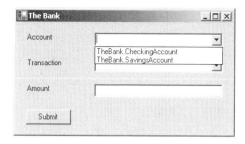

Submit the transaction

1   In the designer, double-click the Submit button to create the Click event method in the code editor.

2   Add this code to the code editor to submit the transaction and report the new account balance:

```vb
' Visual Basic
Private Sub submit_Click(ByVal sender As System.Object, _
ByVal e As System.EventArgs) Handles submit.Click
    Dim selectedAccount As BankAccount
    Dim item As Object = Me.account.SelectedItem
    selectedAccount = CType(item, BankAccount)
    Select Case action.Text
        Case "Deposit"
            selectedAccount.Deposit(Decimal.Parse(amount.Text))
        Case "Withdraw"
            selectedAccount.Withdraw(Decimal.Parse(amount.Text))
    End Select
    MessageBox.Show(String.Format("{0}: {1:C}", _
        selectedAccount.ID, selectedAccount.Balance))
End Sub
```

```csharp
// Visual C#
private void submit_Click(object sender, System.EventArgs e) {
    BankAccount selectedAccount;
    object item = this.account.SelectedItem;
    selectedAccount = (BankAccount)item;
    switch (action.Text) {
        case "Deposit" :
            selectedAccount.Deposit(decimal.Parse(amount.Text));
            break;
        case "Withdraw" :
            selectedAccount.Withdraw(decimal.Parse(amount.Text));
            break;
    }
    MessageBox.Show(String.Format("{0}: {1:C}",
        selectedAccount.ID, selectedAccount.Balance));
}
```

As with the SortedList and ArrayList classes, you can add any type of object to the ComboBox, but the ComboBox treats them all as being of type *System.Object*. (Remember that all classes implicitly derive from *System.Object*.) That means that what is returned from *ComboBox. SelectedItem* can be directly assigned only to a *System.Object* reference.

Because your code has control over the Account combo box, you have restricted the items of the combo box to be of type CheckingAccount or SavingsAccount. Therefore you can cast the *System.Object* item in the *submit_Click* method to a BankAccount object. Once you have a BankAccount object, you can call any of its properties and methods.

When you cast an object from one type to another, no changes occur in the instance itself. The only thing that changes is the view of the object. The preceding code doesn't convert *account.SelectedItem* from a *System.Object* into a SavingsAccount object. The cast only directs the compiler to treat the instance as a SavingsAccount instead of a *System.Object*. There is, after all, only one instance of SavingsAccount. It's just that the account combo box is storing a *System.Object* reference to it, and the Form is storing a SavingsAccount reference to it.

When you have a base class reference to an instance, you can access only the properties and methods defined on the base class. In this example, you couldn't call the *AddInterest* method using the *selectedAccount* variable. You'll see how to do that in the next section.

3   Press F5 to run the application. Make some deposits and withdrawals with the accounts, and you'll see the common and specialized behaviors of the CheckingAccount and SavingsAccount classes.

Find the type of the object

1   Open Form1 in the designer.

2   Add another button to Form1. Set its Name property to *addInterest*, its Text property to *Add interest*, and its Visible property to *False*.

3   Double-click the button to create the Click event method in the code editor.

4   In the form designer, double-click the account ComboBox control to create the *account_SelectedIndexChanged* method in the code editor.

5   Add the following code to the *account_SelectedIndexChanged* method to display the Add Interest button if the selected account is the savings account.

```
' Visual Basic
Private Sub account_SelectedIndexChanged(ByVal sender As _
System.Object, ByVal e As System.EventArgs) _
Handles account.SelectedIndexChanged
    If TypeOf (account.SelectedItem) Is SavingsAccount Then
        addInterest.Visible = True
    Else
        addInterest.Visible = False
    End If
End Sub

// Visual C#
private void account_SelectedIndexChanged(object sender,
System.EventArgs e) {
    if (account.SelectedItem is SavingsAccount) {
        addInterest.Visible = true;
    }
    else {
        addInterest.Visible = false;
    }
}
```

6 Add the following code to the Click event method of the Add Interest button to call the *AddInterest* method of SavingsAccount.

```vb
' Visual Basic
Private Sub addInterest_Click(ByVal sender As System.Object, _
ByVal e As System.EventArgs) Handles addInterest.Click
    If TypeOf (account.SelectedItem) Is SavingsAccount Then
        Dim theSavings As SavingsAccount = _
            CType(account.SelectedItem, SavingsAccount)
        theSavings.AddInterest()
        MessageBox.Show(String.Format("{0}: {1:C}", _
            theSavings.ID, theSavings.Balance))
    End If
End Sub
```

```csharp
// Visual C#
private void addInterest_Click(object sender, System.EventArgs e) {
    SavingsAccount theSavings = account.SelectedItem as SavingsAccount;
    if (theSavings != null) {
        theSavings.AddInterest();
        MessageBox.Show(String.Format("{0}: {1:C}", theSavings.ID,
            theSavings.Balance));
    }
}
```

This method checks the type of the selected item before casting it to a SavingsAccount object. C# has a keyword, *as*, that tests and casts the reference in one step. The *as* keyword is an operator that returns null if the object cannot be cast as the selected type.

7 Press F5 to run the application. The results are shown here:

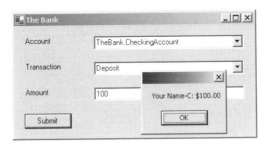

Inherit from a Control:
The RoundButton Class

You can use inheritance to create new classes from .NET Framework classes, as well as from classes you have written yourself. In this next section, you will create a new class by deriving from a class that you didn't develop.

You create a round button control by using *System.Windows.Forms.Button* as the base class. This task requires only that you override the *OnPaint* method of the Button class.

Creating the RoundButton Class

To create a derived class from a .NET class, you declare the class and indicate the base class, just as you did with the bank account classes.

Create the project

1   Create a new Windows Control Library project and name it ARoundButton.

2   Open Form1 in the code editor.

Add the RoundButton class

● If you're using Visual Basic, add the class declaration at the end of the source file. If you're using Visual C#, add the class declaration at the end of the file, but before the closing brace of the RoundButton namespace.

```
' Visual Basic
Public Class RoundButton
    Inherits Button

End Class

// Visual C#
public class RoundButton : Button {
}
```

Overriding the *OnPaint* Method

By overriding the *OnPaint* method, you direct the runtime to draw a round button, instead of the usual rectangular button.

Create the *OnPaint* method

1   If you're using Visual Basic, click RoundButton (Overrides) in the Class List, and then click OnPaint in the Method Name list. The following empty method definition is added to the class. You can also simply type this method into the editor.

```
' Visual Basic
Protected Overrides Sub OnPaint(ByVal pevent As _
System.Windows.Forms.PaintEventArgs)

End Sub
```

If you're using Visual C#, in the Class View expand the Bases And Interfaces nodes of the RoundButton class button until you find the ButtonBase class. Expand the ButtonBase node, right-click the *OnPaint* method, point to Add and click Override on the shortcut menu. The following empty method definition is added to the class. You can also simply type this method into the editor.

```
// Visual C#
protected override void OnPaint(
System.Windows.Forms.PaintEventArgs pevent) {
}
```

The *OnPaint* method is called each time the control is drawn on the form. The base class draws the familiar rectangle. By overriding the *OnPaint* method, you can determine the appearance of the button.

2   Add the following code to draw the round button. Not only will the button be round when it's painted on the form, but the clickable area of the button will be round as well.

```
' Visual Basic
Protected Overrides Sub OnPaint(ByVal pevent As _
System.Windows.Forms.PaintEventArgs)
    Me.Size = New Size(50, 50)
    Dim aCircle As System.Drawing.Drawing2D.GraphicsPath = _
        New System.Drawing.Drawing2D.GraphicsPath()
    aCircle.AddEllipse(New System.Drawing.RectangleF(0, 0, 50, 50))
    Me.Region = New Region(aCircle)
End Sub

// Visual C#
protected override void OnPaint(
System.Windows.Forms.PaintEventArgs pevent) {
    this.Size = new Size(50,50);
    System.Drawing.Drawing2D.GraphicsPath aCircle =
        new System.Drawing.Drawing2D.GraphicsPath();
    aCircle.AddEllipse(new System.Drawing.RectangleF(0, 0, 50, 50));
    this.Region = new Region(aCircle);
}
```

To make a control assume a particular shape, in this case round, you must define its Region property so that it achieves that shape. You can create a shape using the GraphicsPath object. The GraphicsPath object allows you to create a shape by drawing. In this example, you create a drawing by adding a circle to GraphicsPath. The size of the button is constrained to 50 by 50 pixels so that the full circle is visible.

Using the Class

The RoundButton class has been defined in the source file and doesn't appear in the Toolbox for dragging on the form. To add a RoundButton instance to Form1, you can use the same methods you used to create buttons in Chapter 4.

Add a RoundButton control to the form

1   Add the following code to the Form1 class to respond to the Click event of the RoundButton object.

```
' Visual Basic
Private Sub roundButton_Click(ByVal sender As System.Object, _
ByVal e As System.EventArgs)
    MessageBox.Show("Hello")
End Sub
```

```
// Visual C#
private void roundButton_Click(object sender, System.EventArgs e) {
    MessageBox.Show("Hello");
}
```

2   In the form designer, double-click Form1 to add the *Form1_Load* method to the code editor.

3   Add the following code to create a RoundButton object and add it to the form.

```
' Visual Basic
Private Sub Form1_Load(ByVal sender As System.Object, _
ByVal e As System.EventArgs) Handles MyBase.Load
    Dim rb As New RoundButton()
    Me.Controls.Add(rb)
    AddHandler rb.Click, AddressOf roundButton_Click
End Sub
```

```
// Visual C#
private void Form1_Load(object sender, System.EventArgs e) {
    RoundButton rb = new RoundButton();
        rb.Click += new System.EventHandler(this.roundButton_Click);
    this.Controls.Add(rb);
}
```

Run the application

●   Press F5 to run the application. Here are the results:

Design Considerations

Inheritance is a powerful tool in object-oriented programming and is used extensively in the .NET Framework. The following points will help you write classes that work better together and are less error-prone.

The *is-a* relationship   Remember that inheritance models the *is-a* relationship between objects. The derived classes should represent objects that truly are special cases of the base object. If you find yourself trying to eliminate properties or methods of the base class, then you don't have an *is-a* relationship. For example, if you're creating a class that derives from the Button class but you're trying to eliminate the Click event, the new class isn't really a Button. It might be something like a button, but it isn't a button.

Polymorphism   If you aren't going to use the classes polymorphically, consider whether you need to use inheritance at all. It might be that your class only needs to contain an instance of the class rather than serve as a base class.

(continued)

continued

Type-checking   In general, type-checking (using the *type of* operator) is a clue that you are using inheritance incorrectly. Analyze your code to determine whether the objects truly represent an *is-a* relationship. Determine whether you're defining the proper properties and methods so that type-checking is unnecessary.

Select or switch statements   If your code is full of select or switch statements, consider whether using inheritance would simplify the code. Consider the following code snippet where you have defined a Shape class with a type property that will be set to *Rectangle* or *Circle*. To draw the Shape object, you might write some code like this:

```
If aShape.Type = "Rectangle" then
    DrawARectangle()
Else
    DrawACircle()
End If
```

Using inheritance, you might create a Shape class with a *Draw* method as the base class. Then you would create Rectangle and Circle classes as derived classes, and override the *Draw* method in each class. Then you would replace the preceding code with the following:

```
' aShape is a reference to the Shape class, but is
' currently referring to either a Rectangle or Circle
aShape.Draw()
```

Single inheritance   Visual Basic and Visual C# provide single inheritance only. That means you can specify only one base class. Sometimes the choice is obvious, such as BankAccount as a base class for SavingsAccount. But if you want to be able to drag a SavingsAccount onto your form as you would a Timer control or a TextBox, you might want to derive from one of the control or component classes. Because derived classes also inherit from their base classes, you could use the control as the base class for BankAccount, and then derive SavingsAccount from BankAccount. Another way to get the behavior of multiple inheritance using single inheritance is with interfaces, as you'll see in Chapter 9.

Quick Reference

To	Do this

Declare a base class	Create any class.
	
	```' Visual Basic```
	```Public BaseClass```
	```End Class```
	
	```// Visual C#```
	```public BaseClass {```
	```}```

Declare a derived class	In Visual Basic, use the *Inherits* keyword.
	
	```' Visual Basic```
	```Public SomeClass```
	``` Inherits BaseClass```
	```End Class```
	
	In C#, use the : character.
	
	```public BaseClass : BaseClass {```
	```}```
	
	Or
	
	Use the Add Class Wizard and select the base class.

Declare a protected field	Add the *protected* keyword.
	
	```' Visual Basic```
	```Public BaseClass```
	``` Protected aField As Integer```
	```End Class```
	
	```// Visual C#```
	```public BaseClass {```
	``` protected int aField;```
	```}```

Call the base class constructor	Use the *MyBase* or *base* keyword.
	```' Visual Basic```
	```Public Sub New()```
	``` MyBase.New()```
	```End Sub```
	
	```// Visual C#```
	```public DerivedClass() : base() {```
	```}```

(continued)

5

Using Inheritance

To	Do this
Override a property	In the base class, add the overridable property to the property declaration.

```
' Visual Basic
Public Overridable ReadOnly_
Property ID() As String
    Get
        Return m_owner
    End Get
End Property
```

```
// Visual C#
virtual public string ID {
    get {
        return m_owner;
    }
}
```

In the derived class, add the *override* keyword to the property declaration.

```
' Visual Basic
Public Overrides ReadOnly_
Property ID() As String
    Get
        Return Me.m_owner & "-S"
    End Get
End Property
```

```
// Visual C#
override public string ID {
    get {
        return this.m_owner + "-S";
    }
}
```

Or

In Visual Basic, click the property to override in the Method Name list in the code editor.

In Visual C#, right-click the base class property in the Class View, and then point to Add and click Override on the shortcut menu.

To	Do this
Override a method	In the base class, add the *Overridable* or *virtual* keyword to the method declaration.

```
' Visual Basic
Public Overridable_
Function Withdraw(ByVal amount As Decimal)_
As Decimal
End Function
```

```
// Visual C#
virtual public decimal
Withdraw(decimal amount) {
}
```

In the derived class, add the *Overrides* or *override* keyword to the method declaration.

```
Public Overrides_
Function Withdraw(ByVal amount As Decimal)_
As Decimal
End Function
```

```
// Visual C#
override public decimal
Withdraw(decimal amount) {
}
```

Or

In Visual Basic, click the method to override in the Method Name list in the code editor.
In Visual C#, right-click the base class method in the Class View, and then point to Add and click Override on the shortcut menu.

To	Do this
Refer to the class instance from within the class	Use the *Me* or *this* keyword.

```
' Visual Basic
Public Overrides ReadOnly_
Property ID() As String
    Get
        Return Me.m_owner & "-S"
    End Get
End Property
```

```
// Visual C#
override public string ID {
    get {
        return this.m_owner + "-S";
    }
}
```

CHAPTER

6

Designing Base Classes as Abstract Classes

**ESTIMATED
TIME
2 hr.**

In this chapter, you'll learn how to

✔ *Create an abstract base class using the* **MustInherit** *or abstract keyword.*

✔ *Create a derived class from an abstract class.*

✔ *Derive from a .NET abstract class to create a typed collection class.*

✔ *Seal a class using the* **NotInheritable** *or sealed keyword.*

✔ *Hide a base class member using the* **Shadows** *or new keyword.*

In Chapter 5, "Using Inheritance to Create Specialized Classes," you created a base class and derived two classes from it. You created methods and properties in the base class, which you specialized in the derived classes. That chapter showed you the basics of inheritance and polymorphism. You can, however, exercise much more control than you saw in Chapter 5. In this chapter, you'll create an abstract class, one from which you must inherit. In the definition of the abstract class, you'll determine the members that the derived class must implement. You'll see that the Microsoft .NET Framework provides several abstract classes, designed solely as base classes for developers to use to create typed collection classes. You'll also learn how to create members of a base class and a derived class that have the same name, yet don't behave polymorphically.

Abstract Classes

In Chapter 5, you created the fully functional base class, BankAccount. You then created two derived classes, SavingsAccount and CheckingAccount. If you think about a real bank (remembering that classes should model the real world), you might wonder whether you could ever open a generic bank account. Most likely, a bank would offer you a selection of kinds of accounts, and you would choose one. The bank manager would be completely unable to create a generic bank account. So it should be for your BankAccount class. The BankAccount class should define the common behavior of a generic bank account, even though you would never create one. You still want to handle accounts polymorphically, perhaps to send out advertisements. So you will still use inheritance to create the account classes.

Another reason not to create a base class that you can instantiate is that you might then be tempted to add functionality to the base class that isn't appropriate for the derived classes. Making this mistake is all the more likely if your design started with one class and then you derived a new class from it. Suppose your bank started by offering only savings accounts; for that purpose, you created a SavingsAccount class. When your bank became successful, you wanted to add a checking account and decided to derive it from SavingsAccount. Because your checking account service was going to pay interest, just like a savings account, the only thing you needed to add was the service charge for processing checks. Then when the incidence of new savings accounts dropped, you decided to offer a new toaster for each new savings account opened. So you added a *GiveToaster* method to the SavingsAccount class. Through inheritance, you must now offer all the new checking account customers a new toaster! The solution to this problem is to create a base class for SavingsAccount and CheckingAccount. Then add the new toaster behavior only in the SavingsAccount class.

Visual Basic and Visual C# both offer a mechanism for enforcing the concept that you create only instances of the derived class. You set this limitation by creating abstract base classes. Abstract classes can't be instantiated, although you can create derived classes from them. You can completely implement an abstract class, or you can simply define what the derived class must implement. You can declare references to the abstract class, but you can't make instances of them. As a result, you don't lose any of the polymorphic behavior of the derived classes.

The BankAccount Class Revisited

In Chapter 5, the BankAccount class was fully functional, which could lead to errors in the program if you ever instantiated the class because its behavior would be neither that of a SavingsAccount class nor a CheckingAccount class. In this chapter, you'll create the BankAccount class as an abstract class. You might recall that the BankAccount classes had an ID property whose format depended on the account type. Because the ID property depends on the type of account, there's no reason to implement this method in the base class, and furthermore, you don't want to implement it in the base class. If you did, the implementation wouldn't be correct for either type of account. Using an abstract property forces you to implement this method. In this chapter, you'll also add the abstract *PrintStatement* method to the base class. The SavingsAccount statement will include the deposits, withdrawals, and interest paid. The CheckingAccount statement will include deposits, withdrawals, and the number of checks written. If this method were implemented in the base class, it would be valid for neither of the derived classes.

You might be thinking at this point, "I can implement the *PrintStatement* method in the base class. I'll just check the type of the instance and then print the correct statement." This solution would work as long as you know all the derived classes of the base class, but doing this would limit the reusability of the base class. In general, base classes shouldn't contain code that depends on the derived classes.

Describing the Design Using the Unified Modeling Language

The Unified Modeling Language (UML) is a graphical tool for describing object-oriented designs. Development tools such as UML allow developers to discuss designs using a common vocabulary. Such tools also decrease ambiguity in a specification. In previous chapters, the class designs have been specified by tables listing the properties and methods. In this and subsequent chapters, I'll use a UML class diagram to specify designs. The basic unit of the class diagram is the box, which represents the class:

The class element has two sections below the name, one to specify the properties and one to specify the methods:

BankAccount

+ID : ReadOnly String
+Balance : ReadOnly Decimal=0
+TotalDeposits : ReadOnly Decimal=0
+TotalWithdrawals : ReadOnly Decimal=0

+Deposit(in amount : Decimal) : Decimal
+Withdrawal(in amount : Decimal) : Decimal
+PrintStatement() : String

The preceding diagram describes the abstract base class you'll implement, BankAccount. The italic title shows that BankAccount is an abstract class. The UML lists the properties and their default values, and it specifies public properties by preceding them with a plus sign. The lower section of the class element lists the public methods defined in the class. The UML also indicates the parameters for the methods and their return values. In UML, the *in* word indicates that the parameter is passed by value in Visual Basic.

The UML also shows the derived classes with the inheritance relationship denoted by an arrow pointing toward the base class, usually placed above the derived class. The derived classes are assumed to inherit everything from the base class, so only the additions are shown in the derived class. Here's the complete UML class diagram for this chapter:

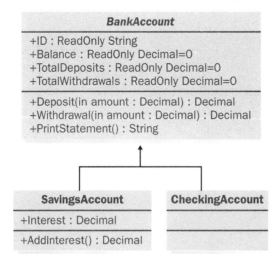

Note that the UML class diagram doesn't specify any of the behavior of the interface. For example, the class diagram doesn't explain the interaction of the

Deposit method and the Balance property. It doesn't explain how the ID property should be implemented in the SavingsAccount and CheckingAccount classes.

You can create UML diagrams yourself using anything from drawing tools to high-end professional development tools. Some tools can generate code from your diagrams or generate diagrams from your code. Even a simple, quickly drawn diagram can convey the basic structure of your object-oriented program.

Creating the Abstract Class

The first class you'll create is the BankAccount class. This class implements some methods and leaves others as abstract. Declaring just one member as abstract makes your entire class abstract.

Create the class

1 Create a new project and name it ABetterBank.

2 On the Project menu, click Add Class. The Add New Item dialog box appears.

3 Name the file BankAccount.vb or BankAccount.cs, depending on the language you're using.

4 Add the *MustInherit* or *abstract* keyword to the class declaration, as you see here:

```
' Visual Basic
Public MustInherit Class BankAccount
```

```
// Visual C#
public abstract class BankAccount
```

Add the nonabstract members

1 Add the following code for the Balance property:

```
' Visual Basic
Private m_balance As Decimal = 0D
Public ReadOnly Property Balance() As Decimal
    Get
        Return m_balance
    End Get
End Property
```

```
// Visual C#
private decimal m_balance;
public decimal Balance {
    get { return m_balance; }
}
```

2 Add the following code for the TotalDeposits property. The TotalDeposits property is the total of all the deposits for the lifetime of the instance.

```vb
' Visual Basic
Private m_totalDeposits As Decimal = 0D
Public ReadOnly Property TotalDeposits() As Decimal
    Get
        Return m_totalDeposits
    End Get
End Property
```

```csharp
// Visual C#
private decimal m_totalDeposits;
public decimal TotalDeposits {
    get { return m_totalDeposits; }
}
```

3 Add the following code for the TotalWithdrawals property. The Total-Withdrawals property is the total of all the withdrawals for the lifetime of the instance.

```vb
' Visual Basic
Private m_totalWithdrawals As Decimal = 0D
Public ReadOnly Property TotalWithdrawals() As Decimal
    Get
        Return m_totalWithdrawals
    End Get
End Property
```

```csharp
// Visual C#
private decimal m_totalWithdrawals;
public decimal TotalWithdrawals {
    get { return m_totalWithdrawals; }
}
```

4 Add the following code for the *Withdraw* and *Deposit* methods:

```vb
' Visual Basic
Public Function Deposit(ByVal amount As Decimal) As Decimal
    m_balance += amount
    m_totalDeposits += amount
    Return (m_balance)
End Function

Public Overridable Function Withdraw(ByVal amount As Decimal) As Decimal
    m_balance -= amount
    m_totalWithdrawals += amount
    Return m_balance
End Function
```

```
// Visual C#
public decimal Deposit(decimal amount) {
    m_totalDeposits += amount;
    return (m_balance += amount);
}

public virtual decimal Withdraw(decimal amount) {
    m_totalWithdrawals += amount;
    return (m_balance -= amount);
}
```

Note that the *Deposit* and *Withdraw* methods maintain the *m_totalDeposits* and *m_totalWithdrawals* fields. The TotalDeposits and TotalWithdrawals properties are read-only. When it's overriding the *Withdraw* method, the derived class code doesn't have access to *m_totalWithdrawals* and *m_totalDeposits* fields because they're private fields of the BankAccount class.

Add the abstract members

1   Add this declaration for the abstract ID property:

```
' Visual Basic
Public MustOverride ReadOnly Property ID() As String
```

```
// Visual C#
public abstract string ID { get; }
```

The declaration isn't followed by an implementation. Because the derived class must implement this property, an implementation would be unnecessary. The addition of the abstract keyword, *MustOverride* or *abstract*, requires that the property be defined in every derived class.

If you declare one of the members of a class using the abstract keyword, you must also declare the class as abstract. An item remains in the Task List until you do this. However, if you declare a class as abstract, you aren't required to declare any of the members as abstract.

A few rules apply if you have multiple levels of inheritance. Suppose, for example, that you use CheckingAccount as a base class for the GoldChecking and SilverChecking classes. If you implement ID in CheckingAccount, you aren't required to implement it again in the GoldChecking and SilverChecking accounts. GoldChecking and SilverChecking can inherit the implementation from CheckingAccount.

2   Add this declaration for the abstract *PrintStatement* method:

```
' Visual Basic
Public MustOverride Function PrintStatement() As String
```

```
// Visual C#
public abstract string PrintStatement();
```

Again, the declaration isn't followed by an implementation, and all the derived classes are required to implement the method.

The abstract BankAccount class is complete. You can't create an instance of BankAccount, although you can create a reference variable to BankAccount. Now create the derived class SavingsAccount.

Writing the SavingsAccount Class

Here's what you do to implement the SavingsAccount class:

- Add a constructor.
- Add the Interest property.
- Add the *AddInterest* method.
- Define the *PrintStatement* method.
- Define the ID property.

Create the class

1   On the Project menu, click Add Class. The Add New Item dialog box appears.

2   Name the file SavingsAccount.vb or SavingsAccount.cs, depending on the language you're using.

3   Add the boldface text to the class declaration to indicate that SavingsAccount inherits from the BankAccount class:

```
' Visual Basic
Public Class SavingsAccount
    Inherits BankAccount
End Class
```

```
// Visual C#
public class SavingsAccount : BankAccount {
    ⋮
}
```

Define the constructor

● Add this code for the constructor. Now that the ID property is defined only in the derived classes, the *m_owner* field is moved to the SavingsAccount class. If you're using C#, replace the parameterless constructor with this constructor:

```
' Visual Basic
Private m_owner As String
Public Sub New(ByVal owner As String)
    m_owner = owner
End Sub
```

```
// Visual C#
private string m_owner;
public SavingsAccount(string owner) {
    m_owner = owner;
}
```

Add the Interest property and the *AddInterest* method

1   Add this code for the Interest property:

```
' Visual Basic
Private m_interest As Decimal = 0.01D
Public Property Interest() As Decimal
    Get
        Return m_interest
    End Get
    Set(ByVal Value As Decimal)
        m_interest = Value
    End Set
End Property
```

```
// Visual C#
private decimal m_interest = 0.01M;
public decimal Interest {
    get { return m_interest; }
    set { m_interest = value; }
}
```

2   Add this code for the *AddInterest* method:

```
' Visual Basic
Private m_totalInterest As Decimal = 0D
Public Function AddInterest() As Decimal
    Dim interest As Decimal = m_interest * Me.Balance
    m_totalInterest += interest
    Me.Deposit(interest)
    Return Me.Balance
End Function
```

(continued)

```
// Visual C#
private decimal m_totalInterest = 0M;
public decimal AddInterest() {
    decimal interest = m_interest * this.Balance;
    m_totalInterest += interest;
    this.Deposit(interest);
    return this.Balance;
}
```

Define the inherited abstract members

1   Add this code to define the *PrintStatement* method. Even though the *PrintStatement* method was only declared and not implemented in the BankAccount class, you still use the *Overrides* or *override* keyword when implementing the method.

```
' Visual Basic
Public Overrides Function PrintStatement() As String
    Dim statement As String = String.Format("{1}{0}" & _
        "Opening balance: $0.00{0}Deposits: {2:C}{0}" & _
        "Withdrawals: {3:C}{0}Interest: {4:C}{0}" & _
        "Ending balance: {5:C}{0}", _
        New Object() {ControlChars.CrLf, Me.ID, _
        Me.TotalDeposits - m_totalInterest, _
        Me.TotalWithdrawals, Me.m_totalInterest, Me.Balance})
    Return statement
End Function
```

```
// Visual C#
public override string PrintStatement() {
    string statement = String.Format("{0}\n" +
        "Opening balance: $0.00\nDeposits: {1:C}\nWithdrawals: {2:C}\n" +
        "Interest: {3:C}\nEnding balance: {4:C}\n",
        new object[] { this.ID, this.TotalDeposits - m_totalInterest,
        this.TotalWithdrawals, this.m_totalInterest, this.Balance});
    return statement;
}
```

You can choose from many ways to build strings in .NET. This method, using one of the overloads of *String.Format*, shows just one. In Visual C#, you can indicate a new line by means of the \n escape character. That escape character isn't recognized in Visual Basic, but you can simply replace the \n character with the formatting expression {0} and match it with *ControlChars.CrLf* in the argument list.

The total deposits to the savings account, maintained in the base class, include the interest payments. The program deducts the interest payments from the total deposits before reporting the deposits. The program reports the interest payments separately.

2   Add this code to define the ID property:

```
' Visual Basic
Public Overrides ReadOnly Property ID() As String
    Get
        Return m_owner & "-S"
    End Get
End Property

// Visual C#
public override string ID {
    get { return m_owner + "-S"; }
}
```

Writing the CheckingAccount Class

Here's what you do to implement the CheckingAccount class:

▪ Override the *Withdraw* method.

▪ Define the *PrintStatement* method.

▪ Define the ID property.

Create the class

1   On the Project menu, click Add Class. The Add New Item dialog box appears.

2   Name the file CheckingAccount.vb or CheckingAccount.cs, depending on the language you're using.

3   Add the boldface text to the class declaration to indicate that BankAccount is the derived class:

```
' Visual Basic
Public Class CheckingAccount
    Inherits BankAccount
End Class

// Visual C#
public class CheckingAccount : BankAccount {
    ⋮
}
```

Define the constructor

● Add this code for the constructor. Now that the ID property is defined only in the derived classes, the *m_owner* field is moved to the CheckingAccount class. If you're using C#, replace the parameterless constructor with this constructor.

```
' Visual Basic
Private m_owner As String
Public Sub New(ByVal owner As String)
    m_owner = owner
End Sub
```

```
// Visual C#
private string m_owner;
public CheckingAccount(string owner) {
    m_owner = owner;
}
```

Define the overridden *Withdraw* method

● Add this code to override the *Withdraw* method:

```
' Visual Basic
Dim m_checks As Integer = 0
Public Overrides Function Withdraw(ByVal amount As Decimal) As Decimal
    m_checks += 1
    Return MyBase.Withdraw(amount + 0.25D)
End Function
```

```
// Visual C#
private int m_checks = 0;
public override decimal Withdraw(decimal amount) {
    m_checks++;
    return (base.Withdraw(amount + 0.25M));
}
```

Define the inherited abstract members

1   Add this code to define the *PrintStatement* method:

```
' Visual Basic
Public Overrides Function PrintStatement() As String
    Dim statement As String = String.Format("{1}{0}" & _
        "Opening balance: $0.00{0}Deposits: {2:C}{0}" & _
        "Withdrawals: {3:C}{0}Checks written: {4}{0}" & _
        "Checking charges: {5:C}{0}Ending balance: {6:C}{0}", _
```

```
        New Object() { ControlChars.CrLf, Me.ID, _
        Me.TotalDeposits, Me.TotalWithdrawals - (m_checks * 0.25D), _
        Me.m_checks, Me.m_checks * 0.25D, Me.Balance})

    Return statement
End Function

// Visual C#
public override string PrintStatement() {
    string statement = String.Format(
        "{0}\nOpening balance: $0.00\nDeposits: {1:C}\n" +
        "Withdrawals: {2:C}\nChecks written: {3}\n" +
        "Checking charges: {4:C}\nEnding balance: {5:C}\n",
        new object[] { this.ID, this.TotalDeposits,
        this.TotalWithdrawals - (m_checks * 0.25M),
        this.m_checks, this.m_checks * 0.25D, this.Balance});

    return statement;
}
```

The withdrawals from the checking account are lumped with the check amounts, so the service charges are deducted from the withdrawals and reported separately.

2   Add this code to define the ID property:

```
' Visual Basic
Public Overrides ReadOnly Property ID() As String
    Get
        Return m_owner & "-C"
    End Get
End Property

// Visual C#
public override string ID {
    get { return m_owner + "-C"; }
}
```

The base and derived classes are complete. The public interface of the classes hasn't changed, except for the addition of the *PrintStatement* method. You can therefore use the same form you used to test the classes in Chapter 5.

Testing the Classes

Even though you changed the implementation of the BankAccount classes, you can still use the same user interface from Chapter 5.

(side tab) 6 Designing Base Classes

Create the user interface

1   In the Solution Explorer, right-click Form1 and click Delete on the shortcut menu. Click OK to confirm the deletion of Form1.

2   On the Project menu, click Add Existing Item.

3   In the Add Existing Item dialog box, navigate to the form you created for the project TheBank in Chapter 5 and click Open. A copy of the form is added to the ABetterBank project folder.

4   If you're using C#, you want to rename the namespace in which the form is contained. Right-click the form in the Solution Explorer, and click View Code on the shortcut menu. Modify the namespace declaration near the top of the file this way:

```
namespace ABetterBank
```

5   Open the form in the form designer by double-clicking Form1.vb or Form1.cs in the Solution Explorer.

6   Drag a Button onto Form1. Set its Name property to *printStatement* and its Text property to *Print*. Here's the complete user interface:

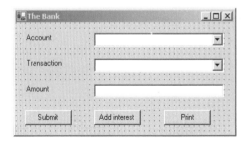

Add the code for the Print button

1   In the designer, double-click the Print button to create the Click event method and edit it in the code editor.

2   Add this code to print the statement for the selected account:

```
' Visual Basic
Private Sub printStatement_Click(ByVal sender As System.Object, _
ByVal e As System.EventArgs) Handles printStatement.Click
    Dim selectedAccount As BankAccount
    Dim item As Object = Me.account.SelectedItem
    selectedAccount = CType(item, BankAccount)
    MessageBox.Show(selectedAccount.PrintStatement())
End Sub
```

```
// Visual C#
private void printStatement_Click(object sender, System.EventArgs e) {
    BankAccount selectedAccount;
    object item = account.SelectedItem;
    selectedAccount = (BankAccount)item;
    MessageBox.Show(selectedAccount.PrintStatement());
}
```

3   Press F5 to run the application. Here are some of the results:

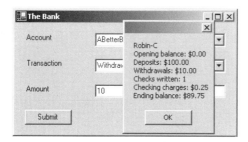

A Typed Collection Class

In Chapter 4, "Working with Methods," you created a Deck class to organize a group of Card instances. In the Deck class, you used the ArrayList class to hold the references to the Card instances. The ArrayList class is extremely flexible because you can add any type of object to it. The disadvantage of using the ArrayList class is that should you accidentally add an object that isn't of the Card class, you might encounter an error when you retrieved the object from the ArrayList class and tried to use it as a Card instance. In no less than three places, this code appears:

```
' Visual Basic
CType(m_cards(0), Card)
```

```
// Visual C#
(Card)m_cards[0]
```

A reasonable way to prevent errors in casting is to create a class that accepts only Card instances and returns only Card instances.

A similar situation exists in Chapter 1, "Writing Your First Object-Oriented Program," with the Library class. In that case, you used the SortedList class.

When you use the SortedList class, the compiler allows any call to the *Add* method as long as there are two arguments. For example, the following code is syntactically correct but would be complete nonsense in our Library application:

```
' Visual Basic
Dim m_shelf As New SortedList()
' Complete nonsense!
m_shelf.Add(14, New System.Windows.Forms.Button())
```

```
// Visual C#
SortedList m_shelf = new SortedList();
// Complete nonsense!
m_shelf.Add(14, new System.Windows.Forms.Button());
```

```
' Visual Basic
theBook = CType(m_shelf(title), Book)
```

```
// Visual C#
theBook = (Book)m_shelf[title];
```

The .NET Framework provides abstract collection classes that you can use as base classes for typed collection classes. A typed collection class allows only one type of object to be added and removed. This means that you can find errors at compile time rather than at run time.

Redesigning the Library Class

The documentation for the *System.Collections.DictionaryBase* class reads, "Provides the abstract (*MustInherit* in Visual Basic) base class for a strongly typed collection of associated keys and values." Here's the UML class diagram for the public interface of DictionaryBase, with members from the *System.Object* class removed:

DictionaryBase
+Count : Integer
+Clear() +GetEnumerator() : IEnumerator +CopyTo(in array : Array, in index : Integer)

What's noticeably absent from the public interface are any methods that add or return items from the collection. The class contains a protected instance member, Dictionary, that will contain the Book instances we want to add to the collection.

Here's the code from the original Library class:

```vbnet
' Visual Basic
Imports System.Collections
Public Class Library
    Private m_shelf As New SortedList()

    Public Sub CheckIn(ByVal newBook As Book)
        m_shelf.Add(newBook.Title, newBook)
    End Sub

    Public Function CheckOut(ByVal title As String) As Book
        Dim theBook As Book
        theBook = CType(m_shelf(title), Book)
        m_shelf.Remove(title)
        Return theBook
    End Function
End Class
```

```csharp
// Visual C#
using System.Collections;
public class Library {
    private SortedList m_shelf = new SortedList();

    public Library() {
    }

    public void CheckIn(Book newBook) {
        m_shelf.Add(newBook.Title, newBook);
    }

    public Book CheckOut(string title) {
        Book theBook;
        theBook = (Book)m_shelf[title];
        m_shelf.Remove(title);
        return theBook;
    }
}
```

The calls to be replaced are shown in boldface type. Using a typed default property or indexer would eliminate the cast that's needed in the original code. Of course, the cast will be forced down into the typed collection that you create, but then you have to write the cast only once. The *Remove* and *Add* methods will be improved because they'll accept only a string as the key and a Book instance as the object. The design of the new BookCollection class is shown in the following UML class diagram. The C# indexer is shown as an Item property.

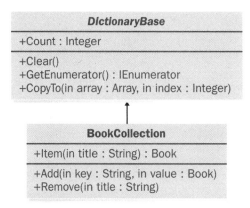

Creating the Class

To create the typed collection class, BookCollection, you'll create a class that inherits from the abstract DictionaryBase class. To make the class functional, you'll add the *Add* and *Remove* methods, and define an Item property or indexer.

Create the project

● Create a new project, and name it ABetterLibrary.

Re-create the Book class

1   On the Project menu, click Add Class. The Add New Item dialog box appears.

2   Name the file Book.vb or Book.cs, depending on the language you're using.

3   Add this code to the Book class for a simplified Book class:

```
' Visual Basic
Public Class Book
    Private m_text As String
    Private m_title As String

    Public ReadOnly Property Title() As String
        Get
            Return m_title
        End Get
    End Property

    Public ReadOnly Property Text() As String
        Get
            Return m_text
        End Get
    End Property
```

```
        Public Sub New(ByVal title As String, ByVal text As String)
            m_title = title
            m_text = text
        End Sub
End Class

// Visual C#
public class Book {
    private string m_text;
    private string m_title;

    public string Title {
        get {
            return m_title;
        }
    }

    public string Text {
        get {
            return m_text;
        }
    }

    public Book(string title, string text) {
        m_title = title;
        m_text = text;
    }
}
```

Create the BookCollection class

1   On the Project menu, click Add Class. The Add New Item dialog box appears.

2   Name the file BookCollection.vb or BookCollection.cs, depending on the language you're using.

Add the *Add* method

1   Modify the class declaration to indicate the base class. Note that there are no items in the Task List because DictionaryBase has no abstract members.

```
' Visual Basic
Public Class BookCollection
    Inherits System.Collections.DictionaryBase
End Class

// Visual C#
public class BookCollection : System.Collections.DictionaryBase {
}
```

2   Add this code for the *Add* method:

```
' Visual Basic
Public Sub Add(aBook as Book)
    Me.Dictionary.Add(aBook.Title, aBook)
End Sub
```

```
// Visual C#
public void Add(Book book) {
    this.Dictionary.Add(book.Title, book);
}
```

Now no one will be able to add anything other than an instance of Book to the collection class. Also, the book is always filed under its title.

Add the *Remove* method

● Add this code for the *Remove* method:

```
' Visual Basic
Public Sub Remove(title As String)
    Me.Dictionary.Remove(title)
End Sub
```

```
// Visual C#
public void Remove(string title) {
    this.Dictionary.Remove(title);
}
```

Add the Item property or indexer

● Add this code for the default Item property or indexer:

```
' Visual Basic
Default Public ReadOnly Property Item (title As String) As Book
    Get
        If Me.Dictionary.Contains(title) Then
            Return CType(Me.Dictionary(title), Book)
        Else
            Return Nothing
        End If
    End Get
End Property
```

```
// Visual C#
public Book this[string title] {
    get {
```

```
                        if (this.Dictionary.Contains(title)) {
                            return (Book)(this.Dictionary[title]);
                        }
                        else {
                            return null;
                        }
                    }
                }
```

Re-create the Library class

1 On the Project menu, click Add Class. The Add New Item dialog box appears.

2 Name the file Library.vb or Library.cs, depending on the language you're using.

3 Add this code to use your BookCollection class rather than the SortedList class. The modified lines are shown in boldface type.

```
' Visual Basic
Public Class Library
    Private m_shelf As New BookCollection()

    Public Sub CheckIn(ByVal newBook As Book)
        m_shelf.Add(newBook)
    End Sub

    Public Function CheckOut(ByVal title As String) As Book
        Dim theBook As Book = m_shelf(title)
        m_shelf.Remove(title)
        Return theBook
    End Function
End Class

// Visual C#
public class Library {
    private BookCollection m_shelf = new BookCollection();

    public Library() {
    }

    public void CheckIn(Book newBook) {
        m_shelf.Add(newBook);
    }

    public Book CheckOut(string title) {
        Book theBook = m_shelf[title];
        m_shelf.Remove(title);
        return theBook;
    }
}
```

Testing the Class

1   Add this code to the Library class to test the classes you have created:

```
' Visual Basic
Public Shared Sub Main()
    Dim aLibrary As New Library()
    aLibrary.CheckIn(New Book("First Book", _
        "Here is the text of the first book."))
    aLibrary.CheckIn(New Book("Second Book", _
        "Here is the text of the second book."))
    Dim firstBook As Book = aLibrary.CheckOut("First Book")
    Console.WriteLine("The text of '{0}' is '{1}'.", _
        firstBook.Title, firstBook.Text)
    aLibrary.CheckIn(firstBook)
End Sub
```

```
// Visual C#
public static void Main() {
    Library aLibrary = new Library();
    aLibrary.CheckIn(new Book("First Book",
        "Here is the text of the first book."));
    aLibrary.CheckIn(new Book("Second Book",
        "Here is the text of the second book."));
    Book firstBook = aLibrary.CheckOut("First Book");
    Console.WriteLine("The text of '{0}' is '{1}'.",
        firstBook.Title, firstBook.Text);
    aLibrary.CheckIn(firstBook);
}
```

2   In the Solution Explorer, right-click the project name, and click Properties on the shortcut menu. The project's Property Pages dialog box appears.

3   In the tree on the left, expand the Common Properties folder and click General.

4   In the Startup Object list, click ABetterLibrary.Library. Click OK.

5   Press F5 to run the application. Here are the results:

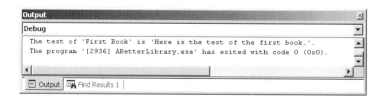

Variations on Inheritance

There are two other variations on inheritance that deserve mention. Sealing classes allows you to prevent inheritance. You can also prevent base members from behaving polymorphically.

Sealing classes   Sometimes you might not want developers to use a class as a base class. You can prevent inheritance by using the *NotInheritable* or *sealed* keyword, as you see here:

```
' Visual Basic
NotInheritable Class NotABaseClass
End Class
```

```
// Visual C#
sealed class NotABaseClass {
}
```

The following code produces an error at compile time:

```
' Visual Basic
Class CantCreateThisClass
    Inherits NotABaseClass
End Class
```

```
// Visual C#
class CantCreateThisClass : NotABaseClass {
}
```

Hiding base class members   In this chapter and Chapter 5, you used the *override* keyword (*Overrides* or *override*) for members in the derived class that were marked as virtual (*MustInherit* or *virtual*) in the base class. Following this practice caused the derived member to be called even if the call was made through a base reference.

Visual Basic and C# also provide keywords, *Shadows* and *new*, to indicate that even though a method in the derived class has the same name as a virtual method in the base class, the derived class method isn't meant to be the override of the base class's virtual method. The effect is that a base reference calls the base method and a derived reference calls the derived method. In the case of Visual Basic, the *Shadows* keyword is applied to all methods of the same name in the base class. In C#, the *new* keyword applies only to members with the same signature (name plus parameters). Here's an example:

```
' Visual Basic
Class BaseClass
```

(continued)

continued

```
        Public Sub BaseMethod()
            Console.WriteLine("BaseMethod in base class.")
        End Sub
End Class

Class DerivedClass
    Inherits BaseClass

    Public Shadows Sub BaseMethod()
        Console.WriteLine("BaseMethod in derived class.")
    End Sub

    Public Shared Sub Main()
        Dim derived As New DerivedClass()
        derived.BaseMethod()

        Dim baseclass As BaseClass = derived
        baseclass.BaseMethod()
    End Sub
End Class

// Visual C#
public class BaseClass {
    public void BaseMethod() {
        Console.WriteLine("BaseMethod in base class.");
    }
}

public class DerivedClass : BaseClass {
    new public void BaseMethod() {
        Console.WriteLine("BaseMethod in derived class.");
    }

    public static void Main() {
        DerivedClass derived = new DerivedClass();
        derived.BaseMethod();

        BaseClass baseclass = derived;
        baseclass.BaseMethod();
    }
}
```

The output from *Main* is

```
BaseMethod in derived class.
BaseMethod in base class.
```

Use *Shadows* and *new* with caution. Developers expect derived classes to act in predictable ways, which generally means that they expect derived classes to act polymorphically.

Quick Reference

To	Do this
Create an abstract class	In Visual Basic, add the *MustInherit* keyword to the class declaration:
	`Public MustInherit Class BankAccount`
	In Visual C#, add the *abstract* keyword to the class declaration:
	`public abstract class BankAccount`
Create an abstract method or property	In Visual Basic, add the *MustOverride* keyword to the declaration:
	`Public MustOverride Function PrintStatement() As String`
	In Visual C#, add the abstract keyword to the declaration:
	`public abstract string PrintStatement();`
Derive from an abstract class	Declare the abstract class as a base class and implement all the abstract class members.
Implement an abstract member	Declare the member with the *override* keyword and implement the member:

	`' Visual Basic`
	`Public Overrides Function PrintStatement() As String`
	`End Function`
	
	`// Visual C#`
	`public override string PrintStatement() {`
	`}`

Prevent a class from becoming a base class	Declare the class with the *NotInheritable* or *sealed* keyword:
	`' Visual Basic`
	`NotInheritable Class NotABaseClass`
	`End Class`
	
	`// Visual C#`
	`sealed class NotABaseClass {`
	`}`

Declare a member in the derived class that doesn't behave polymorphically	Declare the member with the *Shadows* or *new* keyword:
	`' Visual Basic`
	`Public Shadows Sub BaseMethod()`
	`End Sub`
	
	`// Visual C#`
	`new public void BaseMethod() {`
	`}`

Designing Base Classes

6

Responding to Changes with Events

7

Responding to Changes with Events and Exceptions

ESTIMATED TIME
3 hr.

In this chapter, you'll learn how to

✔ *Add a custom control to the Toolbox.*

✔ *Declare an event for your control class.*

✔ *Respond to events from your class using event handlers.*

✔ *Create a delegate.*

✔ *Add and remove event handlers.*

✔ *Derive an EventArgs class.*

✔ *Derive a custom exception class from the ApplicationException class.*

✔ *Throw your custom exception.*

The Microsoft Windows user interface is event driven. The control flow of the program is primarily based on events of the Windows Form control. In this chapter, you'll create a control that appears in the Toolbox. You can drag this control onto a form just as you would any of the built-in Windows controls. The control will have events that you can choose to respond to or ignore in your code. You'll use exceptions to indicate that something has gone wrong during execution. Exceptions can't be ignored. Using exception handling, your code can try to repair the problem or it can exit the program.

Fire on the Tracks! An Event-Driven Application

Your task in this chapter is to create a quick diversion for a young relative:

> A train runs along a track across the screen. At regular intervals but random locations, the track catches fire. The old fire goes out when the new fire appears so that there's always one fire on the track at any point in time. You can adjust the speed of the train using a slider control. The object of the game is to get the train to the end of the track without running into a fire.

A cursory textual analysis of the problem leads to the following class design. In this case, the screen object is represented by the Windows Form class, which contains a track, train, and fire objects. The train moves along the track at a speed set by a slider control, and the fire appears at different points on the track at a set frequency.

The classes are shown in the following UML diagram, which introduces a new UML element, the solid diamond. The solid diamond indicates a relationship called "composition" in object-oriented terminology. Composition is a relationship where some objects are "parts of" another object. It carries the sense that the one object can't exist without the others. All the objects are created and destroyed as a unit.

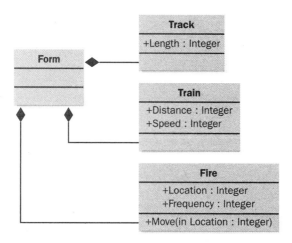

This analysis captures only what's static in the problem, such as the location of the train on the track at a point in time or the distance the train has traveled. It doesn't describe how or when the train moves or when the fire will appear and where. It doesn't describe how the form knows that the train should move or the fire should appear. For that information, you need events, signals from one object to another that something has happened. Here are the events that you need:

- A CaughtOnFire event for the Track class. This event, generated by the track, will be received by the form so that the code in the form can move the fire on the track. The Frequency property will be moved to the Track class to indicate how often the track should raise a CaughtOnFire event.

- A DistanceChanged event for the Train class. This event will be generated periodically to let the form know where the train is on the track. The location of the train depends on the speed of the train and how long it has been running.

Using the CaughtOnFire and DistanceChanged events, the form code can coordinate the behavior of the track, the train, and the fire. In UML, events are modeled as signals, which are similar to classes. In the illustration below, a dashed arrow labeled <<send>> indicates that a particular class, Track, generates a particular event, CaughtOnFire. The event can carry information in parameters. In this case, the CaughtOnFire event carries information about the location of the fire. The UML also provides a syntax for indicating which classes receive the events. The Form class receives both the CaughtOnFire and DistanceChanged events.

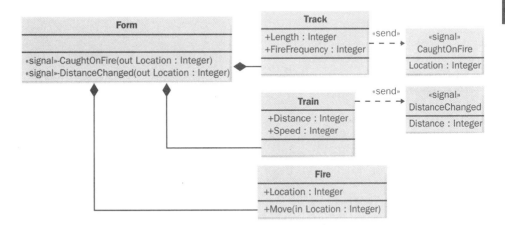

Your last design decision is how to implement the user interface, given the object model. You know that you want a track, a train, and a fire to appear as visual elements on the form. The properties of these visual elements are closely tied to the classes. In fact, you can implement the classes as derived classes of the generic Windows control, the UserControl class, which means that the visual display and behavior of an object are all contained in one class. Additionally, the control can be added to the Toolbox, and then dragged onto the form in the form designer. Here's the complete design:

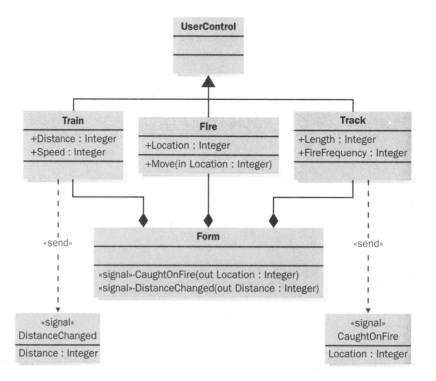

Implementing the Track Class

The first class you'll implement is the Track class. This class derives from the UserControl class, and you draw the track yourself, both the rails and the ties. After you implement the Track class, you can implement the Train class that runs on it.

Create the class

1   Create a new Windows Application project and name it TrainGame.

2   On the Project menu, click Add User Control. The Add New Item dialog box appears.

3   Name the file Track.vb or Track.cs, depending on the language you're using.

Your new user control is empty. You'll define the shape and color of your control by overriding the *OnPaint* method.

Add the properties

1   Right-click the new control and click View Code on the shortcut menu.

2   Add the following code to the Track class for the FireFrequency property. This property determines how often, in seconds, the location of the fire changes.

```vb
' Visual Basic
Private m_fireFrequency As Integer = 1
Public Property FireFrequency() As Integer
    Get
        Return m_fireFrequency
    End Get
    Set(ByVal Value As Integer)
        If Value >= 1 Then
            m_fireFrequency = Value
        End If
    End Set
End Property
```

```csharp
// Visual C#
private int m_fireFrequency = 1;
public int FireFrequency {
    get { return m_fireFrequency; }
    set {
        if (value >= 1) {
            m_fireFrequency = value;
        }
    }
}
```

3   You don't need to add any code for the Length property of the track. Because the Track class inherits from the UserControl class, it already has a Size property, with Height and Width. You'll see more about how this works out in the section about painting the Track control.

Draw the track

The train travels along the track, as you see in the illustration that follows. Your code needs to draw the rails and railroad ties. You might want to shorten or extend the track, so the code should be able to draw tracks of different lengths. You could also accommodate different heights of the track, but the code you write draws a track with a fixed height. Drawing the track is a two-step process:

- Draw the outline of the track using the GraphicsPath class.
- Fill in the outline using the Graphics class.

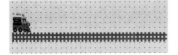

You draw the outline of the track as a series of pieces of track. You create the outline as two horizontal bars and one vertical bar. When you fit the pieces end-to-end and fill them in, you have the track:

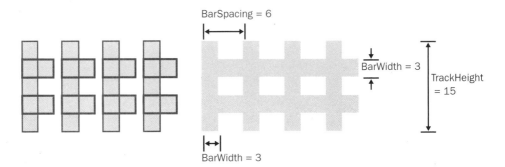

1   Add constants to the Track class to control the size of the track and the spacing of the bars. The preceding diagram shows the relevant measurements in pixels.

```
' Visual Basic
Private Const TrackHeight As Integer = 15          ' Must be divisible by 5
Private Const BarWidth As Integer = TrackHeight \ 5 'Equal to rail width
Private Const BarSpacing As Integer = BarWidth * 2
```

```
// Visual C#
private const int TrackHeight = 15;                // Must be divisible by 5
private const int BarWidth = TrackHeight / 5;   // Equal to rail width
private const int BarSpacing = BarWidth * 2;
```

This code introduces the *Const* and *const* keywords. The constant modifier indicates that the value of the variable can't be modified. Constant values can be of any type, but the compiler must be able to evaluate the expression to the right of the equal sign. Because the compiler doesn't allocate memory for class instances, the expression can't contain a *New* or *new* statement. The result is that constant reference values will be Nothing or null, or a string.

You use the constant field in this case so that you can change the size and proportions of your track by changing these values. All the drawing commands will use these fields, instead of integer literals, such as *"15"*. Using the constant modifier will let the compiler help you by preventing you from accidently changing these values in your code.

2 On the View menu, click Designer to view the control in the form designer. Double-click the control to create the Load event method in the code editor. Add this code to fix the Height property of the Track control to 15 pixels.

```
' Visual Basic
Me.Height = 15
```

```
// Visual C#
this.Height = 15;
```

3 Override the *OnSizeChanged* method to set the Height property of the Track control to 15 pixels and to constrain the width of the control to a multiple of the value assigned to BarSpacing. The height of the control corresponds to the width of the track and the width corresponds to the length of the track. You can type in the code that follows or use the shortcuts provided by Visual Studio. In Visual Basic, click Overrides for the Track class in the Class Name list and OnSizeChanged in the Method Name list. In Visual C#, use the Class View to browse to the Control base class, right-click OnSizeChanged, point to Add, and then click Override. The inheritance tree for the Track class is an amazing eight levels deep. To find the *OnSizeChanged* method, keep opening the Bases and Interfaces nodes until you reach the Control base class. There you will find the *OnSizeChanged* method. The code added to this method, which depends on integer division, is shown here:

```
' Visual Basic
Protected Overrides Sub OnSizeChanged(ByVal e As System.EventArgs)
    Me.Height = TrackHeight
    ' Width must be divisible by BarSpacing
    Dim nBars As Integer = Me.Width \ BarSpacing
    Me.Width = nBars * BarSpacing
End Sub
```

```
// Visual C#
protected override void OnSizeChanged(System.EventArgs e) {
    this.Height = TrackHeight;
    // width must be divisible by BarSpacing
    int nBars = this.Width / BarSpacing;
    this.Width = nBars * BarSpacing;
}
```

4 Override the *OnPaint* method. The code in the *OnPaint* event method is called each time the control is called to paint itself. Add the following code to the *OnPaint* method to draw the track outline and then fill it in with the color brown.

```vb
' Visual Basic
Protected Overrides Sub OnPaint(ByVal e As _
System.Windows.Forms.PaintEventArgs)
    MyBase.OnPaint(e)
    Dim gp As New System.Drawing.Drawing2D.GraphicsPath()
    gp.FillMode = Drawing.Drawing2D.FillMode.Winding
    Dim height As Integer = TrackHeight \ 5
    Dim nBars As Integer = Me.Width \ BarSpacing
    Dim bar As Integer
    For bar = 0 To nBars - 1
        gp.AddRectangle(New System.Drawing.Rectangle( _
            bar * BarSpacing, height, BarSpacing, height))
        gp.AddRectangle(New System.Drawing.Rectangle( _
            bar * BarSpacing, height * 3, BarSpacing, height))
        gp.AddRectangle(New System.Drawing.Rectangle( _
            bar * BarSpacing, 0, BarWidth, TrackHeight))
    Next
    e.Graphics.FillPath(System.Drawing.Brushes.SaddleBrown, gp)
End Sub
```

```csharp
// Visual C#
protected override void OnPaint(System.Windows.Forms.PaintEventArgs e) {
    base.OnPaint(e);
    System.Drawing.Drawing2D.GraphicsPath gp =
        new System.Drawing.Drawing2D.GraphicsPath();
    gp.FillMode = System.Drawing.Drawing2D.FillMode.Winding;
    int height = TrackHeight / 5;
    int nBars = this.Width / BarSpacing;
    for (int bar = 0; bar < nBars; bar++) {
        gp.AddRectangle(new System.Drawing.Rectangle(bar * BarSpacing,
            height, BarSpacing, height));
        gp.AddRectangle(new System.Drawing.Rectangle(bar * BarSpacing,
            height * 3, BarSpacing, height));
        gp.AddRectangle(new System.Drawing.Rectangle(bar * BarSpacing,
            0, BarWidth, TrackHeight));
    }
    e.Graphics.FillPath(System.Drawing.Brushes.SaddleBrown,gp);
}
```

Test the *OnPaint* method

1 Press Ctrl+Shift+B to build the project.

2 Open Form1 in the form designer.

3 Drag a Track control from the Windows Forms area of the Toolbox onto Form1. Resize the Track control. You can make it longer, but you can't change the track height.

Debugging the *OnPaint* Method

If the track doesn't draw itself as you expect, here are some hints for debugging.

- Instead of *e.Graphics.FillPath*, use *e.Graphics.DrawPath*. This draws only the outline of the shapes.
- Experiment with the *GraphicsPath.FillMode* property. This property controls how overlapping shapes are drawn.
- Enlarge the control to make sure you aren't drawing beyond the edge of the control. Remember, the GraphicsPath origin is relative to the control, not the form. Drawing a shape at location (0,0) places the shape at the upper left corner of the control.
- First write the code with hard-coded values, such as *12*, and then replace them with calculated values, such as *2 * BarSpacing*.

Now you're ready to add the CaughtOnFire event.

Creating the CaughtOnFire Event

To raise an event in Visual Basic or Visual C#, you must the declare the event as a field of the class. The declaration contains the name and signature (the parameters and their types) of the event. In .NET, event signatures follow these conventions:

- The first parameter is of type *System.Object* and is the object that raised the event.
- The second parameter is an instance of a class that derives from the EventArgs class. This class carries information about the event that might be useful to the client code. Even though the first parameter is the object that raised the event, the client code might be dependent on information in the EventArgs class. So this extra information carried by the second parameter should be carefully thought out.
- The name of the parameter that derives from the EventArgs class ends in *EventArgs*.

Create the CaughtOnFireEventArgs class

This class contains information about the location of the fire on the track.

1   Add the CaughtOnFireEventArgs class declaration at the end of the Track class definition. In Visual C#, this would be after the closing brace of the Track class, but before the closing brace of the namespace. This class is derived from System.EventArgs.

```
' Visual Basic
Public Class CaughtOnFireEventArgs
    Inherits System.EventArgs
End Class
```

```
// Visual C#
public class CaughtOnFireEventArgs : System.EventArgs {
}
```

2   Add a Location property that indicates how far along the track, in pixels, the new fire is located.

```
' Visual Basic
Private m_location As Integer = 0
Public ReadOnly Property Location() As Integer
    Get
        Return m_location
    End Get
End Property
```

```
// Visual C#
private int m_location = 0;
public int Location {
    get {
        return m_location;
    }
}
```

3   Add the constructor. Because the CaughtOnFireEventArgs class is instantiated only when a fire exists, the constructor requires the *location* parameter.

```
' Visual Basic
Public Sub New(ByVal location As Integer)
    m_location = location
End Sub
```

```
// Visual C#
public CaughtOnFireEventArgs(int location) {
    m_location = location;
}
```

Declare the event

1   In Visual Basic, you simply need to declare the event and its parameters. Add this code to the Track class:

```
' Visual Basic
Public Event CaughtOnFire(ByVal sender As Object, _
    ByVal e As CaughtOnFireEventArgs)
```

The *event handler*, the method that the client code calls when the event is raised, must have the same signature.

2   In Visual C#, you need to take these two steps to declare an event:

■   Declare a delegate. A delegate declares and gives a name to a method signature. By convention, the name of the delegate ends in EventHandler.

■   Declare an event whose type is that of the delegate declared in the preceding step.

Add this code to the Track class:

```
// Visual C#
public delegate void CaughtOnFireEventHandler(object sender,
    CaughtOnFireEventArgs e);
public event CaughtOnFireEventHandler CaughtOnFire;
```

3   To make the CaughtOnFire event the default event for the class, add the DefaultEvent attribute code shown in boldface to the Track class.

```
' Visual Basic
<System.ComponentModel.DefaultEvent("CaughtOnFire")> Public Class Track
    Inherits System.Windows.Forms.UserControl
    ⋮
End Class
```

```
// Visual C#
[System.ComponentModel.DefaultEvent("CaughtOnFire")]
public class Track : System.Windows.Forms.UserControl {
    ⋮
}
```

When you double-click the Track control on the form after you have added this attribute, the CaughtOnFire event method is created in the code editor.

Attributes

Attributes allow you to add information to the elements of your code, and you can use them to affect how the code executes at run time and design time. The attribute information is stored in the compiled assembly as part of the *metadata*. The metadata isn't the code itself, but information about the code. This metadata can be queried at run time or design time in a process called *reflection*. In this case, the Visual Studio development environment uses the DefaultEvent attribute to determine which event handler to add to the code when you double-click the Track control in the form designer.

Your Track control now has a CaughtOnFire event. You'll be able to respond to this event in the form, but first your class has to raise the event in the right circumstances.

Raise the event

The only property you have defined in the Track class is the FireFrequency property. This property indicates how often, in seconds, the track should catch on fire. Each time a fire starts, the CaughtOnFire event should be raised. You'll use a Timer control to signal the Track class that it needs to start a fire.

1 In the Solution Explorer, double-click the Track file to open the control in the form designer.

2 In the Windows Forms area of the Toolbox, double-click the Timer control. The IDE adds a Timer control to the component tray at the bottom of the form designer window and won't be visible at run time.

3 Set the Enabled property of the Timer to *True*.

4 Add code shown in boldface to the *Set* method of the Track's FireFrequency property to set the timer interval. The FireFrequency property indicates how often, in seconds, the Track code should start a fire. The timer interval is expressed in milliseconds. If you want a fire to appear every three seconds, you would set the FireFrequency property to 3, and this code would set the interval of the timer to 3000 milliseconds.

```
' Visual Basic
Private m_fireFrequency As Integer = 1
Public Property FireFrequency() As Integer
    Get
        Return m_fireFrequency
    End Get
```

```vb
    Set(ByVal Value As Integer)
        If Value > 1 Then
            m_fireFrequency = Value
            Timer1.Interval = m_fireFrequency * 1000 ' New code
        End If
    End Set
End Property
```

```csharp
// Visual C#
public int FireFrequency {
    get { return m_fireFrequency; }
    set {
        if (value >= 1) {
            m_fireFrequency = value;
            timer1.Interval = m_fireFrequency * 1000; // New code
        }
    }
}
```

5 View the Track control in the form designer, and double-click the Timer control to create the Tick event method in the Track class.

6 Add code to select a random location on the track and raise the CaughtOnFire event.

```vb
' Visual Basic
Private Sub Timer1_Tick(ByVal sender As Object, _
ByVal e As System.EventArgs) Handles Timer1.Tick
    Dim randomNumber As New System.Random()
    RaiseEvent CaughtOnFire(Me, _
        New CaughtOnFireEventArgs(randomNumber.Next(0, Me.Width)))
End Sub
```

```csharp
// Visual C#
private void timer1_Tick(object sender, System.EventArgs e) {
    if (CaughtOnFire != null) {
        System.Random randomNumber = new System.Random();
        CaughtOnFire(this, new CaughtOnFireEventArgs(
            randomNumber.Next(0,this.Width)));
    }
}
```

Visual Basic provides a keyword, *RaiseEvent*, to raise the event. To raise the event, you must supply the sender parameter, in this case *Me*, and an instance of CaughtOnFireEventArgs. The client code (the code that contains an instance of the Track class), must then create an event handler to respond to the event, just as the Track class has a method to respond to the Tick event of the Timer.

C# uses a different model for raising events. The public delegate *CaughtOnFire* represents a list of methods that should be called when the event is raised. When the *CaughtOnFire* method is called, each method added to the delegate is called. How this works will become more clear when you see the code that responds to the event in the form.

The call, *randomNumber.Next*, returns a random number between 0 and the width of the control, thus guaranteeing that the fire is actually on the track.

7   Press Ctrl+Shift+B to compile your project.

Put the fire on the track

The project design includes a class for the fire. On close inspection, you see that the Fire class adds nothing to the basic user control class, which has a location. A PictureBox control would be sufficient for displaying the fire on the track.

1   In the Solution Explorer, double-click Form1 to open it in the form designer.

2   From the Windows Forms area in the Toolbox, drag a PictureBox control onto the form.

3   Set the Name property of the PictureBox control to *fire*, and the SizeMode property to *AutoSize*.

4   Click the ellipsis (...) next to the Image property to select an image for the fire. You can use Fire.ico in the \Chapter07 folder on the companion CD.

5   Position the PictureBox control so that it's sitting on the track. Your form looks like this:

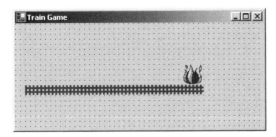

6   Select the Track control and set the FireFrequency property to *3*.

7   Double-click the Track control to create the CaughtOnFire event method in the code editor.

8   Add code to move the fire to the location specified by the *CaughtOnFireEventArgs* parameter.

```vb
' Visual Basic
Private Sub Track1_CaughtOnFire(ByVal sender As System.Object, ByVal e _
As TrainGame.CaughtOnFireEventArgs) Handles Track1.CaughtOnFire
    fire.Location = New System.Drawing.Point(Track1.Left + e.Location, _
        Track1.Top - fire.Height)
End Sub
```

```csharp
// Visual C#
private void track1_CaughtOnFire(object sender,
TrainGame.CaughtOnFireEventArgs e) {
    fire.Location = new System.Drawing.Point(track1.Left
        + e.Location, track1.Top - fire.Height);
}
```

9   Press F5 to run the application, and watch the fire jump along the track.
You can set the FireFrequency property in the Properties window for the
Track control to have fires appear less often.

You now have a working track and fire. All you need to add is a train. The
next section doesn't use any new syntax but does demonstrate coordinating
events from two objects: the train and the track.

Implementing the Train Class

Like the Track class, the Train class inherits from the UserControl class. The
Train class takes advantage of the Image property to display a train image. An
event, DistanceChanged, is triggered when the distance changes. You update the
distance periodically by using a Timer control.

Create the class

1   On the Project menu, click Add User Control. The Add New Item dialog box
appears.

2   Name the file Train.vb or Train.cs, depending on the language you're using.

Add the properties

1   In the Solution Explorer, right-click Train and click View Code on the shortcut menu.

2   Add the following code for the Speed property. The speed is in pixels per
second.

```vb
' Visual Basic
Private m_speed As Integer = 0
Public Property Speed() As Integer
    Get
```

(continued)

```vb
        Return m_speed
    End Get
    Set(ByVal Value As Integer)
        If Value >= 0 Then
            m_speed = Value
        End If
    End Set
End Property
```

```
' Visual C#
private int m_speed = 0;
public int Speed {
    get {
        return m_speed;
    }
    set {
        if (value >= 0) {
            m_speed = value;
        }
    }
}
```

3   Add the following code for the Distance property. Distance is in pixels traveled. Because the distance is determined by the speed and time traveled, this property is read-only. Recall that the *Timer.Tick* event handler calculates the value for the *m_distance* field.

```vb
' Visual Basic
Private m_distance As Integer = 0
Public ReadOnly Property Distance() As Integer
    Get
        Return m_distance
    End Get
End Property
```

```csharp
// Visual C#
private int m_distance = 0;
public int Distance {
    get {
        return m_distance;
    }
}
```

Add the methods

No methods are specified in the design, but it would be convenient to move the train back to the start location at the end of a game so that you can play multiple games. Add the following code to define a *ReStart* method to move the train back to the start of the track:

```
' Visual Basic
Public Sub ReStart()
    m_distance = 0
End Sub

// Visual C#
public void ReStart() {
    m_distance = 0;
}
```

Add the DistanceChanged event

The program calculates the distance traveled by the train each tenth of a second, by using a *Timer.Tick* event.

1   In the Solution Explorer, right-click Train and click View Designer on the shortcut menu.

2   In the Windows Forms area of the Toolbox, double-click the Timer control to add a Timer control.

3   Set the Interval property of the Timer to 100, and the Enabled property to True.

4   Double-click the timer to create the Tick event handler for the Train class.

5   Add the following code to create the DistanceChangedEventArgs class. The DistanceChangedEventArgs class contains a property for the current location of the train. Add the code for this class after the Train class code in the same source file. In Visual C#, this class should be within the TrainGame namespace.

```
' Visual Basic
Public Class DistanceChangedEventArgs
    Inherits System.EventArgs

    Private m_distance As Integer
    Public ReadOnly Property Distance() As Integer
        Get
            Return m_distance
        End Get
    End Property

    Public Sub New(ByVal distance As Integer)
        m_distance = distance
    End Sub
End Class
```

(continued)

```csharp
// Visual C#
public class DistanceChangedEventArgs : System.EventArgs {
    private int m_distance;
    public int Distance {
        get { return m_distance; }
    }

    public DistanceChangedEventArgs(int distance) {
        m_distance = distance;
    }
}
```

6   Declare the event, and in C#, also declare the delegate. Add this code to the Train class:

```vb
' Visual Basic
Public Event DistanceChanged(ByVal sender As Object, _
ByVal e As DistanceChangedEventArgs)
```

```csharp
// Visual C#
public delegate void DistanceChangedEventHandler(object sender,
    DistanceChangedEventArgs e);
public event DistanceChangedEventHandler DistanceChanged;
```

7   Add code to the timer's Tick event method to calculate the new location, if it has changed, and raise an event for the client code. The event is raised only if the location has changed, thus the test for *m_speed* > 0. Remember that when you're raising the event in C#, you must first test that any methods are "listening."

```vb
' Visual Basic
Private Sub Timer1_Tick(ByVal sender As System.Object, _
ByVal e As System.EventArgs) Handles Timer1.Tick
    If m_speed > 0 Then
        m_distance += Convert.ToInt32(Convert.ToInt32(m_speed) _
            * (Convert.ToDouble(Timer1.Interval) / 1000F))
        RaiseEvent DistanceChanged(Me, _
            New DistanceChangedEventArgs(m_distance))
    End If
End Sub
```

```csharp
// Visual C#
private void timer1_Tick(object sender, System.EventArgs e) {
    if (m_speed > 0) {
        m_distance += (int)((double)m_speed *
            ((double)timer1.Interval / 1000F));
```

```
        if (DistanceChanged != null) {
            DistanceChanged(this,new DistanceChangedEventArgs(m_distance));
        }
    }
}
```

8 Add this attribute code to make the DistanceChanged event the default event for the class:

```
' Visual Basic
<System.ComponentModel.DefaultEvent("DistanceChanged")> Public Class Train
    Inherits System.Windows.Forms.UserControl
    ⋮
End Class

// Visual C#
[System.ComponentModel.DefaultEvent("DistanceChanged")]
public class Train : System.Windows.Forms.UserControl
{
    ⋮
}
```

The train class is complete. You can find the Train control in the Windows Forms tab of the Toolbox.

● Press Ctrl+Shift+B to build the project.

Implementing the User Interface

Your form already contains the track and the fire. You need just a few more controls and a little code to complete the project.

Add the controls

1 View Form1 in the form designer, and from the Windows Forms area of the Toolbox, drag a TrackBar control onto the form.

2 Set the following properties of the TrackBar control:

Property	Value
Name	*throttle*
Minimum	*0*
Maximum	*50*
Orientation	*Vertical*
SmallChange	*5*
LargeChange	*10*
TickFrequency	*10*

3   Drag a Train control onto the form and place it on the track.

4   Click the ellipsis button (...) next to the BackgroundImage property and select an image for the train. A train image is provided in the \Chapter07 folder on the companion CD.

5   Modify the Size property of the control to fit the train image. For the image on the companion CD, use 32, 32.

6   Drag a Button control onto the form. Set its Text property to *New game* and its Name property to *reset*.

Program the events

1   Double-click the Train control to create the DistanceChanged event handler for the form.

2   Add the following code to move the train down the track as the location changes. If the train gets to the end of the track, stop it by setting the speed to *0*.

```
' Visual Basic
Private Sub Train1_DistanceChanged(ByVal sender As System.Object, ByVal _
e As TrainGame.DistanceChangedEventArgs) Handles Train1.DistanceChanged
    Train1.Left = Track1.Left + e.Distance
    If Train1.Right >= Track1.Right Then
        Train1.Speed = 0
        throttle.Value = 0
    End If
End Sub

// Visual C#
private void train1_DistanceChanged(object sender,
TrainGame.DistanceChangedEventArgs e) {
    train1.Left = track1.Left + e.Distance;
    if (train1.Right >= track1.Right) {

        train1.Speed = 0;

throttle.Value = 0;
    }
}
```

3   In Visual Basic, click Throttle in the Class Name list and the ValueChanged event in the Method Name list. In Visual C#, view Form1 in the form designer and select the TrackBar control. In the Properties window, click the Events button, and double-click the ValueChanged event.

4 Add the following code to change the speed of the train so that it moves down the track:

```
' Visual Basic
Private Sub throttle_ValueChanged(ByVal sender As Object, ByVal e _
As System.EventArgs) Handles throttle.ValueChanged
    If Train1.Right < Track1.Right Then
        Train1.Speed = throttle.Value
    Else
        throttle.Value = 0
    End If
End Sub
```

```
// Visual C#
private void throttle_ValueChanged(object sender, System.EventArgs e) {
    if (train1.Right < track1.Right) {
        train1.Speed = throttle.Value;
    }
    else {
        throttle.Value = 0;
    }
}
```

5 Double-click the New Game button to create the Click event handler for Form1. Add the following code to move the train back to the start of the track:

```
' Visual Basic
Private Sub reset_Click(ByVal sender As System.Object, ByVal e _
As System.EventArgs) Handles reset.Click
    Train1.ReStart()
    throttle.Value = 0
    ' explicitly set speed, although trackbar_ValueChanged will do it
    Train1.Speed = 0
    Train1.Left = Track1.Left
End Sub
```

```
// Visual C#
private void reset_Click(object sender, System.EventArgs e) {
    train1.ReStart();
    throttle.Value = 0;
    // explicitly set speed, although trackbar_ValueChanged will do it
    train1.Speed = 0;
    train1.Left = track1.Left;
}
```

Test the program

1   Press F5 to run the application. Use the TrackBar control to adjust the speed of the train so that you don't run over the fire. You can adjust how often the fire moves to increase your chances of getting the train to the end of the track without incident. Here's the program:

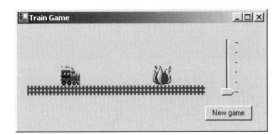

2   Using the CaughtOnFire and DistanceChanged events, you can add other functionality to the program. You could change the train bitmap for the occasions that the train catches on fire, for example, or you could give the user a reward if he or she reaches the end of the track without running into a fire.

Setting Up Event Methods Without Using the Designer

In the TrainGame example, you created a user control with events. When you dragged the Train control onto the form, the events were available in the Method Name list for Visual Basic projects and in the Properties window for Visual C# projects. You don't have to use the designer to connect your event methods to your class instances; you can do it simply by using code statements. Setting up event methods in code allows you to

    ■   Create control instances at run time and respond to their events

    ■   Change the event handler for a particular event at run time

In Visual Basic, you can choose from two ways to set up event methods. One way uses the *Handles* keyword. The other way uses the *AddHandler* statement. To use the *Handles* keyword, you must declare the instance with the *WithEvents* keyword as a field of a class. The catch is that you can't use the *New* keyword in the declaration, so the class must be instantiated elsewhere in the class, most likely in the constructor. Once you declare the class using the *WithEvents* keyword, the events become available for the instance in the Method Name list of the code editor, which is the method used by the form designer. If you were to create a new Windows Application project, add one Button control, and double-click the control, you'd find the following code in the form, after expanding the section labeled Windows Form Designer Generated Code in the code editor.

```
' Visual Basic
' Only code relevant to the button is shown.
Public Class Form1
    Inherits System.Windows.Forms.Form

    Public Sub New()
        MyBase.New()
        'Call to InitializeComponent standard for a Windows Form
        InitializeComponent()
    End Sub

    ' Button is declared using WithEvents.
    Friend WithEvents Button1 As System.Windows.Forms.Button

    ' Button is instantiated in this method.
    Private Sub InitializeComponent()
        Me.Button1 = New System.Windows.Forms.Button()
    End Sub

    ' Handles keyword used to associate method with event.
    Private Sub Button1_Click(ByVal sender As System.Object, _
        ByVal e As System.EventArgs) Handles Button1.Click
    End Sub
End Class
```

If you wanted to add controls at run time, you wouldn't be able to declare them as fields of the class. In this case, you can use the *AddHandler* statement to associate a method with an event, as shown in the following code. The following *Button1_Click* method adds a new button to the form and assigns the *newButton_Click* method as the event handler for the button's Click event.

```
Private Sub Button1_Click(ByVal sender As System.Object, _
ByVal e As System.EventArgs) Handles Button1.Click
    Dim newButton As New Button()
    Me.Controls.Add(newButton)
    AddHandler newButton.Click, AddressOf newButton_Click
End Sub
```

(continued)

```
Private Sub newButton_Click(ByVal sender As System.Object, _
ByVal e As System.EventArgs)
    MessageBox.Show("You clicked the new button!")
End Sub
```

You can't add an event handler by name; you must use its run-time address. The *AddressOf* keyword returns this address. If, at a later time in the application, you want the Click event of the new Button to execute a different method, you can use the *RemoveHandler* statement.

```
RemoveHandler newButton.Click, AddressOf newButton_Click
```

Visual C# gives you only one way to connect events to methods. C# uses the operators += and −= to add and remove event handlers to and from an event. If you were to create a new Windows Application project, add one Button control, and double-click the control, you'd find the following code in the form, after expanding the section labeled Windows Form Designer Generated Code in the code editor. Because events are declared as delegate fields in the class, you need to create an instance of the delegate of the same type as the event, as you can see here:

```
// Visual C#
// Only code relevant to the button is shown.
public class Form1 : System.Windows.Forms.Form {
    private System.Windows.Forms.Button button1;

    public Form1() {
        // Call to InitializeComponent standard for a Windows Form.
        InitializeComponent();
    }

    // Button is instantiated in this method.
    private void InitializeComponent() {
        this.button1 = new System.Windows.Forms.Button();
        // += operator used to associate method with event.
        this.button1.Click += new
            System.EventHandler(this.button1_Click);
    }

    private void button1_Click(object sender, System.EventArgs e) {
    }
}
```

More on Delegates

When you created the delegate for the CaughtOnFire event in the Track class, you were actually creating an extension of the *System.Delegate* class. The only operations defined for the delegate outside the Track class (in the form code) are the += and −= operators, which add and remove event handlers. The event handlers are added as instances of the delegate class you defined, which is why you'll see the following syntax to add the event handler in the generated code of the form:

```
this.train1.DistanceChanged += new TrainGame.Train.
    DistanceChangedEventHandler(this.train1_DistanceChanged);
```

You can create controls at run time and use the += and −= operators to add and remove handlers at run time. The following *button1_Click* method adds a new button to the form.

```
private void button1_Click(object sender, System.EventArgs e) {
    Button newButton = new Button();
    this.Controls.Add(newButton);
    newButton.Click += new EventHandler(this.newButton_Click);
}

private void newButton_Click(object sender, System.EventArgs e) {
    MessageBox.Show("You clicked the new button!");
}
```

Exceptions—When Things Go Wrong

In the last section, you programmed events for things that you expect to happen to your object. Trains are expected to change location as they drive along, but sometimes things happen that aren't expected. In .NET programming, these exceptional situations are handled using *exceptions*, a programming construct for handling error conditions. A program is said to "throw an exception" when errors occur. You can write code to "catch" the exception, so that execution of your program doesn't stop completely. Additionally, you can create custom exceptions for your application to provide specific information to your program and your user about what has gone wrong.

Generate an exception

This small application demonstrates an exception being thrown.

1   Create a new Windows application and name it ThrowSystemException.

2   Add a Button control to the form.

3   Double-click the Button control to create the Click event handler, and add the following code, which attempts to access the tenth integer in an array of five integers.

```
' Visual Basic
Private Sub Button1_Click(ByVal sender As System.Object, _
ByVal e As System.EventArgs) Handles Button1.Click
    Dim numbers() As Integer = {1, 2, 3, 4, 5}
    MessageBox.Show(numbers(9))
End Sub
```

```
// Visual C#
private void button1_Click(object sender, System.EventArgs e) {
    int[] numbers = { 1, 2, 3, 4, 5};
    MessageBox.Show(numbers[9].ToString());
}
```

4   Press F5 to run the application and click the Button control. The following message box is displayed. Click Break, and then click Stop Debugging from the Debug menu to stop the program.

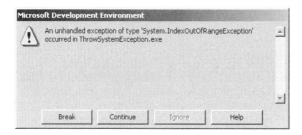

System.IndexOutOfRangeException is thrown because the index, 9, is out of range of the array, which is 0 through 4.

You can prevent error messages from popping up like this by trapping the exceptions using exception handling.

5   Modify the code for the Click event as you see here:

```
' Visual Basic
Private Sub Button1_Click(ByVal sender As System.Object, _
ByVal e As System.EventArgs) Handles Button1.Click
    Dim numbers() As Integer = {1, 2, 3, 4, 5}
    Try
```

```
            MessageBox.Show(numbers(9))
        Catch ex As Exception
            MessageBox.Show("Something went wrong: " & ex.Message)
        End Try
    End Sub

    // Visual C#
    private void button1_Click(object sender, System.EventArgs e) {
        int[] numbers = { 1, 2, 3, 4, 5};
        try {
            MessageBox.Show(numbers[9].ToString());
        }
        catch (Exception ex) {
            MessageBox.Show("Something went wrong: " + ex.Message);
        }
    }
```

6 Press F5 to run the program. In this case, no system error message appears on the screen, and you don't have the opportunity to choose whether to quit or continue. When you catch an exception this way, the code you write is responsible for that decision.

Writing Your Own Exception Class

You can generate exceptions using the throw keyword (*Throw* in Visual Basic, *throw* in Visual C#). The .NET convention is to throw objects that derive from the *System.Exception* class. More specifically, applications should throw objects that derive from *System.ApplicationException*, which itself derives from *System.Exception*.

The following small application shows how you can derive an exception class, throw the exception under the right conditions, and catch the exception using a *try* block. This application uses a Person class with FirstName and LastName properties. The class provides one constructor that expects the name in "First Last" format. Should the constructor parameter not follow that format, the constructor will throw a *NameFormatIncorrectException*.

Create the project

1 Create a new Windows Application and name it PersonList.

2 Drag a ListBox control onto the form. Set the Name property to *personList* and the Sorted property to *True*.

3 Drag a TextBox control onto the form. Set the Name property to *personsName* and the Text property to (*blank*).

4 Drag a Button control onto the form. Set the Name property to *addPerson* and the Text property to *Add*.

Create the exception class

1   Right-click Form1 and click View Code on the shortcut menu.

2   Add the following code after the Form1 class to declare the exception class.

```
' Visual Basic
Public Class NameFormatIncorrectException
    Inherits System.ApplicationException
End Class
```

```
// Visual C#
public class NameFormatIncorrectException : System.ApplicationException {
}
```

The ApplicationException class has two properties of interest. The first is the Message property, which contains a string that describes the error that has occurred. The second is the Inner property. If you're throwing an exception because you caught an exception, you can pass on that exception in the Inner property.

3   Add this code for the overloaded constructors:

```
' Visual Basic
Public Sub New()
    MyBase.New()
End Sub

Public Sub New(ByVal message As String)
    MyBase.New(Message)
End Sub

Public Sub New(ByVal message As String,_
ByVal innerException As Exception)
    MyBase.New(message, InnerException)
End Sub
```

```
// Visual C#
public NameFormatIncorrectException() : base() {
}

public NameFormatIncorrectException(string message) : base(message) {
}

public NameFormatIncorrectException(string message,
Exception innerException) :
    base(message, innerException) {
}
```

The exception classes in .NET have three constructors, all of which can call a matching base constructor. One is parameterless, and its message is blank. The second takes one exception, the message text. The third sets both the message text and the inner exception.

The exception class is complete.

Create the Person class

1   Add the following code to declare the Person class after the NameFormatIncorrectException class and add the FirstName and LastName properties.

```
' Visual Basic
Public Class Person
    Private m_first As String
    Private m_last As String

    Public Property FirstName() As String
        Get
            Return m_first
        End Get
        Set(ByVal Value As String)
            m_first = Value
        End Set
    End Property

    Public Property LastName() As String
        Get
            Return m_last
        End Get
        Set(ByVal Value As String)
            m_last = Value
        End Set
    End Property
End Class

// Visual C#
public class Person {
    private string m_first;
    private string m_last;

    public string FirstName {
        get { return m_first; }
        set { m_first = value; }
    }

    public string LastName {
        get { return m_last; }
        set { m_last = value; }
    }
}
```

2   Add the following code for the overridden *ToString* method. This property is used to display the Person class instance in the ListBox control.

```
' Visual Basic
Public Overrides Function ToString() As String
    Return m_last & ", " & m_first
End Function
```

```
// Visual C#
public override string ToString() {
    return m_last + ", " + m_first;
}
```

3   Add the constructor that takes a name in "First Last" format and parses it into the FirstName and LastName properties:

```
' Visual Basic
Public Sub New(ByVal firstlast As String)
    Try
        Dim splitCharacters As String = " "
        Dim names() As String = _
            firstlast.Split(splitCharacters.ToCharArray())
        m_first = names(0)
        m_last = names(1)
    Catch ex As Exception
        Throw New NameFormatIncorrectException( _
        "Cannot find the first name and last name in the string: " _
        & firstlast, ex)
    End Try
End Sub
```

```
// Visual C#
public Person(string firstlast) {
    try {
        string splitCharacters = " ";
        string[] names = firstlast.Split(splitCharacters.ToCharArray());
        m_first = names[0];
        m_last = names[1];
    }
    catch (Exception ex) {
        throw new NameFormatIncorrectException("Cannot find the first " +
        "name and last name in the string: " + firstlast, ex);
    }
}
```

Add the code for the user interface

1   Open the form in the designer and double-click the Add button to create the Click event.

2 Add the following code to add a new person to the list. You can have multiple catch blocks in a *try* block so that you can capture specific types of exceptions.

```vb
' Visual Basic
Private Sub addPerson_Click(ByVal sender As System.Object, _
ByVal e As System.EventArgs) Handles addPerson.Click
    Try
        personList.Items.Add(New Person(personsName.Text))
    Catch nameException As NameFormatIncorrectException
        If Not IsNothing(nameException.InnerException) Then
            MessageBox.Show(nameException.Message & ControlChars.CrLf _
                & nameException.InnerException.Message)
        Else
            MessageBox.Show(nameException.Message)
        End If
    Catch ex As Exception
        MessageBox.Show(ex.Message)
    End Try
    personsName.Text = ""
End Sub
```

```csharp
// Visual C#
private void addPerson_Click(object sender, System.EventArgs e) {
    try {
        personList.Items.Add(new Person(personsName.Text));
    }
    catch (NameFormatIncorrectException nameException) {
        if (nameException.InnerException != null) {
            MessageBox.Show(nameException.Message + "\n" +
            nameException.InnerException.Message);
        }
        else {
            MessageBox.Show(nameException.Message);
        }
    }
    catch (Exception ex) {
        MessageBox.Show(ex.Message);
    }
    personsName.Text = "";
}
```

Test the application

● Press F5 to run the application. Entering a string like *Bob Smith* in the TextBox correctly adds Smith, Bob to the ListBox. Entering a string like *Bob* results in a thrown exception.

Quick Reference

To	Do this

Declare an event for your control class	In Visual Basic, declare the event name and its signature.
	
	```Public Event CaughtOnFire(ByVal sender As Object, _\n ByVal e As CaughtOnFireEventArgs)```
	
	In Visual C#, declare the delegate type of the event, and then declare the delegate of that type.
	
	```public delegate void CaughtOnFireEventHandler(object sender,\n CaughtOnFireEventArgs e);\npublic event CaughtOnFireEventHandler CaughtOnFire;```

Add an event handler using the designer and code editor	Visual Basic Declare a class field of the object using the *WithEvents* keyword. In the Class Name list click the class. In the Method Name list click the event. The event handler is added to the code. Visual C# In the form designer, select the control. In the Properties window, click the Events button. Double-click the event, and the event handler is added to the code.

Add and remove event handlers at run time	In Visual Basic, use the *AddHandler* and *RemoveHandler* statements.
	
	```AddHandler newButton.Click, AddressOf newButton_Click\nRemoveHandler newButton.Click, AddressOf newButton_Click```
	
	In Visual C#, use the += and −= operators.
	
	```newButton.Click += new EventHandler(this.newButton_Click);\nnewButton.Click -= new EventHandler(this.newButton_Click);```

Derive an EventArgs class	Create a class that inherits from *System.EventArgs*, and add the properties to pass information about the event.
	
	```' Visual Basic\nPublic Class CaughtOnFireEventArgs\n Inherits System.EventArgs\nEnd Class```
	
	```// Visual C#\npublic class CaughtOnFireEventArgs : System.EventArgs {\n}```

Derive a custom exception class from the Application-Exception class	Custom exceptions should derive from the *System.Application* class, and provide the three constructors. ```' Visual Basic\nPublic Class NewException\n Inherits System.ApplicationException\n Public Sub New()\n MyBase.New()\n End Sub```

To	Do this

```
        Public Sub New(ByVal message As String)
            MyBase.New(Message)
        End Sub

        Public Sub New(ByVal message As String,_
        ByVal innerException As Exception)
            MyBase.New(message, InnerException)
        End Sub
End Class

// Visual C#
public class NewException: System.ApplicationException {
    public NewException () : base() {
}

    public NewException (string message) : base(message) {
}

    public NewException (string message,
    Exception innerException) :
    base(message, innerException) {
}
}
```

To	Do this
Throw your custom exception	When the code determines that the error condition occurs, throw a new instance of the exception, using one of the three constructors.

```
' Visual Basic
Throw New NewException("Error text")

// Visual C#
throw new NewException("Error Message");
```

Catch your custom exception	Add a catch statement to the *try* block for the custom exception.

```
' Visual Basic
Try
    ' Normal execution
Catch ne As NewException
    ' Respond to NewException
Catch ex As Exception
    ' Respond to all other exceptions
End Try

// Visual C#
try {
    // Normal execution
}
catch (NewException ne) {
    // Respond to NewException
}
catch (Exception ex) {
    // Respond to all other exceptions
}
```

Putting It All Together with Components

ESTIMATED TIME
3 hr. 30 min.

In this chapter, you'll learn how to

✔ *Turn a class into a component.*

✔ *Create a class library.*

✔ *Select and use a namespace for your control library.*

✔ *Add design-time support for your control and component classes, including Toolbox icons, Properties window categories, and description strings.*

In the previous chapters, you learned about the basic constructs of object-oriented programs in the .NET Framework, including fields, properties, methods, constructors, events, and inheritance. You now have a solid basis for designing your object-oriented projects. It's time to use that knowledge to think about how a developer would use the classes you've created in the Visual Studio .NET development environment. You want to create objects that are easy to use and, when appropriate, can be used by simply dragging them from the Toolbox onto a form. When a developer selects your custom control or component in the form designer, you'd like the control's properties to display help text in the Properties window, and you want the control to have its own icon in the Toolbox. In this chapter, you'll write a complete application that uses classes, events, exceptions, and inheritance. You'll design these classes with other developers in mind—the developers who will use your classes.

The Memory Game

Your task in this chapter is to design and implement a memory card game. You have a design directive to utilize the visual design support of the Visual Studio .NET environment. When you develop with components and controls, you can move some of the developer's work from coding to the design-time environment. Consider the ListBox control. If you drag a ListBox control onto a form and click the ellipsis button (...) next to the Items property, the ListBox collection editor appears, allowing you to add items to the list box. You can also add items to the list box by using the *ListBox.Items.Add* method, but many users prefer the more visual method offered by the collection editor.

The Memory game will present the player with a grid of cards placed face down. The player can select two cards at a time by clicking them. When clicked, the cards will turn face up. If the two cards have matching face values, they are removed from the game. If the cards do not match, they turn face down again. When all the cards have been removed, a message box appears, congratulating the player and reporting the number of times cards were turned over in the course of the game. The game is shown here:

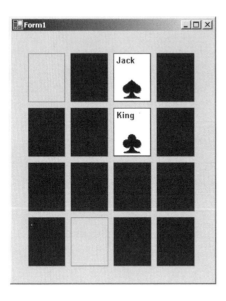

In Chapter 4, "Working with Methods," you created three classes for card games: Card, Hand, and Deck. You instantiated the Hand and Deck classes in code, and then used those classes to manipulate a set of Card instances, which you also instantiated in code. To create the Deck you wanted, you used a constructor that used arrays of Suit and FaceValue enumeration values for the cards in the deck. This time around, you again want to create a Deck, but you want to do so by dragging a Deck component from the Toolbox to the form and then setting the suits and face values by using the Properties window. In addition to instantiating the Deck in a constructor, the form class contained a lot of code for manipulating the Card instances. In a more object-oriented program, that manipulation might be better handled in a class that represents a game.

Designing the Game

You'll use two projects to build the Memory game. The first is a control library, GamesLibrary, which contains the controls and components needed to implement the Memory game. The second project is the game project, which uses the controls in the library to implement the game. The following UML diagram describes the game:

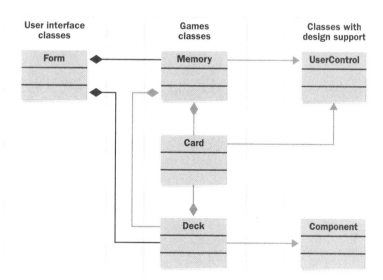

This diagram divides the primary classes of the design into three categories. The user interface class is the familiar *System.Windows.Forms* class. This class contains the visual elements that the game player can interact with. The games classes should be familiar to you from the exercises in Chapter 4.

The classes with design support provide functionality that you can take advantage of at design time. For example, the Memory class, which represents the Memory game, derives from the UserControl class. Thus you can add the Memory control to the Toolbox and create an instance by just dragging one onto the form. From that point, you can set the properties of the Memory control in the Properties window.

The Component class is similar to the UserControl class in that you can add the component to the Toolbox and drag an instance onto a form. One difference is that the component instance is added to the component tray, rather than being a visual element of the form. Another difference is that in the Windows Forms Designer generated code, the component instance is added to the form's components container, rather than to the form's Controls collection.

Showing Composition and Aggregation in UML

The solid diamond in the UML diagram indicates a relationship called *composition* in object-oriented terminology. Composition means that one object can't exist without another object. As an example, a car without an engine isn't really a car. If the engine stops working, the car stops working—or you at least need to get a new engine to get the car running.

This diagram introduces a new UML element, the open diamond. The open diamond indicates a relationship called *aggregation*. Aggregation implies that one object can use another object, but can be created without it: a car can have a driver, but even without a driver it's still a car.

You might not necessarily agree with the assignment of open and closed diamonds in the diagram. Designers often disagree about the distinctions between composition and aggregation.

The Games Class Library

The first project is a class library that contains the Card, Deck, and Game classes. You'll add this library as a reference to the project that runs the Memory game.

Create the GamesLibrary project

1   On the File menu, point to New, and then click Project.

2   In the Projects Types tree, click Visual Basic Projects or Visual C# Projects.

3   In the Templates list, click Windows Control Library.

4   In the Name box, type *GamesLibrary* and then click OK.

Changing the Namespace

In the .NET Framework, classes are contained in namespaces. A namespace defines a scope for a class. The projects in this book so far have had one namespace, which is identical to the project name, but this can be changed. In the .NET Framework, namespaces are named in a particular way, by convention: *Company.Technology*. In this library, your company LotsOfFun has created several games classes. Thus your classes will be contained in the namespace *LotsOfFun.Games*.

Change the namespace

1   In the Solution Explorer, right-click the GamesLibrary project and click Properties on the shortcut menu. The GamesLibrary Property Pages dialog box appears.

Notice that the setting for Output Type is Class library. The output of this project will be a .dll file. You can use objects defined in a class library file, but you cannot execute a .dll file.

2   Click General under Common Properties in the list. In the Root Namespace box for Visual Basic or the Default Namespace box for Visual C#, type *LotsOfFun.Games*, and click OK. Subsequent classes added to the project will be added to this namespace.

3   If you are using Visual C#, right-click UserControl1.cs in the Solution Explorer, and then click View Code on the shortcut menu. Locate the namespace declaration near the top of the file and replace GamesLibrary with *LotsOfFun.Games*.

Putting It All Together 8

Creating the Card Control

The Card control inherits from the UserControl class. In Chapter 4, you used the Button control as the basis for the user interface of the Card. Then you used the Tag property to save the Card class associated with the Button control. That wasn't the best object-oriented solution, because you had to cast the Tag property to use the Card instance. In this project, you could create the Card control by inheriting from Button, adding Suit and FaceValue properties, and then controlling the Text and Image properties. You'll get a better result by inheriting from the UserControl class because the Button control has several properties you don't want the user to have access to, such as Text and Image. You want to control those properties so that they reflect the Suit and FaceValue properties at all times.

In addition to the Suit and FaceValue properties you implemented for Card in Chapter 4, you'll add the FaceUp property to the Card class. This value determines whether the Card control is displayed face up (suit and value showing) or face down (back of the card showing). Other additions to the class are used for design-time support of the Card control. These additions include help strings for the properties, a Property window category for the properties, and a Toolbox icon. Finally, you will use the control's Paint event to dynamically update the control's appearance when the Suit and FaceValue are set in the designer.

Add the Card control to the project

1   Right-click UserControl1 in the Solution Explorer, and then click Rename on the shortcut menu. Rename the file *Card.vb* or *Card.cs*, depending on the language you're using.

2   Right-click Card in the Solution Explorer, and then click View Code on the shortcut menu.

3   Rename the class Card. If you're using Visual C#, locate the constructor and change its name to *Card*, too.

4   Right-click Card in the Solution Explorer, and then click View Designer on the shortcut menu.

5   Right-click the control in the designer and click Properties on the shortcut menu.

6   In the Properties window, expand Size and set the Width to 60 and the Height to 75.

Define the Toolbox icon for the Card control

1 Create a 16-by-16-pixel bitmap for your project, name it *Card.bmp*, and save it in the project directory. An icon is available on the companion CD in the \Chapter08 folder. The file must be named Card.bmp, so that Visual Studio will use it as the Toolbox icon for the Card class.

2 In the Solution Explorer, right-click the GamesLibrary project, point to Add, and then click Add Existing Item on the shortcut menu.

3 In the Add Existing Item dialog box, click Image Files in the Files Of Type list.

4 Select Card.bmp and click Open.

5 In the Solution Explorer, right-click the Card.bmp file and click Properties on the shortcut menu.

6 In the Properties window, set the Build Action property of the bitmap file to *Embedded Resource*. When the project is built, the bitmap will be added to the assembly file, which is the file created when you compile the program. The bitmap's name, Card, will cause it to be used as the Toolbox icon of the Card control.

Add the Suit and FaceValue enumerations

1 Add the Suit enumeration to the *LotsOfFun.Games* namespace. In the Solution Explorer, right-click Card and click View Code on the shortcut menu to see the class code in the code editor. In Visual Basic, add this code just above the Card class. In Visual C#, this code goes inside the namespace block, but outside the Card class.

```
' Visual Basic
Public Enum Suit
    Hearts
    Diamonds
    Clubs
    Spades
End Enum

// Visual C#
public enum Suit {
    Clubs, Spades, Diamonds, Hearts
};
```

2   Add the FaceValue enumeration after the Suit enumeration.

```
' Visual Basic
Public Enum FaceValue
    Ace
    Two
    Three
    Four
    Five
    Six
    Seven
    Eight
    Nine
    Ten
    Jack
    Queen
    King
End Enum

// Visual C#
public enum FaceValue {
    Ace, Two, Three, Four, Five, Six, Seven, Eight, Nine, Ten,
    Jack, Queen, King
};
```

Add the Suit, FaceValue, and FaceUp properties

The Suit, FaceValue, and FaceUp properties all use attributes to customize their appearance in the Properties window. These attributes come from the *System.ComponentModel* namespace. An *Imports* or *using* statement for the namespace allows you to use the attributes without the qualified name.

1   If you're using Visual Basic, right-click the GamesLibrary project in the Solution Explorer, and click Properties on the shortcut menu. Click Imports under Common Properties and type *System.ComponentModel* into the Namespace box. Click Add Import, and then click OK. If you're using Visual C#, the corresponding *using* statement is added to each source file.

```
// Visual C#
using System.ComponentModel;
```

2   Add the following code for the FaceValue property to the Card class:

```
' Visual Basic
Private m_faceValue As FaceValue = FaceValue.Ace
<Category("Game"), Description("Face value of the card.")> _
Public Property FaceValue() As FaceValue
    Get
```

```
              Return m_facevalue
        End Get
        Set(ByVal Value As FaceValue)
            m_facevalue = Value
            Me.Refresh()
        End Set
    End Property
```

```
// Visual C#
private FaceValue m_faceValue = FaceValue.Ace;
[Category("Game")]
[Description("Face value of the card.")]
public FaceValue FaceValue {
    get { return m_faceValue; }
    set {
        m_faceValue = value;
        this.Refresh();
    }
}
```

This is the same code you wrote in Chapter 4, with additions to support the fact that the Card is also a UserControl. The call to *Refresh* uses the Paint event to redraw the card whenever the Suit changes. You'll write the Paint event handler in the next section. The property also has two attributes, Category and Description. Visual Studio .NET uses these attributes when the properties are displayed in the Properties window.

3 Add the following code for the Suit property:

```
' Visual Basic
Private m_suit As Suit = Suit.Hearts
<Category("Game"), Description("Suit (Hearts, Spades, Diamonds, Clubs)")> _
Public Property Suit() As Suit
    Get
        Return m_suit
    End Get
    Set(ByVal Value As Suit)
        m_suit = Value
        Me.Refresh()
    End Set
End Property
```

```
// Visual C#
private Suit m_suit = Suit.Hearts;
[Category("Game")]
[Description("Suit (Hearts, Spades, Diamonds, Clubs)")]
public Suit Suit {
```

(continued)

```
        get { return m_suit; }
        set {
            m_suit = value;
            this.Refresh();
        }
    }
```

4   Add the following code for the FaceUp property:

```
' Visual Basic
Private m_faceUp As Boolean = True
<Category("Game"), Description("Is the card face up?")> _
Public Property FaceUp() As Boolean
    Get
        Return m_faceUp
    End Get
    Set(ByVal Value As Boolean)
        m_faceUp = Value
        Me.Refresh()
    End Set
End Property

// Visual C#
private bool m_faceUp = true;
[Category("Game")]
[Description("Is the card face up?")]
public bool FaceUp {
    get { return m_faceUp; }
    set {
        m_faceUp = value;
        this.Refresh();
    }
}
```

Add the constructors and the *Paint* method

1   The Chapter08 folder on the companion CD has four icons for the four possible suits in a deck. Copy the icons to the GamesLibrary project folder.

2   Add the following code shown in boldface to the parameterless constructor and a field to the class to hold the suit images. If you're using Visual Basic, you'll have to expand the Windows Forms Designer Generated Code region to find the parameterless constructor. The constructor loads the images for the suits into an ArrayList. This loads a set of images for each Card instance. Don't delete the call to *InitializeComponent* in the constructor. This call is necessary to initialize the control. You'll need to replace *PATH* in the code with the path to the folder where you have stored the icons on your system.

```
' Visual Basic
Dim m_images As New SortedList()
Public Sub New()
    MyBase.New()
    ' This call is required by the Windows.Forms Form Designer.
    InitializeComponent()

    m_images.Add(Suit.Clubs, New Icon("PATH\clubs.ico"))
    m_images.Add(Suit.Diamonds, New Icon("PATH\diamonds.ico"))
    m_images.Add(Suit.Hearts, New Icon("PATH\hearts.ico"))
    m_images.Add(Suit.Spades, New Icon("PATH\spades.ico"))
End Sub

// Visual C#
SortedList m_images = new SortedList();
public Card()
{
    // This call is required by the Windows.Forms Form Designer.
    InitializeComponent();

    m_images.Add(Suit.Clubs, new Icon("PATH\\clubs.ico"));
    m_images.Add(Suit.Diamonds, new Icon("PATH\\diamonds.ico"));
    m_images.Add(Suit.Hearts, new Icon("PATH\\hearts.ico"));
    m_images.Add(Suit.Spades, new Icon("PATH\\spades.ico"));
}
```

3 Add the constructor that takes a Suit and a FaceValue as parameters. Note that this constructor calls the base constructor to set up the image fields.

```
' Visual Basic
Public Sub New(ByVal newSuit As Suit, ByVal newValue As FaceValue)
    Me.New()
    m_suit = newsuit
    m_faceValue = newvalue
End Sub

// Visual C#
public Card(Suit suit, FaceValue faceValue) : this() {
    m_suit = suit;
    m_faceValue = faceValue;
}
```

4 If you're using Visual Basic, click Base Class Events in the Class Name list of the code editor. Then click Paint in the Method Name list to create the declaration for the Paint event handler.

If you're using Visual C#, double-click Card.cs in the Solution Explorer to open the control in the designer. In the designer, right-click the control and then click Properties on the shortcut menu. Click the Events toolbar button in the Properties window, and then double-click the Paint event. A Paint event handler is added to the Card class.

5   Add code to the Paint event handler to draw the card either face down or face up.

```vb
' Visual Basic
Private Sub Card_Paint(ByVal sender As Object, ByVal e As _
System.Windows.Forms.PaintEventArgs) Handles MyBase.Paint
    Dim g As Graphics = Me.CreateGraphics()
    g.DrawRectangle(System.Drawing.Pens.Black, 0, 0, _
        Me.ClientRectangle.Width - 1, Me.ClientRectangle.Height - 1)
    If Me.FaceUp Then
        Me.BackColor = Color.White
        g.DrawString(Me.m_faceValue.ToString(), New  _
            System.Drawing.Font("Arial", 10, _
            System.Drawing.FontStyle.Bold), _
            System.Drawing.Brushes.Black, 3, 3)
        g.DrawIcon(CType(Me.m_images(m_suit), Icon), 14, 40)
    Else
        Me.BackColor = Color.Blue
    End If
End Sub
```

```csharp
// Visual C#
private void Card_Paint(object sender,
System.Windows.Forms.PaintEventArgs e)
{
    Graphics g = this.CreateGraphics();
    g.DrawRectangle(System.Drawing.Pens.Black,0,0,
        this.ClientRectangle.Width-1, this.ClientRectangle.Height-1);
    if (this.m_faceUp) {
        this.BackColor = Color.White;
        g.DrawString(this.m_faceValue.ToString(),
        new System.Drawing.Font("Arial",10,System.Drawing.FontStyle.Bold),
        System.Drawing.Brushes.Black,3,3);
        g.DrawIcon((Icon)(this.m_images[m_suit]),14,40);
    }
    else {
        this.BackColor = Color.Blue;
    }
}
```

Write the SizeChanged event handler

You can respond to the SizeChanged event to prevent the user from changing the size of the control. You'll want to do this, because drawing code you wrote in the Paint event handler depends on the control maintaining a constant size.

1   If you're using Visual Basic, click Base Class Events in the Class Name list, and then click SizeChanged in the Method Name list in the code editor. This creates the declaration for the SizeChanged event handler.

If you're using Visual C#, right-click Card.cs in the Solution Explorer, and then click View Designer on the shortcut menu. In the designer, right-click the control and click Properties on the shortcut menu. Click the Events toolbar button in the Properties window. In the Properties window, double-click the SizeChanged property. This creates the declaration for the SizeChanged event handler.

2   Add the following code to prevent the user from changing the size of the control. The constant size of the control is exposed as a public member, because the Memory control will use it to lay out the cards. (In Chapter 11, "Using Shared and Static Members," you'll learn how to do this without exposing fields.)

```
' Visual Basic
Public Const FixedWidth As Integer = 60
Public Const FixedHeight As Integer = 75
Private Sub Card_SizeChanged(ByVal sender As Object, _
ByVal e As System.EventArgs) Handles MyBase.SizeChanged
    Me.Size = New Size(FixedWidth, FixedHeight)
End Sub

// Visual C#
public const int FixedWidth = 60;
public const int FixedHeight = 75;
private void Card_SizeChanged(object sender, System.EventArgs e)
{
    this.Size = new Size(FixedWidth, FixedHeight);
}
```

3   On the Build menu, click Build.

The Card class is now complete and you can test it.

Creating the Memory Game Project

The Card class is contained in a class library, which means it provides classes you can use in other projects. You can't run a class library assembly, so you will use a Windows Application project for instantiating the display of a Card control.

Add a new project to the solution

By adding a new project to the solution, you can work on the class library and use the objects it contains at the same time.

1 On the File menu, point to Add Project, and then click New Project.

2 In the Projects Types tree, click Visual Basic Projects or Visual C# Projects. In the Templates list, click Windows Application.

3 In the Name box, type *Memory* and then click OK.

Add a reference to the Games library

Even though the two projects are in the same solution, you can't use the controls defined in the Games library until you've added a reference to the library in the Memory project.

1 Right-click the Memory project in the Solution Explorer and click Add Reference on the shortcut menu. The Add Reference dialog box appears.

2 On the .NET tab, click the Browse button. The Select Component dialog box appears. Browse to the obj\debug folder of the GamesLibrary project.

3 Select GamesLibrary.dll and click Open.

4 In the Add Reference dialog box, click OK to add the reference to the Memory project.

Add the Card control to the Toolbox

When you add the Card control to the Toolbox, you can simply add a Card control by dragging it onto a form. Follow these steps to add the control to the Toolbox:

1 Double-click Form1 of the Memory project in the Solution Explorer.

2 Right-click the Toolbox and click Add Tab on the shortcut menu. A new tab appears at the bottom of the Toolbox.

3 Type *Games* for the name of the new tab and press Enter.

4 Click the new Games tab.

5 Right-click in the Games tab and click Customize Toolbox on the shortcut menu.

6 Click the .NET Framework Components tab.

7 Click the Browse button and browse to the GamesLibrary.dll file, as you did in the previous section.

8 Select the check box for the Card component in the *LotsOfFun.Games* namespace.

9 Click OK. The Card control icon is added to the Toolbox, as shown here.

10 Drag a card onto the form. Experiment with changing the suit and value of the card. Here's the Jack of Diamonds:

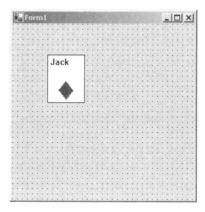

11 The Properties window follows. Note that property descriptions are displayed at the bottom of the Properties window, and that the Card properties are shown together in the Game category of the Properties window. Also note that the Text property isn't in the Properties window.

Creating the Deck Component

You'll implement the Deck as a component, which means that you'll be able to add a Deck component icon to the Toolbox. When you drag the Deck component to the form, an instance will be placed in the component tray, similar to the Timer control. By making the Deck a component, you can use the graphical tools of the Visual Studio .NET design environment to set the properties of the component.

This implementation of Deck behaves differently than the version you wrote in Chapter 4. In that version, the parameterless constructor created a 52-card deck, and a second constructor allowed you to specify the suits and face values that would appear in the deck. In this implementation, the parameterless constructor again creates a 52-card deck, but there is no constructor that takes parameters. Instead, the Deck class will support a Suits property and a FaceValues property. The user can therefore use a collection editor—similar to the collection editor for the ListBox control—to choose the values at design time. When the user changes either the Suit value or the FaceValue property, the Card instances are created to match the new values.

Add the Deck component to the project

1   Right-click the GamesLibrary project in the Solution Explorer, point to Add, and then click Add Component on the shortcut menu. The Add New Item dialog box appears.

2   Name the new component *Deck.vb* or *Deck.cs*, depending on the language you're using.

3   Right-click in the designer and click View Code on the shortcut menu.

Examine the code for the Deck. You'll see the important elements of a component:

- The key feature of a component is that it can be hosted (or sited) in a container for design-time support. Thus, you'll find this constructor:

```
' Visual Basic
Public Sub New(Container As System.ComponentModel.IContainer)
    MyClass.New()

    'Required for Windows.Forms Class Composition Designer support
    Container.Add(me)
End Sub
```

```
// Visual C#
public Deck(System.ComponentModel.IContainer container) {
    /// <summary>
    ///
 Required for Windows.Forms Class Composition Designer support
    /// </summary>
    container.Add(this);
    InitializeComponent();
    //
    // TODO: Add any constructor code after InitializeComponent call
    //
}
```

- The second feature, also seen in the UserControl, is that the component contains a component field, so that the component can host other components:

```
' Visual Basic
Private components As System.ComponentModel.Container
```

```
// Visual C#
private System.ComponentModel.Container components = null;
```

Define the Toolbox icon for the Deck component

To define the icon for the Deck component, add a bitmap named Deck.bmp to the project.

1   Create a 16-by-16-pixel bitmap for your project, name it *Deck.bmp*, and save it in the project directory. An icon is available on the companion CD in the \Chapter08 folder. The file must be named Deck.bmp.

2   In the Solution Explorer, right-click the GamesLibrary project, point to Add, and then click Add Existing Item in the shortcut menu.

3   In the Add Existing Item dialog box, change Files Of Type to Image Files.

4   Select Deck.bmp and click Open.

5   In the Solution Explorer, right-click the Deck.bmp file and click Properties on the shortcut menu.

6   In the Properties window, set the Build Action property of the bitmap file to *Embedded Resource*. This will cause the bitmap to be added to the assembly file.

Add the Suits and FaceValues properties

In Chapter 4, you passed the suits and face values for the deck as parameters to the constructor. In this case, you want to allow the user to define the suits and face values after dropping the Deck component onto the form, so that the values won't be defined when the control is created.

1   Add the following code for the Suits property. The Suits property is an array of Suit enumeration values. At design-time, the development environment will be able to examine the type of the array and provide a collection editor for entering the values. You will define the *MakeDeck* method in the next section. Whenever the suits in the deck are changed, a new set of cards is created.

```
' Visual Basic
Dim m_suits() As Suit = {Suit.Clubs, Suit.Diamonds, Suit.Hearts, _
    Suit.Spades}
<Category("Game"), Description("The suits in the deck.")> _
Public Property Suits() As Suit()
    Get
        Return m_suits
    End Get
    Set(ByVal Value As Suit())
        m_suits = Value
        Me.MakeDeck()
    End Set
End Property

// Visual C#
private Suit[] m_suits = {Suit.Clubs, Suit.Diamonds, Suit.Hearts,
    Suit.Spades};
[Category("Game")]
[Description("The suits in the deck.")]
public Suit[] Suits {
    get { return m_suits; }
    set {
        m_suits = value;
        this.MakeDeck();
    }
}
```

2 Add the following code for the FaceValues property. Like the code you added for the Suits property, this code is an array of enumeration values.

```vb
' Visual Basic
Dim m_faceValues() As FaceValue = {FaceValue.Ace, FaceValue.Two, _
    FaceValue.Three, FaceValue.Four, FaceValue.Five, FaceValue.Six, _
    FaceValue.Seven, FaceValue.Eight, FaceValue.Nine, FaceValue.Ten, _
    FaceValue.Jack, FaceValue.Queen, FaceValue.King}
<Category("Game"), Description("The face values in the deck.")> _
Public Property FaceValues() As FaceValue()
    Get
        Return m_faceValues
    End Get
    Set(ByVal Value As FaceValue())
        m_faceValues = Value
        Me.MakeDeck()
    End Set
End Property
```

```csharp
// Visual C#
private FaceValue[] m_faceValues = {FaceValue.Ace, FaceValue.Two,
    FaceValue.Three, FaceValue.Four, FaceValue.Five, FaceValue.Six,
    FaceValue.Seven, FaceValue.Eight, FaceValue.Nine, FaceValue.Ten,
    FaceValue.Jack, FaceValue.Queen, FaceValue.King};
[Category("Game")]
[Description("The face values in the deck.")]
public FaceValue[] FaceValues {
    get { return m_faceValues; }
    set {
        m_faceValues = value;
        this.MakeDeck();
    }
}
```

Add and modify the constructors

● Add the following call to the two existing constructors. Add this code as the last line of code in each constructor. If you're using Visual Basic, expand the code region labeled Component Designer Generated Code to find the two constructors.

```vb
' Visual Basic
MakeDeck()
```

```csharp
// Visual C#
MakeDeck();
```

Add the *MakeDeck* and *Shuffle* methods

The *MakeDeck* private method creates the cards using the Suits and FaceValues properties. It's called whenever either the Suits or FaceValues property is changed.

1   Add the following code for the *MakeDeck* method. This is the same method you used in the Chapter 4 exercise, except that it uses the *m_suits* and *m_faceValues* fields instead of taking two parameters. Because the deck might have cards from a previous call to *MakeDeck*, those cards are removed.

```
' Visual Basic
Dim m_cards As New System.Collections.ArrayList()
Private Sub MakeDeck()
    ' Dispose of the existing cards.
    Dim count As Integer
    For count = 0 To m_cards.Count - 1
        CType(m_cards(count), Card).Dispose()
    Next
    m_cards.Clear()

    ' Add the new cards.
    Dim asuit, avalue As Integer
    For asuit = 0 To suits.Length - 1
        For avalue = 0 To m_faceValues.Length - 1
            m_cards.Add(New Card(m_suits(asuit), m_faceValues(avalue)))
        Next
    Next
End Sub
```

```
// Visual C#
System.Collections.ArrayList m_cards = new System.Collections.ArrayList();
private void MakeDeck() {
    // Dispose of the existing cards.
    for (int count = 0; count < m_cards.Count; count++ ) {
        ((Card)m_cards[count]).Dispose();
    }
    m_cards.Clear();

    // Add the new cards.
    for (int asuit = 0; asuit < m_suits.Length; asuit++) {
        for (int avalue = 0; avalue < m_faceValues.Length; avalue++) {
            m_cards.Add(new Card(m_suits[asuit], m_faceValues[avalue]));
        }
    }
}
```

The *Dispose* Method

The .NET runtime supports automatic garbage collection. When you create an instance of a class, a certain amount of memory is reserved for and used by the instance. At some later time in the program, you might not need that instance anymore, and you'll want to release the memory for use by other instances in your program or other programs. The .NET runtime tracks the use of objects in your program. When the runtime determines that you have no reference variables that point to a class instance, that memory is released. One of the limitations of this garbage collection is that you can't force memory to be released. You might want to release class instances, though, if they're using resources that are limited, such as the number of open files. You'll find that some objects in the .NET Framework provide a *Dispose* method that releases any of these resources. When you use a class that supports the *Dispose* method, you should call that method on any reference that you know you're going to release. Be aware that once you call *Dispose* on an instance, that instance becomes invalid.

2 Add the following code for the *Shuffle* method. This code is unchanged from the code in Chapter 4.

```
' Visual Basic
Public Sub Shuffle()
    Dim rgen As New System.Random()
    Dim newdeck As New System.Collections.ArrayList()
    While (m_cards.Count > 0)
        ' Choose one card at random.
        Dim removeindex As Integer = rgen.Next(0, m_cards.Count - 1)
        Dim removeobject As Object = m_cards(removeindex)
        m_cards.RemoveAt(removeindex)
        ' Add the removed card to the new collection.
        newdeck.Add(removeobject)
    End While

    ' Replace the old deck with the new deck.
    m_cards = newdeck
End Sub
```

(continued)

```
// Visual C#
public void Shuffle() {
    System.Random rgen = new System.Random();
    System.Collections.ArrayList newdeck =
    new System.Collections.ArrayList();
    while (m_cards.Count > 0) {
        // Remove one from m_cards.
        int toremove = rgen.Next(0, m_cards.Count - 1);
        Card remove = (Card)m_cards[toremove];
        m_cards.Remove(remove);
        // Add it to the new deck.
        newdeck.Add(remove);
    }

    // Replace old deck with new deck.
    m_cards = newdeck;
}
```

Add the Count and indexer properties

You can now implement the Count and indexer properties, which use the *ArrayList* field. Again, this code is unchanged from Chapter 4, except for additions to support the Properties window.

1   Add the following code for the Count property:

```
' Visual Basic
<Category("Game"), Description("Number of cards in the deck.")> _
Public ReadOnly Property Count() As Integer
    Get
        Return m_cards.Count
    End Get
End Property
```

```
// Visual C#
[Category("Game")]
[Description("Number of cards in the deck.")]
public int Count {
    get { return m_cards.Count; }
}
```

2   Add the following code for the default property in Visual Basic and the indexer property in Visual C#:

```
' Visual Basic
Default Public ReadOnly Property Cards(ByVal indexer As Integer) As Card
    Get
        If ((indexer >= 0) And (indexer < m_cards.Count)) Then
            Return CType(m_cards(indexer), Card)
```

```
        Else
            Throw New ArgumentOutOfRangeException("Index out of range.")
        End If
    End Get
End Property

// Visual C#
public Card this[int indexer] {
    get {
        if ((indexer >= 0) && (indexer < m_cards.Count)) {
            return((Card)m_cards[indexer]);
        }
        else {
            throw new ArgumentOutOfRangeException("Index out of range.");
        }
    }
}
```

3   On the Build menu, click Build Solution.

4   Refresh the GamesLibrary reference in the Memory project. Expand References under Memory in the Solution Explorer, right-click GamesLibrary and click Remove on the shortcut menu.

5   Right-click References and click Add Reference on the shortcut menu. Click Browse on the .NET tab, select the GamesLibrary.dll in the GamesLibrary\obj\debug folder and click Open. Click OK to close the Add Reference dialog box.

Testing the Control

You can now add a Deck component to the Memory game. As with the Card control, you'll first add the component to the Toolbox. Then all you have to do is drag it onto the form.

Add the Deck component to the Toolbox

1   Double-click Form1 in the Solution Explorer to open it in the form designer.

2   Right-click the Games tab of the Toolbox and click Customize Toolbox on the shortcut menu. The Customize Toolbox dialog box appears.

3   Click the .NET Framework Components tab and then click Browse.

4   Browse to and select the GamesLibrary.dll file, found in the obj\debug folder of the project folder. Click Open.

5   Select the Deck component in the list and click OK. The Deck component is added to the Games tab of the Toolbox.

Add a Deck component to the form

1 Drag a Deck component onto the form. An instance named *Deck1* or *deck1* (depending on the language you're using) is added to the component tray of Form1.

Right-click the Deck1 control in the component tray and click Properties on the shortcut menu. Notice, in the Properties window, the Suits property of the Deck component. The ellipsis indicates that you can set the Suits array using a designer.

2 Explore the designer support by clicking the ellipsis button next to the Suits property. The Suit Collection Editor appears, as shown here:

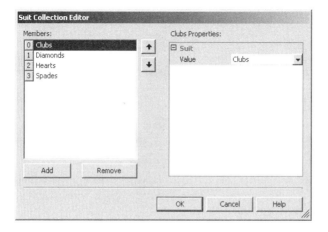

3 Click Add to add a Suit value to the list.

4 Use the Value drop-down list in the Properties pane to select the Suit, as shown here:

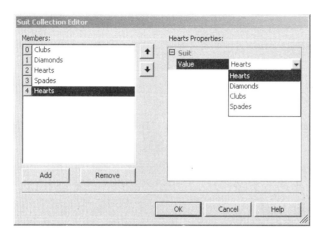

5 After you add and delete Suit items and FaceValue items from the component, notice that the read-only Count property changes to reflect the number of Card instances in the Deck component.

Creating the Memory Control

The Memory control will use the Card control and the Deck component to implement the simple Memory game. The entire Memory game is encapsulated in the Memory control. When you assign a Deck instance to the game and call the *Play* method, the game is ready to run.

Add the Memory control to the project

1 Right-click the GamesLibrary project in the Solution Explorer, point to Add, and then click Add User Control on the shortcut menu. The Add New Item dialog box appears.

2 Name the new component *Memory.vb* or *Memory.cs*, depending on the language you're using.

Define the Toolbox icon for the Memory control

To define the icon for the Memory control, add a bitmap named Memory.bmp to the project.

1 Create a 16-by-16-pixel bitmap for your project, name it *Memory.bmp*, and save it in the project directory. An icon is available on the companion CD in the Chapter08 folder. The file must be named Memory.bmp.

2 In the Solution Explorer, right-click the GamesLibrary project, click Add, and then click Add Existing Item in the shortcut menu.

3 In the Add Existing Item dialog box, change the Files Of Type to Image files.

4 Select the Memory.bmp file and click Open.

5 In the Solution Explorer, right-click the Memory.bmp file and click Properties on the shortcut menu.

6 In the Properties window, set the Build Action property of the bitmap file to *Embedded Resource*.

Add the Rows, Columns, and Deck properties

1 Edit the Memory class code by right-clicking in the designer and clicking View Code on the shortcut menu.

2 Add the following code to the Memory class for the Rows property. When the number of rows or columns changes, the control needs to be redrawn. The call to *Refresh* will redraw the control. The initial value is *2*, which is more reasonable than the usual *0*.

```vbnet
' Visual Basic
Private m_rows As Integer = 2
<Category("Game"), Description("Number of rows in the grid.")> _
Public Property Rows() As Integer
    Get
        Return m_rows
    End Get
    Set(ByVal Value As Integer)
        If Value > 0 Then
            m_rows = Value
            Me.Refresh()
        End If
    End Set
End Property
```

```csharp
// Visual C#
private int m_rows = 2;
[Category("Game")]
[Description("Number of rows in the grid.")]
public int Rows {
    get { return m_rows; }
    set {
        if (value > 0) {
            m_rows = value;
            this.Refresh();
        }
    }
}
```

3   Add the following code for the Columns property:

```vbnet
' Visual Basic
Private m_columns As Integer = 2
<Category("Game"), Description("Number of columns in the grid.")> _
Public Property Columns() As Integer
    Get
        Return m_columns
    End Get
    Set(ByVal Value As Integer)
        If Value > 0 Then
            m_columns = Value
            Me.Refresh()
        End If
    End Set
End Property
```

```
// Visual C#
private int m_columns = 2;
[Category("Game")]
[Description("Number of columns in the grid.")]
public int Columns {
    get { return m_columns; }
    set {
        if (value > 0) {
            m_columns = value;
            this.Refresh();
        }
    }
}
```

4 Add the following code for the Deck property:

```
' Visual Basic
Private m_deck As Deck
<Category("Game"), _
Description("The deck used to fill the grid with cards.")> _
Public Property Deck() As Deck
    Get
        Return m_deck
    End Get
    Set(ByVal Value As Deck)
        m_deck = Value
    End Set
End Property
```

```
// Visual C#
private Deck m_deck;
[Category("Game")]
[Description("The deck used to fill the grid with cards.")]
public Deck Deck {
    get { return m_deck; }
    set { m_deck = value; }
}
```

Override the *OnPaint* method to draw the Memory control

● Add the following code to override the *OnPaint* method. The *OnPaint* method draws outlines for where the cards will be when the game is played. This gives the developer a visual guide to what the game will look like at run time. The Card is a fixed size, and the public constants FixedHeight and FixedWidth are used to draw the card outlines.

```vb
' Visual Basic
Private Const m_spacing As Integer = 10
Protected Overrides Sub OnPaint(ByVal e As _
System.Windows.Forms.PaintEventArgs)
    Dim height As Integer = LotsOfFun.Games.Card.FixedHeight
    Dim width As Integer = LotsOfFun.Games.Card.FixedWidth
    Me.Width = (width + m_spacing) * m_columns + m_spacing
    Me.Height = (height + m_spacing) * m_rows + m_spacing

    ' Just draw the outline of the cards; the actual Card
    ' instances are added when Play is called.
    Dim g As Graphics = Me.CreateGraphics()
    Dim row, column As Integer
    For row = 0 To m_rows - 1
        For column = 0 To m_columns - 1
            g.DrawRectangle(System.Drawing.Pens.Gray, _
            column * (width + m_spacing) + m_spacing, _
            row * (height + m_spacing) + m_spacing, width, height)
        Next
    Next
End Sub
```

```csharp
// Visual C#
private const int m_spacing = 10;
protected override void OnPaint(System.Windows.Forms.PaintEventArgs e) {
    int height = LotsOfFun.Games.Card.FixedHeight;
    int width = LotsOfFun.Games.Card.FixedWidth;
    this.Width = (width + m_spacing) * m_columns + m_spacing;
    this.Height = (height + m_spacing) * m_rows + m_spacing;
    //this.Refresh();

    // Just draw the outline of the cards; the actual Card
    // instances are added when Play is called.
    Graphics g = this.CreateGraphics();
    for (int row = 0; row < m_rows; row++) {
        for (int column = 0; column < m_columns; column++) {
            g.DrawRectangle(System.Drawing.Pens.Gray,
            column * (width + m_spacing) + m_spacing,
            row * (height + m_spacing) + m_spacing, width, height);
        }
    }
}
```

The *OnPaint* Method and the Paint Event

You have two choices for painting your control: You can override the *OnPaint* method or you can add an event handler for the control's Paint event. If you override the *OnPaint* method, you prevent the *OnPaint* method of the base class from executing. If you use the Paint event, the base *OnPaint* method is called and the Paint event handler is called. Using the Paint event carries a possible performance penalty, since it involves this additional event call. The choice is yours.

Implement the playing features of the game

The basic design of the game is implemented this way:

1   Shuffle the cards in the deck and display them on the Game control. Their locations will match the design-time drawing of the control. Note that Card instances are added to the Memory control, not to the form that is hosting the Memory control. The Form class has no access to the Card instances through the Memory control.

2   Use the Click event of the Card control to change the FaceUp property of the card.

3   After each card is clicked, determine whether a pair has been clicked. If so, remove the pair from the Memory control. If the cards don't match, turn them face down.

4   Continue allowing the user to click the cards until all the cards have been removed from the Memory control. When the last pair is removed, raise a GameOver event that reports the number of Card clicks needed to win the game.

Support the GameOver event

1   Add the following code to the Memory class for the Clicks property that maintains a count of the times a card was clicked in the game:

```
' Visual Basic
Private m_clicks As Integer = 0

// Visual C#
private int m_clicks = 0;
```

2   Add the EventArgs class after the Memory class. This class is used to return the number of clicks needed to win the game. In Visual C#, this class goes in the *LotsOfFun.Games* namespace.

```
' Visual Basic
Public Class GameOverEventArgs
    Inherits System.EventArgs

    Private m_clicks As Integer
    Public Sub New(ByVal clicks As Integer)
        m_clicks = clicks
    End Sub

    Public ReadOnly Property Clicks() As Integer
        Get
            Return m_clicks
        End Get
    End Property
End Class

// Visual C#
public class GameOverEventArgs : System.EventArgs {
    private int m_clicks;

    public GameOverEventArgs(int clicks) {
        m_clicks = clicks;
    }

    public int Clicks {
        get { return m_clicks; }
    }
}
```

3   Add the event declaration to the Memory class. In the case of Visual C#, the event declaration includes the delegate declaration.

```
' Visual Basic
Public Event GameOver(sender As Object, e as GameOverEventArgs)

// Visual C#
public delegate void
    GameOverHandler(object sender, GameOverEventArgs e);
public event GameOverHandler GameOver;
```

4   Add the DefaultEvent attribute, shown in boldface, to the class declaration:

```
' Visual Basic
<DefaultEvent("GameOver")> _
Public Class Memory
    Inherits System.Windows.Forms.UserControl
```

```
// Visual C#
[DefaultEvent("GameOver")]
public class Memory : System.Windows.Forms.UserControl
```

Implement the game play

In the client code, the developer adds a Memory control to the form and sets the Rows, Columns, and Deck properties. At run time, the *Play* method is called to populate the control with Card instances.

One of the challenges in implementing the game play is tracking the Card instances. The instances are initially created and contained in the Deck component, and they are never removed from the Deck component. To display the Cards during game play, add them to the Controls collection of the Memory control. When the player selects a pair, those cards are removed from the collection of the Memory control. Since you control (through your code) the controls in the Controls collection, you'll know the game is over when the Controls collection has no controls in it.

1   Add the following code for the DeckGridIncompatibilityException class, after the GameOverEventArgs class. This exception is thrown if the number of cards in the deck doesn't match the number of slots in the Memory game layout.

```
' Visual Basic
Public Class DeckGridIncompatibilityException
    Inherits System.ApplicationException

    Public Sub New()
        MyBase.New()
    End Sub

    Public Sub New(ByVal message As String)
        MyBase.New(Message)
    End Sub

    Public Sub New(ByVal message As String, _
    ByVal innerException As Exception)
        MyBase.New(message, InnerException)
    End Sub
End Class

// Visual C#
public class DeckGridIncompatibilityException
    : System.ApplicationException {
```

(continued)

```
public DeckGridIncompatibilityException() : base() {
}

public DeckGridIncompatibilityException(string message)
    : base(message) {
}

public DeckGridIncompatibilityException(string message,
    Exception innerException) : base(message, innerException) {
}
}
```

2   Add the following *CardOver* method to the Memory class for the Click event handler for the Card instances. This method will be called each time a player clicks a Card control during a game. Since the Card instances are added at run time, you can't just double-click them in the designer to create the event handler in the code editor. You use the *AddHandler* method in Visual Basic—or the += operator in Visual C#—to assign the event handler to the Card's click event.

```vb
' Visual Basic
Private Sub CardOver(ByVal sender As Object, ByVal e As System.EventArgs)
    Dim theCard As Card = CType(sender, Card)
    theCard.FaceUp = Not theCard.FaceUp
    theCard.Refresh()
    m_clicks += 1
    CheckForPair()
    If (Me.Controls.Count = 0) Then
        RaiseEvent GameOver(Me, New GameOverEventArgs(m_clicks))
    End If
End Sub
```

```csharp
// Visual C#
private void CardOver(object sender, System.EventArgs e) {
    Card card = (Card)sender;
    card.FaceUp = !card.FaceUp;
    card.Refresh();
    m_clicks++;
    CheckForPair();
    if ((this.Controls.Count == 0) && (GameOver != null)) {
        GameOver(this, new GameOverEventArgs(m_clicks));
    }
}
```

3   Add the following code for the *Play* method. It calls a private method to check for and remove pairs from the game.

```vb
' Visual Basic
Public Sub Play()
    ' Reset controls and clicks before starting the next game.
    Dim aControl As Control
    For Each aControl In Me.Controls
        RemoveHandler aControl.Click, AddressOf Me.CardOver
    Next
    Me.Controls.Clear()

    ' If m_deck is null, the grid is empty, and there is
    ' no game play.
    If Not IsNothing(m_deck) Then
        ' The deck should have the right number of cards
        ' before the game can begin.
        If (m_deck.Count <> (m_rows * m_columns)) Then
            Throw New DeckGridIncompatibilityException(String.Format( _
                "Cards: {0} Cells: {1}", m_deck.Count, m_rows * m_columns))
        End If

        ' Add the cards from the deck to the game.
        m_clicks = 0
        m_deck.Shuffle()
        Dim cardCounter As Integer = 0
        Dim row, column As Integer
        For row = 0 To m_rows - 1
            For column = 0 To m_columns - 1
                Dim aCard As Card = CType(m_deck(cardCounter), Card)
                aCard.FaceUp = False
                AddHandler aCard.Click, AddressOf Me.CardOver
                Me.Controls.Add(aCard)
                aCard.Left = column * (Card.FixedWidth + m_spacing) _
                    + m_spacing
                aCard.Top = row * (Card.FixedHeight + m_spacing) _
                    + m_spacing
                cardCounter += 1
            Next
        Next
    End If
End Sub

// Visual C#
public void Play() {
    // Reset controls and clicks before starting the next game.
    foreach (Control control in this.Controls) {
        control.Click -= new System.EventHandler(this.CardOver);
    }
    this.Controls.Clear();
```

(continued)

```csharp
// If m_deck is null, the grid is empty, and there is
// no game play.
if (m_deck != null) {
    // The deck should have the right number of cards
    // before the game can begin.
    if (m_deck.Count != (m_rows * m_columns)) {
        throw new DeckGridIncompatibilityException(String.Format(
            "Cards: {0} Cells: {1}", m_deck.Count, m_rows * m_columns));
    }

    // Add the cards from the deck to the game.
    m_clicks = 0;
    m_deck.Shuffle();
    int cardCounter = 0;
    for (int row = 0; row < m_rows; row++) {
        for (int column = 0; column < m_columns; column++) {
            Card card = m_deck[cardCounter];
            card.FaceUp = false;
            card.Click += new System.EventHandler(this.CardOver);
            this.Controls.Add(card);
            card.Left = column * (Card.FixedWidth + m_spacing)
                + m_spacing;
            card.Top = row * (Card.FixedHeight + m_spacing)
                + m_spacing;
            cardCounter++;
        }
    }
}
}
```

4   Add the following code for the *CheckForPair* method. This method first counts the number of cards that are face up. If two cards are face up and the face values don't match, the cards are turned face down. If the cards match, they're removed from the Controls collection of the Memory control, and thus aren't displayed. Remember that Card instances are still contained in the Deck instance. For that reason, the *Dispose* method isn't called. The CardOver event handler is removed. It will be added again if another game is played. If this event handler wasn't removed and the game was restarted, the Card control would have the *CardOver* method attached twice and the *CardOver* method would be called twice for each click. The call to Sleep allows the player to have a look at the cards before they're turned over or removed.

```vbnet
' Visual Basic
Private Sub CheckForPair()
    System.Threading.Thread.Sleep(500)
    Dim nFaceUp As Integer = 0
    Dim cards(1) As Card
```

```
        Dim count As Integer
        For count = 0 To Me.Controls.Count - 1
            Dim aCard As Card = CType(Me.Controls(count), Card)
            If aCard.FaceUp Then
                cards(nFaceUp) = aCard
                nFaceUp += 1
            End If
        Next

        If nFaceUp = 2 Then
            If (cards(0).FaceValue = cards(1).FaceValue) Then
                Me.Controls.Remove(cards(0))
                Me.Controls.Remove(cards(1))
                RemoveHandler cards(0).Click, AddressOf Me.CardOver
                RemoveHandler cards(1).Click, AddressOf Me.CardOver
                Me.Refresh()
            Else
                cards(0).FaceUp = False
                cards(1).FaceUp = False
            End If
        End If
End Sub

// Visual C#
private void CheckForPair() {
    System.Threading.Thread.Sleep(500);
    int nfaceup = 0;
    Card[] cards = new Card[2];
    for (int i = 0; i < this.Controls.Count; i++) {
        Card card = (Card)this.Controls[i];
        if (card.FaceUp) {
            cards[nfaceup] = card;
            nfaceup++;
        }
    }

    if (nfaceup == 2) {
        if (cards[0].FaceValue == cards[1].FaceValue) {
            this.Controls.Remove(cards[0]);
            this.Controls.Remove(cards[1]);
            cards[0].Click -= new System.EventHandler(this.CardOver);
            cards[1].Click -= new System.EventHandler(this.CardOver);
            this.Refresh();
        }
        else {
            cards[0].FaceUp = false;
            cards[1].FaceUp = false;
        }
    }
}
```

Build the solution

1   On the Build menu, click Rebuild Solution.

2   Refresh the GamesLibrary reference in the Memory project. Expand References under Memory in the Solution Explorer, right-click GamesLibrary and click Remove on the shortcut menu.

3   Right-click References and click Add Reference on the shortcut menu. Click Browse on the .NET tab, select the GamesLibrary.dll in the GamesLibrary\obj\ debug folder and click Open. Click OK to close the Add Reference dialog box.

The *LotsOfFun.Games* library is now complete. You can now finish the programming for the Memory game.

The Memory Game Application

To program the game, you'll add a Deck component and a Memory control to the user interface form. You'll use the designer to set the properties of the Deck component and the Memory control and add a little code to start the game running.

Add the *LotsOfFun.Games* controls to the Toolbox

1   Open Form1 from the Memory project, and delete any controls that you added for testing.

2   Right-click the Games tab of the Toolbox and click Customize Toolbox on the shortcut menu. The Customize Toolbox dialog box appears.

3   On the .NET Framework Components tab, click Browse and navigate to and select the GamesLibrary.dll in the obj\debug folder. Click Open to add the controls and component in the library to the .NET Framework Components tab.

4   Click Assembly By Name to sort the list and then select the check boxes for the latest version of the Card, Deck, and Memory components. Clear the check boxes for any older versions of the components and controls you find in the list, and then click OK.

Create the user interface

1   Drag a Deck and a Memory component to the form.

2   Right-click the Deck component, Deck1, and click Properties on the shortcut menu. Deck1 is created with 52 cards.

3   Click the ellipsis button next to the FaceValues property to display the FaceValue Collection Editor.

4   Remove members until only the Ace, Jack, Queen, and King remain and then click OK. With four suits and four face values, a deck of 16 cards will be generated at run time.

5   Select the Memory control.

6   Set the Rows property to 4.

7   Set the Columns property to 4.

8   Set the Deck property to Deck1.

9   Resize Form1 and move the Memory control until it appears as shown here:

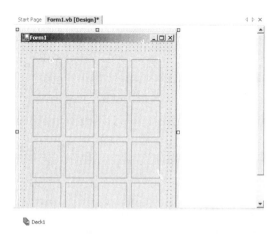

Program the game play

1   In the designer, double-click the form to create the Load event handler. Use this event to start the game, as shown in this code:

```
' Visual Basic
Private Sub Form1_Load(ByVal sender As System.Object, _
ByVal e As System.EventArgs) Handles MyBase.Load
    Me.Memory1.Play()
End Sub

// Visual C#
private void Form1_Load(object sender, System.EventArgs e) {
    this.memory1.Play();
}
```

2   In the designer, double-click the Memory control to create the GameOver event handler. Add the following code to tell the user how many clicks it took to win the game, and to ask if the user would like to play again.

```vbnet
' Visual Basic
Private Sub Memory1_GameOver(ByVal sender As System.Object, ByVal e _
As LotsOfFun.Games.GameOverEventArgs) Handles Memory1.GameOver
    Dim result As DialogResult
    result = MessageBox.Show("You win in " & e.Clicks & _
        " turns." & ControlChars.CrLf & "Play again?", _
        "Game over", MessageBoxButtons.YesNo)
    If (result = DialogResult.Yes) Then
        Me.Memory1.Play()
    End If
End Sub
```

```csharp
// Visual C#
private void memory1_GameOver(object sender,
LotsOfFun.Games.GameOverEventArgs e) {
    DialogResult result;
    result = MessageBox.Show("You win in " + e.Clicks +
        " turns.\nPlay again?", "Game over", MessageBoxButtons.YesNo);
    if (result == DialogResult.Yes) {
        this.memory1.Play();
    }
}
```

3   In the Solution Explorer, right-click the Memory project and click Set As Startup Project on the shortcut menu.

4   Press F5 to run the program and play the game, shown here:

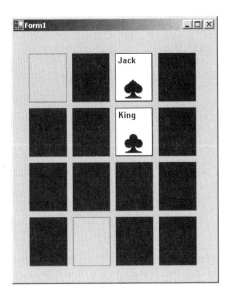

Quick Reference

To	Do this
Create a component	Right-click the GamesLibrary project in the Solution Explorer, point to Add, and then click Add Component on the shortcut menu. The Add New Item dialog box appears.
Assign a Toolbox bitmap to a component or control	Add a 16-by-16-pixel bitmap to the project that has the same name as the control. Set the Build Action property of the bitmap to *EmbeddedResource*.

Assign a Properties window category to a property	Add the Category attribute to the property declaration. In Visual Basic, this must be on the same line.
	
	`' Visual Basic`
	`<Category("Game")>`
	
	`// Visual C#`
	`[Category("Game")]`

Assign a Properties window description to a property	Add the Description attribute to the property declaration. In Visual Basic, this must be on the same line.
	
	`' Visual Basic`
	`<Description("Face value")>`
	
	`// Visual C#`
	`[Description("Face value")]`

Create a class library	Select the Class Library template when creating a new project.
Add a control or component to the Toolbox	Right-click the Toolbox and click Customize Toolbox in the shortcut menu. Click the .NET Framework Components tab. Click Browse, navigate to and select the class library, and then click Open. On the .NET Framework Components tab, select the items you want to add to the Toolbox and click OK.

9

Providing Services Using Interfaces

ESTIMATED TIME
2 hr. 45 min.

In this chapter, you'll learn how to

✔ *Create an interface.*

✔ *Implement an interface that you created.*

✔ *Implement the IComparable interface.*

✔ *Implement the IEnumerable and IEnumerator interfaces.*

✔ *Implement the IFormattable interface.*

✔ *Use an inner class.*

In Chapters 5 and 6, you used inheritance to make new classes out of existing classes. When classes are related by inheritance, you can refer to a derived instance through a base reference value. This polymorphic behavior isn't limited to derived classes. Visual Basic .NET and Visual C# provide another construct, the interface, that also behaves polymorphically. In the Microsoft .NET Framework, interfaces are commonly used to provide services for a class. The interface can support something your object can do, but that service doesn't fall into the *is-a* relationship found in inheritance.

An IMoveable Interface

An interface is like an abstract class with all abstract members. The interface serves as a contract that defines what methods, properties, and events a class must implement. In this chapter, you'll create an interface, implement it in a class, and use the class polymorphically through an interface reference.

Your first task is to create an IMoveable interface and implement it in a Pawn class. This interface might be useful if you were moving objects around as part of a game. The classes in the the project can be so different that they aren't related by inheritance, but they do share the ability to be moved around. The IMoveable interface provides a standard interface for relocating objects. This interface is described in the following UML diagram:

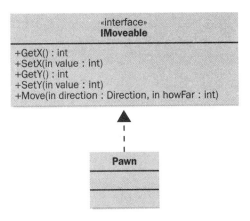

This diagram introduces a new UML element for an interface. Technically, the property, as the construct that contains a *get* and a *set* method, isn't supported by UML. In earlier exercises, I've used the upper section of the class diagram, called the attributes section, to specify the properties. The attributes section contains the data members of a case, which often have a one-to-one correspondence with the properties. Other languages don't have the property construct and thus list the private data members in the attributes section, while the *get* and *set* methods are shown in the methods section. The property construct fits nicely with the attributes section in a class element, but this correspondence breaks down in the case of an interface element because the interface element, as defined by the UML, doesn't have an attribute section. Because interfaces carry no implementation, they don't have instance data, only methods. So to fit the property concept into the UML interface, the getters and setters are shown as *Get* and *Set* methods. The IMoveable interface contains two properties, X and Y, and a *Move* method that takes two parameters for direction (up, down, left, right) and distance.

The following diagram is a shorthand style of representing interfaces in UML. This style is used more commonly than the extended version shown previously.

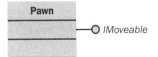

Define the IMoveable interface

This short example is a console application rather than a Windows application. The output of the program appears in the command prompt window. The interface defines the location of the object as X and Y properties and includes a *Move* method for moving the object around.

1 On the File menu, point to New, and then click Project.

2 Click Visual Basic or Visual C# in the Project Types tree.

3 In the Templates list, click Console Application.

4 Name the application MoveIt, and click OK.

5 On the Project menu, click Add New Item.

6 In the Add New Item dialog box, click Code File in the Templates list, name the new file IMoveable.vb or IMoveable.cs, and click Open.

7 Add the following code to declare the IMoveable interface. If you're using Visual C#, add a namespace declaration so that the IMoveable interface is in the same namespace as the other classes in the project.

```
' Visual Basic
Public Interface IMoveable
End Interface

// Visual C#
namespace MoveIt {
    public interface IMoveable {
    }
}
```

8 Add an enumeration to indicate which direction the object is to move. Add this enumeration immediately before the interface. Although Visual Basic allows the definition of nonpublic enumerations inside the interface, Visual C# does not.

```
' Visual Basic
Public Enum Direction
    Up
    Down
    Left
    Right
End Enum

// Visual C#
public enum Direction { Up, Down, Left, Right };
```

9 Add the two property declarations to the interface definition. The *public* keyword isn't allowed in interface definitions. The purpose of the interface is to define what methods, properties, and events a class will support. Private members don't make sense in this context. The Visual Basic definition allows the Readonly and Writeonly modifiers of properties. In the case of Visual C#, you need to show which of the accessors need to be implemented.

```
' Visual Basic
Property X() As Integer
Property Y() As Integer
```

```
// Visual C#
int X {
    get;
    set;
}
```

```
int Y {
    get;
    set;
}
```

10 Add the *Move* declaration to the interface:

```
' Visual Basic
Sub Move(ByVal aDirection As Direction, ByVal howFar As Integer)
```

```
// Visual C#
void Move(Direction direction, int howFar);
```

The interface is complete. To make it usable, you need to implement the interface in a class.

Implement the IMoveable interface in the Pawn class

In the Pawn class, you implement the X and Y properties and the *Move* method.

1 On the Project menu, click Add Class. Name the new class Pawn.

2 Modify the class to indicate that it will implement the IMoveable interface.

```
' Visual Basic
Public Class Pawn
    Implements IMoveable
End Class
```

```
// Visual C#
public class Pawn : IMoveable {
}
```

Visual C# uses the same syntax for declaring base classes and interfaces. Visual Basic uses the *Implements* keyword to indicate the interfaces of a class. Notice that after you type the *Implements* keyword, IntelliSense displays a list of interfaces. The icon next to the interface name is similar to the UML symbol.

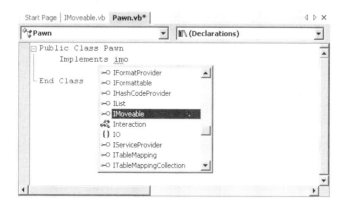

3   If you're using Visual Basic, click IMoveable in the Class Name list. In the Method Name list, click Move. The declaration for the *Move* method is added to the class. Repeat this procedure for the X and Y properties of IMoveable.

If you're using Visual C#, in the Class View, expand the Pawn class and Bases And Interfaces. Right-click the IMoveable interface in the Class View, point to Add, and then click Implement Interface on the shortcut menu. The declarations for all the members are added to the class. In addition, the code is enclosed in region statements that make that section of code collapsible.

4   Add a field for the X property, and implement the X property:

```
' Visual Basic
Private m_x As Integer = 0
Public Property X() As Integer Implements MoveIt.IMoveable.X
    Get
        Return m_x
    End Get
    Set(ByVal Value As Integer)
        m_x = Value
    End Set
End Property
```

(continued)

```
// Visual C#
private int m_x;
public int X {
    get { return m_x; }
    set { m_x = value; }
}
```

Notice that Visual Basic uses the *Implements* keyword again to specify which interface member is being implemented. The *Implements* keyword is followed by the qualified name of the method. The fully qualified name takes the form *Namespace.ClassName.MemberName*. Unless you have added a namespace declaration or changed the default project properties, the namespace is the same as the project name. The Visual C# compiler makes the determination without the special keyword by using the signature.

You don't use the *Overrides* or *override* keyword when you're implementing the interface member. The code isn't overriding a base class member. The interface is strictly a contract about what will be found in the class interface.

5   Add a field for the Y property, and implement the Y property. For Visual Basic, you add the keyword *Implements* and the qualified name of the member implemented. In Visual C#, the compiler matches the class method to the interface method.

```
' Visual Basic
Private m_y As Integer = 0
Public Property Y() As Integer Implements MoveIt.IMoveable.Y
    Get
        Return m_y
    End Get
    Set(ByVal Value As Integer)
        m_y = Value
    End Set
End Property
```

```
// Visual C#
private int m_y;
public int Y {
    get { return m_y; }
    set { m_y = value; }
}
```

6   Add code for the *Move* method:

```
' Visual Basic
Public Sub Move(ByVal aDirection As MoveIt.Direction, ByVal howFar _
As Integer) Implements MoveIt.IMoveable.Move
    Select Case aDirection
        Case Direction.Up
```

```
                m_y += howFar
        Case Direction.Down
                m_y -= howFar
        Case Direction.Left
                m_x -= howFar
        Case Direction.Right
                m_x += howFar
    End Select
End Sub

// Visual C#
public void Move(Direction direction, int howFar) {
    switch (direction) {
        case Direction.Up :
            m_y += howFar;
            break;
        case Direction.Down :
            m_y -= howFar;
            break;
        case Direction.Left :
            m_x -= howFar;
            break;
        case Direction.Right :
            m_x += howFar;
            break;
    }
}
```

7   Add one method to the Pawn class that's not part of the IMoveable interface:

```
' Visual Basic
Private m_captured As Boolean = False
Public Property Captured() As Boolean
    Get
        Return m_captured
    End Get
    Set(ByVal Value As Boolean)
        m_captured = Value
    End Set
End Property

// Visual C#
private bool m_captured = false;
public bool Captured {
    get { return m_captured; }
    set { m_captured = value; }
}
```

That completes the implementation of the IMoveable interface in the Pawn class.

Test the IMoveable interface

When you created the project as a console application, Visual Studio .NET created a start-up method. Now you add code to that method to test the Pawn class.

1   If you're using Visual Basic, double-click Module1.vb in the Solution Explorer to open the file in the code editor.

If you're using Visual C#, double-click Class1.cs in the Solution Explorer to open the file in the code editor.

2   Add code to the *Main* method. Note that mover is declared as IMoveable yet instantiated as Pawn. You can't instantiate an interface; it does not have implementation.

```vb
' Visual Basic
Sub Main()
    Dim mover As IMoveable = New Pawn()
    mover.X = 10
    mover.Y = 10
    Console.WriteLine("X:{0}  Y:{1}", mover.X, mover.Y)
    Console.WriteLine("Moving up 5 spaces.")
    mover.Move(Direction.Up, 5)
    Console.WriteLine("X:{0}  Y:{1}", mover.X, mover.Y)

    Dim aPawn As Pawn = CType(mover, Pawn)
    Console.WriteLine("Is the pawn captured? {0}", aPawn.Captured)
End Sub
```

```csharp
// Visual C#
static void Main(string[] args)
    IMoveable mover = new Pawn();
    mover.X = 10;
    mover.Y = 10;
    Console.WriteLine("X:{0}  Y:{1}", mover.X, mover.Y);
    Console.WriteLine("Moving up 5 spaces.");
    mover.Move(Direction.Up, 5);
    Console.WriteLine("X:{0}  Y:{1}", mover.X, mover.Y);

    Pawn pawn = (Pawn)mover;
    Console.WriteLine("Is the pawn captured? {0}", pawn.Captured);
}
```

Using a reference to an interface is similar to using a reference to a base class. The reference variable *mover* has access only to the members of IMoveable, though you can set it to refer to an instance of Pawn. To access the Pawn members of the *mover* reference, you must cast the reference to

Pawn. In a larger application, the *mover* reference could be pointing to some other game piece, such as a King or a Queen. As you type the code, look closely at the IntelliSense lists to see these differences.

3   Press Ctrl+F5 to run the program. If you press F5, the output flashes briefly. Running the program with Ctrl+F5 gives you a chance to examime the output. Here's the output:

.NET Framework Interfaces

The .NET Framework defines several interfaces from which you can choose to implement your classes. These interfaces usually buy you some extra functionality for your object. Most of the interfaces contain only a few members, and many contain only one. Others are more complex. For the complex interfaces, you're often able to inherit from a .NET Framework class that implements the interface. Some of the interfaces are described in the following table:

Interface	Benefits
IComparable	Defines sorting of class instances. It's useful if you want to use the class as a key value in SortedList or support the *Sort* method of the ArrayList.
IEnumerable and IEnumerator	These two classes work together to support using *For Each* or *foreach* with your class.
IFormattable	Allows you to define custom formatting strings for your class.
IList	Allows your class to serve as a data source for controls such as ListBox and DataGrid. The base implementation is List.
ICloneable	Allows you to define exactly how your object is copied.
IComponent	Provides your class with design-time support as a component. The base implementation is Component.
IDataErrorInfo	Allows you to attach data error information to a class. Supporting this interface allows you to use the Windows Forms DataError control.

9

Providing Services

In the next few sections, you'll create a simple class that represents a point. You'll use this class as a basis for implementing the IComparable, IEnumerable, IEnumerator, and IFormattable interfaces. These interfaces make your class more user friendly for other developers.

Implementing the IComparable Interface

The IComparable interface allows you to define an order for class instances. If your class represents an object that carries a meaningful interpretation of more or less, first or last, or larger or smaller, it's reasonable to define the IComparable interface for your class. IComparable has one member, the *CompareTo* method. In this example, you implement a class that represents a point and compare points based on distance from the origin.

Create the SortablePoint class

1   Create a new Windows application project, and name it Points.

2   Add a new class to the project, and name the class SortablePoint.

3   Add the X and Y properties to the SortablePoint class:

```
' Visual Basic
Private m_x As Integer = 0
Public Property X() As Integer
    Get
        Return m_x
    End Get
    Set(ByVal Value As Integer)
        m_x = Value
    End Set
End Property

Private m_y As Integer = 0
Public Property Y() As Integer
    Get
        Return m_y
    End Get
    Set(ByVal Value As Integer)
        m_y = Value
    End Set
End Property

// Visual C#
private int m_x = 0;
public int X {
    get { return m_x; }
    set { m_x = value; }
}
```

```
private int m_y = 0;
public int Y {
    get { return m_y; }
    set { m_y = value; }
}
```

4   Add the constructors. If you're using Visual C#, you don't need to add the parameterless constructor.

```
' Visual Basic
Public Sub New()
End Sub

Public Sub New(ByVal x As Integer, ByVal y As Integer)
    m_x = x
    m_y = y
End Sub

// Visual C#
public SortablePoint() {
}

public SortablePoint(int x, int y) {
    m_x = x;
    m_y = y;
}
```

Add the IComparable interface

1   Add the IComparable interface to the class declaration:

```
' Visual Basic
Public Class SortablePoint
    Implements IComparable
    ' Code for the class is here.
    ⋮
End Class

// Visual C#
public class SortablePoint : IComparable {
    // Code for the class is here.
    ⋮
}
```

2   If you're using Visual Basic, click IComparable in the Class Name list. In the Method Name list, click CompareTo. The declaration for the *CompareTo* method is added to the class.

If you're using Visual C#, in the Class View, expand the SortablePoint class and Bases And Interfaces. Right-click the IComparable interface in the Class View, point to Add, and then click Implement Interface. The declaration for the *CompareTo* method is added to the class.

```
' Visual Basic
Public Function CompareTo(ByVal obj As Object) As Integer _
    Implements System.IComparable.CompareTo
End Function
```

```
// Visual C#
#region Implementation of IComparable
public int CompareTo(object obj) {
    return 0;
}
#endregion
```

The *CompareTo* method compares the one class instance, *Me* or *this*, to another instance of the class, *obj*. If the two instances are equal, according to the class's definition of sorting, *CompareTo* returns 0. If the *Me* or *this* instance is larger (comes second), *CompareTo* returns a positive integer. If the *Me* or *this* instance is smaller (comes first), *CompareTo* returns a negative integer.

3   Add code to the *CompareTo* function and create a helper function, *SquaredDistance*. Points are compared two at a time, so it doesn't matter what value is returned by the *CompareTo* method, as long as a positive number is returned if the *Me* or *this* point is farther away than the other point. The *SquaredDistance* method returns the squared distance of the point from the origin. If the *CompareTo* method used the actual distance to compare distances, the code would have to work with *System.Double* values. Working with *System.Double* values has three disadvantages. First, it negatively affects performance. Second, because of the way doubles are stored, it's more work to test for equivalence. Third, the code has to convert the difference back into an integer, the return type of *CompareTo*.

```
' Visual Basic
Public Function CompareTo(ByVal obj As Object) As Integer _
Implements System.IComparable.CompareTo
    Return Me.SquaredDistance() - _
        CType(obj, SortablePoint).SquaredDistance()
End Function

Private Function SquaredDistance() As Integer
    Return (m_x * m_x) + (m_y * m_y)
End Function
```

```
// Visual C#
#region Implementation of IComparable
    public int CompareTo(object obj) {
    return this.SquaredDistance() -
        ((SortablePoint)obj).SquaredDistance();
}

private int SquaredDistance() {
    return (m_x * m_x) + (m_y * m_y);
}
#endregion
```

Test the interface

The straightforward way to test the IComparable interface would be to create a list of points, sort them, and then print out the sorted points to check that they're in order. Instead of doing that, this procedure generates a group of randomly placed points. You draw the points on the form and let the color density vary according to the sort order.

1 Open Form1 in the designer, and drag a Button control onto the form. Set the Text property to *Draw*.

2 Double-click the Draw button to create the Click event handler.

3 Add this code to generate points, sort them, and display them on the form. The ArrayList's *Sort* method uses the *IComparable.CompareTo* method to sort the SortablePoint instances. The intensity of the color depends on the point's position among the sorted points. The higher the value, the less intense the color.

```
' Visual Basic
Private Sub Button1_Click(ByVal sender As System.Object, _
ByVal e As System.EventArgs) Handles Button1.Click
    Dim points As New ArrayList()
    Dim rgen As New System.Random()
    Dim pt As SortablePoint
    Dim count As Integer
    Dim graph As Graphics = Me.CreateGraphics
    Dim aColor As Color
    For count = 0 To 249
        points.Add(New SortablePoint(rgen.Next(200), rgen.Next(200)))
    Next

    points.Sort()

    For count = 0 To 249
        pt = CType(points(count), SortablePoint)
```

(continued)

```
            aColor = System.Drawing.Color.FromArgb(25, 25, count)
            Dim brush As New System.Drawing.SolidBrush(aColor)
            graph.FillEllipse(brush, pt.X, pt.Y, 10, 10)
            brush.Dispose()
        Next
    End Sub

    // Visual C#
    private void button1_Click(object sender, System.EventArgs e) {
        ArrayList points = new ArrayList();
        System.Random rgen = new System.Random();
        SortablePoint pt;
        Graphics graph = this.CreateGraphics();

        for (int count = 0; count < 250; count++) {
            points.Add(new SortablePoint(rgen.Next(200), rgen.Next(200)));
        }

        points.Sort();

        for (int count = 0; count < 250; count++) {
            pt = (SortablePoint)(points[count]);
            Color color = System.Drawing.Color.FromArgb(25, 25, count);
            System.Drawing.SolidBrush brush =
                new System.Drawing.SolidBrush(color);
            graph.FillEllipse(brush, pt.X, pt.Y, 10,10);
            brush.Dispose();
        }
    }
```

4   Press F5 to run the program. Each time you click the Draw button, 250 more points are added to the form. Because the points aren't drawn in the Paint event, the points won't stay on the form if you minimize and then maximize it. To get a clear indication that the points are being sorted, comment out the call to *Sort,* and then run the program.

Implementing the IEnumerable and IEnumerator Interfaces

In the preceding example, you generated the points, added them to an ArrayList object, sorted them, and then drew them on the form. In this next example, you create a class, SortedPointList, that holds a group of points. Instead of using a *for* loop to access the members of the ArrayList class and then casting each item to the SortablePoint type, you'll be able to use a *For Each* (or *foreach* in Visual C#) block that returns only a SortablePoint object.

The IEnumerable interface has one member, the *GetEnumerator* method. The *GetEnumerator* method returns an instance of a class that implements the IEnumerator interface. The IEnumerator interface has three members, the *Reset* and *MoveNext* methods and the Current property. The three members work together to enumerate the members of the SortedPointList class, points, as you see here:

```
' Visual Basic
Dim enumerator As IEnumerator = points.GetEnumerator()
dim pt As SortablePoint
While enumerator.MoveNext
    pt = CType(enumerator.Current, SortablePoint)
    ' Use the SortablePoint instance here.
End While
```

```
// Visual C#
IEnumerator enumerator = points.GetEnumerator();
SortablePoint pt;
while (enumerator.MoveNext()) {
    pt = (SortablePoint)enumerator.Current;
    // Use the SortablePoint instance here.
}
```

Create the SortedPointList class

1   Add a new class to the project, and name it SortedPointList.

2   Modify the class to add the IEnumerable interface:

```
' Visual Basic
Public Class SortedPointList
    Implements IEnumerable
End Class
```

```
// Visual C#
public class SortedPointList : IEnumerable {
}
```

3   If you're using Visual Basic, add the parameterless constructor:

```
' Visual Basic
Public Sub New()
End Sub
```

4   If you're using Visual C#, add a *using* statement for the *System.Collections* namespace:

```
// Visual C#
using System.Collections;
```

5   Add an instance of ArrayList and a method named *AddRandomPoints*, which adds a number of randomly generated points to the ArrayList class. This code is nearly identical to the Click event handler code for the Draw button in the previous section.

```
' Visual Basic
Private m_points As New ArrayList()
Public Sub AddRandomPoints(ByVal howMany As Integer, _
ByVal maximum As Integer)
    m_points.Clear()
    Dim rgen As New System.Random()
    Dim count As Integer
    For count = 0 To howMany - 1
        m_points.Add( _
            New SortablePoint(rgen.Next(maximum), rgen.Next(maximum)))
    Next
    m_points.Sort()
End Sub

// Visual C#
private ArrayList m_points = new ArrayList();
public void AddRandomPoints(int howMany, int maximum) {
    m_points.Clear();
    System.Random rgen = new System.Random();
    for (int count = 0; count < howMany; count++) {
        m_points.Add(new SortablePoint(rgen.Next(maximum),
            rgen.Next(maximum)));
    }
    m_points.Sort();
}
```

Add the IEnumerator inner class

1   Declare a new class inside the PointList class, named PointEnumerator, that implements the IEnumerator interface.

```vb
' Visual Basic
Private Class PointEnumerator
    Implements IEnumerator
End Class
```

```csharp
// Visual C#
private class PointEnumerator : IEnumerator {
}
```

The PointEnumerator class is called an *inner class* because it's defined within another class. An instance of this class is created and returned by the *GetEnumerator* method. The user of the PointEnumerator instance needs to know only that the class implements the IEnumerator interface. So the only class that needs to know about the PointEnumerator class is the SortedPointList class.

2   If you're using Visual Basic, click IEnumerator in the Class Name list. In the Method Name list, click Reset. The declaration for the *Reset* method is added to the class. Repeat this procedure for the *MoveNext* method and the Current property in the IEnumerator interface.

If you're using Visual C#, in Class View, expand the SortedPointList class, the PointEnumerator class, and Bases And Interfaces. Right-click the IEnumerator interface, point to Add, and then click Implement Interface on the shortcut menu. The declarations for the IEnumerator methods are added to the class as you see here:

```vb
' Visual Basic
Private Class PointEnumerator
    Implements IEnumerator

    Public ReadOnly Property Current() As Object _
        Implements System.Collections.IEnumerator.Current
        Get

        End Get
    End Property

    Public Function MoveNext() As Boolean _
        Implements System.Collections.IEnumerator.MoveNext
    End Function

    Public Sub Reset() Implements System.Collections.IEnumerator.Reset
    End Sub
End Class
```

(continued)

```
// Visual C#
#region Implementation of IEnumerator
public void Reset() {
}

public bool MoveNext() {
    return true;
}

public object Current {
    get {
        return null;
    }
}
}
#endregion
```

3   Add these fields to the class PointEnumerator. The first member refers to the *m_points* collection of the SortedPointsList instance. The *m_position* is the current position in the enumeration. The *m_initialCount* is the count of points in *m_points* when the enumerator is instantiated. By convention in the .NET Framework, the enumerator's *MoveNext* and *Current* members should fail if the collection being enumerated changes during enumeration. In this example, you'll use the initial count of points to test whether the ArrayList class has changed.

```
' Visual Basic
Dim m_points As ArrayList
Dim m_position As Integer = -1
Dim m_initialCount As Integer

// Visual C#
ArrayList m_points;
int m_position = -1;
int m_initialCount;
```

4   Add the constructor to the class to initialize the points list:

```
' Visual Basic
Public Sub New(ByVal points As ArrayList)
    m_points = points
    m_initialCount = points.Count
End Sub

// Visual C#
public PointEnumerator(ArrayList points) {
    m_points = points;
    m_initialCount = points.Count;
}
```

5 Add this code for the *Reset* method. You implement the enumerator by adding 1 to *m_position* with each call to *MoveNext*. The Current property returns the item in the ArrayList *m_points* at the *m_position* index. Because the first value in the enumeration is found by calling the *MoveNext* method, the *Reset* method needs to hold the value of the index right before the first element in the ArrayList. The first element in ArrayList is at index 0, so the *Reset* method sets *m_position* to −1.

```
' Visual Basic
Public Sub Reset() Implements System.Collections.IEnumerator.Reset
    m_position = -1
End Sub
```

```
// Visual C#
public void Reset() {
    m_position = -1;
}
```

6 Add the following code for the *MoveNext* method. The first test determines whether SortablePoint instances have been added or deleted from the *m_points* ArrayList. If not, *m_position* is incremented. Otherwise, the code throws an exception, *InvalidOperationException*.

```
' Visual Basic
Public Function MoveNext() As Boolean _
Implements System.Collections.IEnumerator.MoveNext
    If (m_initialCount = m_points.Count) Then
        m_position += 1
        If (m_position >= m_points.Count) Then
            Return False
        Else
            Return True
        End If
    Else
        Throw New InvalidOperationException( _
            "Collection has changed during enumeration.")
    End If
End Function
```

```
// Visual C#
public bool MoveNext() {
    if (m_initialCount == m_points.Count) {
        m_position++;
        if (m_position >= m_points.Count) {
            return false;
        }
```

(continued)

Providing Services

```
        else {
            return true;
        }
    }
    else {
        throw new InvalidOperationException(
        "Collection has changed during enumeration.");
    }
    return true;
}
```

7 Add this code for the Current property:

```
' Visual Basic
Public ReadOnly Property Current() As Object _
Implements System.Collections.IEnumerator.Current
    Get
        If (m_initialCount <> m_points.Count) Then
            Throw New InvalidOperationException( _
                "Collection has changed during enumeration.")
        ElseIf (m_position >= m_points.Count) Then
            Throw New InvalidOperationException( _
                "Enumeration value is invalid.")
        Else
            Return m_points(m_position)
        End If
    End Get
End Property
```

```
// Visual C#
public object Current {
    get {
        if (m_initialCount != m_points.Count) {
            throw new InvalidOperationException(
            "Collection has changed during enumeration.");
        }
        else if (m_position >= m_points.Count) {
            throw new InvalidOperationException(
            "Enumeration value is invalid.");
        }
        else {
            return m_points[m_position];
        }
    }
}
```

Now that you've defined the enumerator for the class, you can implement the *GetEnumerator* method in the SortedPointList class.

Add the IEnumerable interface

1   If you're using Visual Basic, click IEnumerable in the Class Name list. In the Method Name list, click GetEnumerator. The declaration for the *GetEnumerator* method is added to the class.

If you're using Visual C#, in the Class View, expand the SortedPointList class and Bases And Interfaces. Right-click the IEnumerable interface in the Class View, point to Add, and then click Implement Interface on the shortcut menu. The declaration for the *GetEnumerator* method is added to the class.

2   Add this code for the *GetEnumerator* method:

```
' Visual Basic
Public Function GetEnumerator() As System.Collections.IEnumerator _
Implements System.Collections.IEnumerable.GetEnumerator
    Return New PointEnumerator(m_points)
End Function
```

```
// Visual C#
#region Implementation of IEnumerable
public System.Collections.IEnumerator GetEnumerator() {
    return new PointEnumerator(m_points);
}
#endregion
```

Test the interfaces

1   Modify the button click code in the Form1 class so that it uses the *For Each* or *foreach* control structure.

```
' Visual Basic
Private Sub Button1_Click(ByVal sender As System.Object, _
ByVal e As System.EventArgs) Handles Button1.Click
    Dim points As New SortedPointList()
    points.AddRandomPoints(250, 200)
    Dim graph As Graphics = Me.CreateGraphics
    Dim count As Integer = 1
    Dim aColor As Color
    Dim pt As SortablePoint

    For Each pt In points
        aColor = System.Drawing.Color.FromArgb(25, 25, count)
        count += 1
        Dim brush As New System.Drawing.SolidBrush(aColor)
```

(continued)

```
        graph.FillEllipse(brush, pt.X, pt.Y, 10, 10)
        brush.Dispose()
    Next
end sub

// Visual C#
private void button1_Click(object sender, System.EventArgs e) {
    SortedPointList points = new SortedPointList();
    points.AddRandomPoints(250, 200);
    Graphics graph = this.CreateGraphics();

    int count = 1;
    foreach(SortablePoint pt in points) {
        Color color = System.Drawing.Color.FromArgb(25,25,count++);
        System.Drawing.SolidBrush brush =
            new System.Drawing.SolidBrush(color);
        graph.FillEllipse(brush, pt.X, pt.Y, 10,10);
        brush.Dispose();
    }
}
```

2   Press F5 to run the program. The results are similar to those of the first example.

Implementing the IFormattable interface

In Chapter 5, you used the following formatting expression to display a *System.Decimal* value as a currency value:

```
' Visual Basic
MessageBox.Show(String.Format("{0:C}", account.Balance))

// Visual C#
MessageBox.Show(String.Format("{0:C}", account.Balance));
```

The System.Decimal data type has defined the format string *C* so that it returns a string representing currency. You can also define custom formatting schemes for the classes you create. In the next task, you'll add two custom formatting options to the SortablePoint class. The first, a long option indicated by *L*, prints the point as (*x, y*). The second, a short option indicated by *S*, prints the point as *x:y*. You'll define three overloads of the *ToString* method to provide consistent formatting behavior for the SortablePoint class. The three overloads are described in the following table.

Overload	Behavior
`ToString()`	```' Visual Basic
Dim p As New SortablePoint(1,2)
Dim s As String = p.ToString()```
`ToString();`	```// Visual C#
Point p = new SortablePoint(1,2);
string s = p.ToString();``` Value of s: (1, 2)
`ToString(format As String)`	```' Visual Basic
Dim p As New SortablePoint(1,2)
Dim plong As String = p.ToString("L")
Dim pshort As String = p.ToString("S")```
`ToString(string format);`	```// Visual C#
Point p = new SortablePoint(1,2);
string plong = p.ToString("L");
string pshort = p.ToString("S");``` Value of plong: (1, 2) Value of pshort: 1:2

`ToString(format As String, _`
`  formatprovider As _`
`  IFormatProvider)`
	``' Visual Basic

Dim p As New SortablePoint(1,2)
Dim s As String =_
String.Format("{0:L}", p)```

`ToString(string format,`
`  IFormatProvider`
`  formatProvider);`
	``// Visual C#

Point p = new SortablePoint(1,2);
string s = string.Format("{0:L}", p);``` Value of s: (1, 2)

The first overload overrides the *ToString* method found in the *System.Object* class. *System.Object* is the base class for every Visual Basic and Visual C# class. The second overload is a *ToString* method defined just for the class. It's neither an override of a base implementation nor an implementation of an interface method. The last overload is the implementation of the *IFormattable.ToString* method, the only member of the IFormattable interface. This is the version of *ToString* that's called if a formatting expression is evaluated. You could also implement an IFormatProvider class to provide additional formatting options for base types. In this example, if this code doesn't recognize the format string, you pass the IFormatProvider interface along to another call to the *ToString* method.

Add the IFormattable interface

1   Add the IFormattable interface to the list of interfaces for the SortablePoint class:

```
' Visual Basic
Public Class SortablePoint
    Implements IComparable, IFormattable
    ⋮
End Class
```

```
// Visual C#
public class SortablePoint : IComparable, IFormattable {
    ⋮
}
```

2   Add this code to implement the *IFormattable.ToString* method. Because the *System.Object* class implements a parameterless *ToString* method, this *ToString* method is an overload. If the SortablePoint class doesn't recognize the formatting string, the individual methods create a string by passing the *formatProvider* to the *ToString* methods of the individual fields.

```
' Visual Basic
Public Function ToString(ByVal format As String, _
ByVal formatProvider As System.IFormatProvider) As String _
Implements System.IFormattable.ToString
    Dim result As String
    Select Case format.ToUpper()
        Case "L"
            result = String.Format("({0}, {1})", m_x, m_y)
        Case "S"
            result = String.Format("{0},{1}", m_x, m_y)
        Case Else
            result = (m_x.ToString(format, formatProvider) & " " _
                & m_y.ToString(format, formatProvider))
    End Select
```

```
        Return result
End Function


// Visual C#
#region Implementation of IFormattable
public string ToString(string format, System.IFormatProvider
    formatProvider) {
    string result;
    switch (format.ToUpper()) {
        case "L" :
            result = string.Format("({0}, {1})", X, Y);
            break;
        case "S" :
            result = string.Format("{0}:{1}", X, Y);
            break;
        default :
            result =  X.ToString(formatProvider) + " "
                + Y.ToString(formatProvider);
            break;
    }
    return result;
}
#endregion
```

Overload the *ToString* method

● Add two more overloads of *ToString* so that the SortablePoint class is formatted consistently in all the *ToString* methods. Each overload calls the *ToString* method implemented for the IFormattable interface. The default *ToString* method for the SortablePoint class returns the long version.

```
' Visual Basic
Public Overrides Function ToString() As String
    Return Me.ToString("L")
End Function

Public Function ToString(ByVal format As String) As String
    Return Me.ToString(format, Nothing)
End Function
```

(continued)

```
// Visual C#
public override string ToString() {
    return this.ToString("L");
}

public string ToString(string format) {
    return this.ToString(format, null);
}
```

Test the IFormattable interface

1   Replace the code in the Click event handler for the Draw button with this code, which creates a few points and then draws them labeled with their coordinates:

```
' Visual Basic
Private Sub Button1_Click(ByVal sender As System.Object, _
ByVal e As System.EventArgs) Handles Button1.Click
    Dim points As New SortedPointList()
    points.AddRandomPoints(5, 200)
    Dim graph As Graphics = Me.CreateGraphics
    Dim pt As SortablePoint

    For Each pt In points
        graph.FillEllipse(System.Drawing.Brushes.Black, pt.X, pt.Y, 10, 10)
        Dim ptlocation As String = String.Format("{0:L}", pt)
        graph.DrawString(ptlocation, New Font("Arial", 8), _
            System.Drawing.Brushes.Black, pt.X + 11, pt.Y)
    Next
End Sub

// Visual C#
private void button1_Click(object sender, System.EventArgs e) {
    SortedPointList points = new SortedPointList();
    points.AddRandomPoints(5, 200);
    Graphics graph = this.CreateGraphics();

    foreach (SortablePoint pt in points) {
        graph.FillEllipse(System.Drawing.Brushes.Black, pt.X, pt.Y,
            10, 10);
        string ptlocation = String.Format("{0:L}", pt);
        graph.DrawString(ptlocation, new Font("Arial", 8),
        System.Drawing.Brushes.Black, pt.X + 11, pt.Y);
    }
}
```

2 Press F5 to run the program. Here's an example of the output:

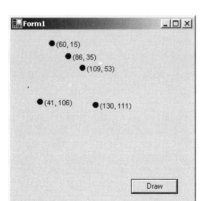

Two Other Uses of Interfaces

In programming with the .NET Framework, you'll implement interfaces primarily to provide services from your class. You might, in addition, use an interface for a project in the following two situations.

Multiple inheritance Classes created in Visual Basic and Visual C# can have only one base class, but they can implement multiple interfaces. Because interfaces behave polymorphically, like base classes, you can use interfaces to simulate multiple inheritance. Suppose you were creating a Backyard class and wanted it to derive from both Lawn and Garden, but Lawn and Garden didn't share a common base class other than System.Object. You could choose to implement an ILawn interface and then implement the ILawn interface in a Lawn class. You then create Garden as a base class. When you create the Backyard class, it inherits from Garden and implements ILawn as you see here:

```
' Visual Basic
Public Class Backyard
    Inherits Garden
    Implements ILawn
End Class

// Visual C#
public class Backyard : Garden, ILawn {
}
```

It would appear that you haven't gained much from this code because you have to reimplement all the members of ILawn. Fortunately, you can use *containment* and *delegation* to reuse some of your work. In the Backyard class, you can create a private instance of the Lawn class. This is *containment*. You then implement the ILawn methods by calling the corresponding method of the private Lawn instance. This is called *delegation*. You're delegating the work of the ILawn interface to the contained Lawn member. Suppose the ILawn class has a *Grow* method and a Height property. Your code might look something like this:

```
' Visual Basic
Public Class Backyard
    Inherits Garden
    Implements ILawn
    Private m_lawn As New Lawn()
    Public Sub Grow() Implements ILawn.Grow
        m_lawn.Grow()
    End Sub
    Public Property Height() As Integer Implements ILawn.Height
        Get
            Return m_lawn.Height
        End Get
        Set(ByVal Value As Integer)
            m_lawn.Height = Value
        End Set
    End Property
End Class
```

```
// Visual C#
public class Backyard : Garden, ILawn {
    private Lawn m_lawn = new Lawn();

    #region Implementation of ILawn
    public void Grow() {
        m_lawn.Grow();
    }

    public int Height {
        get { return m_lawn.Height; }
        set { m_lawn.Height = value; }
    }
    #endregion
}
```

Data views   In Chapter 3 you created an array of SourceFile classes that you were able to use as a data source in a DataGrid control. In general, you want the data model to fit the data well, and then you want to provide methods to support a user interface. You may also want to limit the amount of control the user interface has over the model. For example, you might not want to allow updates.

You can prevent updates by implementing an interface on your class. When you create a reference to the data model for the user interface, you provide only a reference to the interface. You could, of course, provide a reference to the full model, but using an interface can let the compiler do some of the work, alerting you when you're attempting to update data.

Quick Reference

To	Do this
Declare an interface	```' Visual Basic
Public Interface InterfaceName
End Interface

// Visual C#
public interface InterfaceName {
}``` |
| Declare an interface property | ```' Visual Basic
Property PropertyName() As Integer

// Visual C#
int PropertyName {
    get;
    set;
}``` |
| Declare an interface method | ```' Visual Basic
Sub Move(ByVal aDirection As Direction, _
ByVal howFar As Integer)

// Visual C#
void Move(Direction direction, int howFar);``` |
| Declare a class that implements an interface | ```' Visual Basic
Public Class ClassName
    Implements InterfaceName
End Class

// Visual C#
public class Pawn : InterfaceName {
}``` |
Support *For Each* or *foreach* for a class	Implement the IEnumerable interface.
Support sorting on a class	Implement the IComparable interface.
Provide custom string formatting for a class	Implement the IFormattable interface.

CHAPTER
10

Using Classes Interchangeably Through Polymorphism

ESTIMATED TIME
3 hr. 30 min.

In this chapter, you'll learn how to

✔ *Use derived classes polymorphically.*

✔ *Override a base class event (Visual C#).*

✔ *Raise an event from the base class (Visual Basic).*

✔ *Create a class that derives from the UserControl class.*

In the first several chapters, you used classes as abstractions of objects in the real world, creating classes to represent books, playing cards, and trains. In Chapter 8, you saw how to use inheritance of the Component class to make client code easier to write. In this chapter, you'll see how to use object-oriented design, and polymorphism in particular, to solve a programming task. Polymorphism allows you to refer to an instance of a derived class through a base reference variable, but when you call a method or use a property, the method or property called is the one defined in the derived class. Thus, derived classes can respond in different ways to the same method call. In this chapter's example, the class is designed to represent an object that solves both the real world problem and the programming problem. You'll see how polymorphism simplifies the programming task and makes the design more easily extensible.

Pattern Maker

Your task in this chapter is to create an application that allows a user to create a set of patterns. The user can draw the patterns by using straight lines or by importing a bitmap file created in another application, such as Paint. The following graphic shows the user interface.

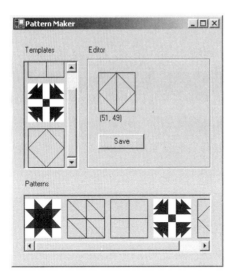

The user selects a pattern by clicking one of the patterns in the Templates panel. When clicked, the pattern is displayed in an editor that allows the user to modify the pattern. The particular type of editor depends on the template type. This application has two types of pattern templates. In the first type, the user modifies the pattern by drawing lines in a square. In the second type, the user selects an existing bitmap file that contains a drawing of a pattern. Both editor types contain a Save button. When the user clicks Save, the modified pattern is saved in the Patterns panel.

Pattern Maker Design

The Pattern Maker application presents two common programming tasks that can be accomplished by using polymorphism. The first challenge is to display the correct editor based on the pattern selected. The second is to create new instances of the patterns.

Designing the Pattern and Editor Classes

The Pattern Maker application supports two different pattern types: a drawn pattern and a bitmap pattern. If you can design the two pattern types to have the same base class, you can write one set of code to work with both types. Additionally, you can add more pattern types without rewriting your code. This polymorphic solution has the following advantages:

- **You can easily add a new pattern type.** You'll write one block of code that deals only with base class references. At run time, you supply the derived class instances. To extend the application, you implement additional derived classes.

■ **The code is less repetitive.** If you didn't use polymorphism in this application, you'd have a block of code that created a new drawn pattern and displayed an editor for it. You'd have an almost identical block of code that did the same thing with the bitmap pattern. Polymorphism allows you to write and debug the code that creates and displays a pattern only once. The differences in how the patterns are created and displayed are handled in the derived class code.

■ **There are fewer class names in the application.** In the Pattern Maker application, you'll have a Pattern base class and DrawnPattern and BitmapPattern derived classes. You'll be able to limit references to DrawnPattern and BitmapPattern to one method of the client code. The rest of the client code will use only references to Pattern instances. This reduces the number of classes you have to keep track of while you're working, thus simplifying the programming task.

What we want to design is a base class—Pattern—that contains the functionality for both a drawn pattern and a bitmap pattern. Ideally, you could extend the Pattern class at a later date with other pattern types, without having to rewrite the Pattern class or the existing derived classes.

The Pattern class you'll implement is able to

■ **Supply its own editor—through a *GetEditor* method—that returns a customized UserControl.** To edit the pattern, all the client code needs to do is ask the Pattern instance for an instance of its editor. Because the editor is derived from UserControl, it merely needs to be added to the Controls collection of a form to be displayed at run time. The editor in this application is also represented by a base class, the PatternEditor class.

■ **Make copies of itself, by way of a *Clone* method.** The user clicks a particular pattern in the Templates panel, and the Pattern instance in the panel simply makes a copy of itself. The client code doesn't need to know the derived type of the class. It just needs to ask for a copy, and then ask the copy for its editor.

The PatternEditor class you'll implement will

■ **Derive from the UserControl class.** This means you'll be able to develop the editor as a unit, and then display it on the form at run time by simply adding an instance to the form's Controls collection.

■ **Implement a Saved event.** The user interface responds to the Saved event by moving the edited pattern to the Patterns pane and removing the editor from the form. Removing the editor is as simple as removing the editor, a UserControl, from the form's Controls collection.

The following graphic shows the relevant UML for the base classes Pattern and PatternEditor:

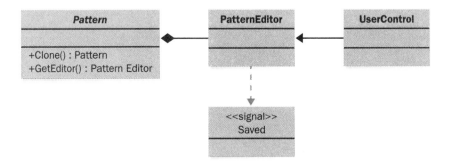

Each pattern type is implemented by deriving from both a Pattern and a PatternEditor class. The UML for the relationship between the base classes and the drawn pattern classes is shown here:

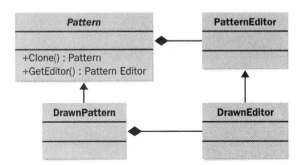

It's important to understand that Pattern and PatternEditor will never be instantiated. Only the derived classes DrawnPattern, DrawnPatternEditor, BitmapPattern (not shown in the preceding diagram), and BitmapPatternEditor are instantiated. Also remember that DrawnPattern creates only DrawnPatternEditor instances and BitmapPattern creates only BitmapPatternEditor instances.

Using these classes, the basic control flow in the form code looks something like this:

1   At startup, the application loads a few template patterns into the Templates panel. The Pattern class implements a *Draw* method to facilitate this. This startup code doesn't use polymorphism because the derived classes must be instantiated specifically.

2   The user clicks one of the templates, which is an instance of either the DrawnPattern or the BitmapPattern class. The event handler for the Click event doesn't determine the derived type of the clicked pattern, but simply accesses the instance through a Pattern reference.

3   A copy of the instance is created by calling the *Clone* method. This call behaves polymorphically.

4   A new PatternEditor instance is created by calling the *GetEditor* method of the selected instance. Again this call behaves polymorphically.

5   The PatternEditor instance, which derives from UserControl, is added to the form's Controls collection and displayed on the form.

6   The user changes the pattern by using the PatternEditor.

7   The user clicks the Save button, which is part of the PatternEditor control. The Click event handler for the Save button saves the changes to the pattern and raises the Saved event to the form.

8   In response to the Saved event, the Pattern instance is added to the Patterns panel and the PatternEditor—a UserControl—is removed from the form's control collection and disposed of.

The Base Classes

The two base classes in this project are the Pattern and PatternEditor classes. These classes have very few members—just the functions needed to create, draw, edit, and save the Pattern instances. These members create the class interface that will be used throughout the client code. The behavior of the calls will be defined in the derived classes. At run time, the client code uses mostly references to the base class, but the behavior will depend on the derived class instantiated.

Create the Pattern class

The Pattern class has only three members and is an abstract class, meaning that it can't be instantiated but instead a new class must derive from it. This leaves the entire implementation to the derived classes, which is appropriate considering how varied the derived classes might be.

1   Create a new Windows Application project. Name it PatternMaker.

2   Add a new class to the project. Name it Pattern.

3   Modify the class declaration to include the following abstract keyword shown in boldface:

```
' Visual Basic
Public MustInherit Class Pattern
End Class
```

```
// Visual C#
public abstract class Pattern {
}
```

4   Add the following abstract members to the class:

```
' Visual Basic
Public MustOverride Sub Draw(ByVal sender As Object, _
    ByVal e As System.Windows.Forms.PaintEventArgs)
Public MustOverride Function GetEditor() As PatternEditor
Public MustOverride Function Clone() As Pattern
```

```
// Visual C#
public abstract void Draw(object sender,
    System.Windows.Forms.PaintEventArgs e);
public abstract PatternEditor GetEditor();
public abstract Pattern Clone();
```

The *Draw* method has the same signature as the *Paint* method for Windows Forms controls. By using the same signature as the *Paint* method, you can add this method as an event handler to the *Paint* method of any control. You'll take advantage of this when you create the user interface portion of the project.

Notice that all the properties and methods of the Pattern class refer only to the Pattern and PatternEditor classes. In the derived classes, the *GetEditor* method returns an instance of either the DrawnPatternEditor or BitmapPatternEditor class. The return type of *GetEditor* is PatternEditor, which allows the derived classes to return any type that derives from PatternEditor. The new instance can be added to the Controls collection of the form because the PatternEditor class derives from UserControl. The *Clone* method returns a copy of the Pattern instance. In the derived classes, the instance returned will be of either the DrawnPattern or BitmapPattern class.

Create the PatternEditor class

PatternEditor is a class—derived from the UserControl class—that implements a Saved event. As I said in Chapter 6, you might typically design base classes as abstract classes. In this case, the class isn't declared as an abstract class because you want to design the derived classes in the Windows Forms Designer. To do this, a class must inherit from a *concrete* (nonabstract) class.

1   Add a UserControl to the project. Name it PatternEditor.

2   If you're using C#, add the SavedEventHandler delegate to the PatternEditor.cs file in the PatternMaker namespace:

```
// Visual C#
public delegate void SavedEventHandler(object sender, EventArgs e);
```

3   Add the declaration for the Saved event to the PatternEditor class. If you're using Visual C#, the event is virtual and will be overridden in the derived classes. Events aren't inheritable in Visual Basic.

```
' Visual Basic
Public Event Saved(sender As Object, e As EventArgs)
```

```
// Visual C#
public virtual event SavedEventHandler Saved;
```

4   If you're using Visual Basic, add the following method to the PatternEditor class to raise the Saved event. Events in the base class can't be raised in the derived class. This method, which will be accessible from the derived classes, raises the Saved event. Also note that it wouldn't work to just implement a Saved event in each derived class. For the event to behave polymorphically, it must be declared in the base class.

```
' Visual Basic
Public Sub RaiseSaved(ByVal sender As Object, ByVal e As EventArgs)
    RaiseEvent Saved(sender, e)
End Sub
```

The Derived Classes

For each pattern type, you implement a pair of classes that derive from Pattern and PatternEditor. The classes derived from PatternEditor will implement only the Saved event. The classes derived from Pattern will implement the abstract members and add members for creating new instances. Any public members that you add to a derived class can be accessed only by using a reference of the derived class type. Because we want to use the classes polymorphically, through a base reference, it doesn't make sense to add public members to the class. But because we ultimately have to create instances of the Pattern-derived classes, each class derived from PatternEditor needs a custom constructor that accepts an instance of the Pattern-derived class and a member to store that instance.

Create the DrawnPattern class

The underlying structure of the drawn pattern is an ordered collection of points in a 60-by-60-pixel grid. The user creates the pattern by drawing a line from one point to the next in connect-the-dots fashion. The following illustration from a test version shows the list of points and the resulting pattern.

1   Add a new class to the project. Name it DrawnPattern.

2   Add an *Imports* or *using* statement at the beginning of the DrawnPattern source file to include the *System.Drawing* namespace. The points will be stored as an array of *System.Drawing.Point*. Adding the *Imports* or *using* statement allows you to use the unqualified name, *Point*, in the code.

```
' Visual Basic
Imports System.Drawing
```

```
// Visual C#
using System.Drawing;
```

3   Modify the class declaration to indicate that the class derives from the Pattern class.

```
' Visual Basic
Public Class DrawnPattern
    Inherits Pattern
End Class
```

```
// Visual C#
public class DrawnPattern : Pattern {
}
```

4   Add the following array and the property to store the points:

```
' Visual Basic
Private m_points() As Point = New Point() {}
Public Property Points() As Point()
    Get
        Return m_points
```

```
    End Get
    Set(ByVal Value As Point())
        m_points = Value
    End Set
End Property

// Visual C#
private Point[] m_points = new Point[0];
public Point[] Points {
    get { return m_points; }
    set { m_points = value; }
}
```

5   Define the *Draw* method. The client code can assign this method as the
    event handler to any control that raises a Paint event.

```
' Visual Basic
Public Overrides Sub Draw(ByVal sender As Object, _
ByVal e As System.Windows.Forms.PaintEventArgs)
    e.Graphics.DrawRectangle(Pens.Black, 0, 0, 60, 60)
    Dim point As Integer
    For point = 0 To m_points.Length - 2
        Dim ptOne As Point = m_points(point)
        Dim ptTwo As Point = m_points(point + 1)
        e.Graphics.DrawLine(System.Drawing.Pens.Black, ptOne, ptTwo)
    Next
End Sub

// Visual C#
public override void Draw(object sender,
System.Windows.Forms.PaintEventArgs e) {
    e.Graphics.DrawRectangle(Pens.Black, 0, 0, 60, 60);
    for(int point = 0; point < m_points.Length - 1; point++) {
        Point ptOne = m_points[point];
        Point ptTwo = m_points[point+1];
        e.Graphics.DrawLine(System.Drawing.Pens.Black, ptOne, ptTwo);
    }
}
```

6   Define the *GetEditor* method. You might get a compile error at this point
    because you haven't yet implemented the DrawnPatternEditor class. (You'll
    do that in the next section.)

```
' Visual Basic
Public Overrides Function GetEditor() As PatternEditor
    Return New DrawnPatternEditor(Me)
End Function
```

(continued)

Using Classes

```
// Visual C#
public override PatternEditor GetEditor() {
    return new DrawnPatternEditor(this);
}
```

7   Define the *Clone* method. This method allocates new memory for all the objects contained in the new instance, and copies the value from the *Me* or *this* instance to the new instance.

```
' Visual Basic
Public Overrides Function Clone() As Pattern
    Dim newPattern As New DrawnPattern
    newPattern.m_points = CType(m_points.Clone(), Point())
    return newPattern
End Function
```

```
// Visual C#
public override Pattern Clone() {
    DrawnPattern newPattern = new DrawnPattern();
    newPattern.m_points = (Point[])m_points.Clone();
    return newPattern;
}
```

That completes the DrawnPattern class.

Create the DrawnPatternEditor class

DrawnPatternEditor is a user control with a Saved event added. The purpose of the control is to give the user a graphical interface for drawing lines in a 60-by-60-pixel square. When the user clicks Save, those points are saved back to the DrawnPattern instance, and the Saved event is raised.

1   Add a UserControl to the project. Name it DrawnPatternEditor.

By creating the class first from the UserControl class, you allow Visual Studio to generate all the override code needed to design a UserControl. In the last step, you'll change the class declaration to indicate the base class is the PatternEditor class.

2   Open the DrawnPatternEditor class in the form designer and set the Size property in the Properties window to 175, 150. The control needs to fit into the space reserved on the main form, which will have a size of 200, 175.

3   Add the following controls and set their properties as shown in the table.

Control	Property	Value
PictureBox	Name	*pictureBox1*
	Size	*62, 62*
	Location	*8, 16*
Label	Name	*label1*
	Location	*8, 88*
	Text	*(blank)*
Button	Name	*save*
	Location	*8, 120*
	Text	*Save*

Your control should look like this:

4 Open the DrawnPatternEditor class in the code editor and add a field for the points that define the drawing. DrawnPatternEditor maintains a separate array of points that are copied back to the DrawnPattern instance when the user clicks the Save button.

```
' Visual Basic
Private m_Points() As Point = New Point() {}
```

```
// Visual C#
private Point[] m_points = new Point[0];
```

5 Add the following field to refer to the DrawnPattern instance being edited. DrawnPatternEditor holds this reference so that it can copy the new set of points back after the user clicks Save.

```
' Visual Basic
Private m_pattern As DrawnPattern
```

```
// Visual C#
private DrawnPattern m_pattern;
```

(continued)

6   Add the following constructor to take one parameter—the DrawnPattern object. The constructor will copy the points from the DrawnPattern object to the DrawnPatternEditor object, save the reference to the DrawnPattern object, and assign a drawing method for the PictureBox control.

```
' Visual Basic
Public Sub New(ByVal pattern As DrawnPattern)
    MyBase.New()
    InitializeComponent()

    ReDim Me.m_Points(pattern.Points.Length - 1)
    pattern.Points.CopyTo(Me.m_Points, 0)
    AddHandler Me.pictureBox1.Paint, AddressOf Me.Draw
    m_pattern = pattern
End Sub
```

```
// Visual C#
public DrawnPatternEditor(DrawnPattern pattern)
{
    InitializeComponent();

    this.m_points = new Point[pattern.Points.Length];
    pattern.Points.CopyTo(this.m_points, 0);
    this.pictureBox1.Paint += new PaintEventHandler(this.Draw);
    m_pattern = pattern;
}
```

7   Add the *Draw* method for the PictureBox control.

```
' Visual Basic
Public Sub Draw(ByVal sender As Object, _
ByVal e As System.Windows.Forms.PaintEventArgs)
    e.Graphics.DrawRectangle(New Pen(Brushes.Black, 1), 0, 0, 60, 60)
    Dim point As Integer
    For point = 0 To m_Points.Length - 2
        Dim one As Point = m_Points(point)
        Dim two As Point = m_Points(point + 1)
        e.Graphics.DrawLine(Pens.Black, one, two)
    Next
End Sub
```

```
// Visual C#
public void Draw(object sender, System.Windows.Forms.PaintEventArgs e) {
    e.Graphics.DrawRectangle(new Pen(Brushes.Black,1),0,0, 60,60);
    for(int point = 0; point < m_points.Length - 1; point++) {
        Point one = m_points[point];
        Point two = m_points[point + 1];
        e.Graphics.DrawLine(Pens.Black, one, two);
    }
}
```

8 Create the event handler for the picture box's MouseMove event and add the following code to display the current mouse coordinates in the label control. In Visual C#, create the event handler by double-clicking the event in the PictureBox's Properties window.

```
' Visual Basic
Private Sub pictureBox1_MouseMove(ByVal sender As Object, _
ByVal e As System.Windows.Forms.MouseEventArgs) _
Handles pictureBox1.MouseMove
    Me.label1.Text = String.Format("({0}, {1})", e.X, e.Y)
End Sub
```

```
// Visual C#
private void pictureBox1_MouseMove(object sender,
System.Windows.Forms.MouseEventArgs e) {
    this.label1.Text = string.Format("({0}, {1})", e.X, e.Y);
}
```

9 Create the event handler for the picture box's MouseDown event and add the following code to add a new point to the pattern and redraw the picture box. In Visual C#, create the event handler by double-clicking the event in the PictureBox's Properties window.

```
' Visual Basic
Private Sub pictureBox1_MouseDown(ByVal sender As Object, _
ByVal e As System.Windows.Forms.MouseEventArgs) _
Handles pictureBox1.MouseDown
    ReDim Preserve m_Points(m_Points.Length)
    m_Points(m_Points.Length - 1) = New Point(e.X, e.Y)
    Me.Refresh()
End Sub
```

```
// Visual C#
private void pictureBox1_MouseDown(object sender,
System.Windows.Forms.MouseEventArgs e) {
    Point[] newPoints = new Point[m_points.Length + 1];
    m_points.CopyTo(newPoints,0);
    newPoints[newPoints.Length-1] = new Point(e.X, e.Y);
    m_points = newPoints;
    this.Refresh();
}
```

10 If you're using Visual C#, add the event declaration to the DrawnPattern-Editor class. Events can't be overridden in Visual Basic.

```
// Visual C#
public override event SavedEventHandler Saved;
```

11 Double-click Save to create the Click event handler and add the following code to save the points back to the DrawnPattern instance and raise the Saved event. The *RaiseSaved* method won't appear in IntelliSense because the base class at this point is UserControl, not PatternEditor.

```
' Visual Basic
Private Sub save_Click(ByVal sender As System.Object, _
ByVal e As System.EventArgs) Handles save.Click
    m_pattern.Points = m_Points
    MyBase.RaiseSaved(Me, New System.EventArgs())
End Sub
```

```
// Visual C#
private void save_Click(object sender, System.EventArgs e) {
    m_pattern.Points = m_points;
    if (this.Saved != null) {
        this.Saved(this, new System.EventArgs());
    }
}
```

12 Modify the class declaration to indicate that the class derives from the PatternEditor class instead of the UserControl class.

```
' Visual Basic
Public Class DrawnPatternEditor
    Inherits PatternEditor
    ⋮
End Class
```

```
// Visual C#
public class DrawnPatternEditor : PatternEditor {
    ⋮
}
```

Create the BitmapPattern class

To create the BitmapPattern class, you'll again implement a pair of classes that derive from the Pattern and PatternEditor classes. The BitmapPattern class maintains the name of the bitmap file for the pattern. BitmapPatternEditor maintains a reference to the BitmapPattern instance and a copy of the bitmap filename. After the user selects a new bitmap file and clicks the Save button, the new filename is saved to the BitmapPattern instance.

1 Add a new class to the project. Name it BitmapPattern.

2 Modify the class declaration to indicate that the class derives from the Pattern class.

```
' Visual Basic
Public Class BitmapPattern
```

```
        Inherits Pattern
End Class

// Visual C#
public class BitmapPattern : Pattern {
}
```

3   Add the following field and property to store the filename of the bitmap:

```
' Visual Basic
Private m_bitmapFile As String = ""
Public Property BitmapFile() As String
    Get
        Return m_bitmapFile
    End Get
    Set(ByVal Value As String)
        m_bitmapFile = Value
    End Set
End Property

// Visual C#
private string m_bitmapFile = "";
public string BitmapFile {
    get { return m_bitmapFile; }
    set { m_bitmapFile = value; }
}
```

4   Define the *Draw* method. Just as with the DrawnPattern class, the user
interface code will use this method to display the pattern.

```
' Visual Basic
Public Overrides Sub Draw(sender As Object, _
e As System.Windows.Forms.PaintEventArgs)
    e.Graphics.DrawImage(new _
        System.Drawing.Bitmap(m_bitmapFile), 0, 0)
End Sub

// Visual C#
public override void Draw(object sender,
System.Windows.Forms.PaintEventArgs e) {
    e.Graphics.DrawImage(new
        System.Drawing.Bitmap(m_bitmapFile), 0, 0);
}
```

5   Define the *GetEditor* method. You might get a compile error at this point
because you have not yet implemented the BitmapPatternEditor class.

```
' Visual Basic
Public Overrides Function GetEditor() As PatternEditor
```

(continued)

```
        Return New BitmapPatternEditor(Me)
    End Function

    // Visual C#
    public override PatternEditor GetEditor() {
        return new BitmapPatternEditor(this);
    }
```

6 Define the *Clone* method.

```
    ' Visual Basic
    Public Overrides Function Clone() As Pattern
        Dim newPattern As New BitmapPattern()
        newPattern.BitmapFile = Me.BitmapFile
        Return newPattern
    End Function

    // Visual C#
    public override Pattern Clone() {
        BitmapPattern newPattern = new BitmapPattern();
        newPattern.BitmapFile = this.BitmapFile;
        return newPattern;
    }
```

Create the BitmapPatternEditor class

The BitmapPatternEditor class needs only Browse and Save buttons and a picture box to display the selected bitmap file.

1 Add a new UserControl class to the project. Name it BitmapPatternEditor.

2 Open BitmapPatternEditor in the designer and set the Size property to 175, 150 in the Properties window.

3 Add the following controls and set their properties as shown in the table.

Control	Property	Value
PictureBox	*Name*	*pictureBox1*
	Size	*61, 61*
	Location	*8, 8*
Button	*Name*	*browse*
	Location	*8, 88*
	Text	*Browse...*
Button	*Name*	*save*
	Location	*96, 88*
	Text	*Save*
OpenFileDialog	*Name*	*openFileDialog1*

The following graphic shows the completed user control:

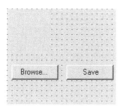

4   Open the BitmapPatternEditor class in the code editor and add a field for the bitmap file. The BitmapPatternEditor class maintains a separate reference to the filename that's copied back to the BitmapPattern instance when the user clicks Save.

```
' Visual Basic
Private m_bitmapFile As String
```

```
// Visual C#
private string m_bitmapFile;
```

5   Add a field to refer to the BitmapPattern instance being edited. Bitmap-PatternEditor maintains this reference so that it can copy the bitmap filename back to BitmapPattern after the user clicks Save.

```
' Visual Basic
Private m_pattern As BitmapPattern
```

```
// Visual C#
private BitmapPattern m_pattern = null;
```

6   Add the following constructor, which takes one parameter, a BitmapPattern instance. The constructor will copy the bitmap filename from BitmapPattern to BitmapPatternEditor, save the reference to DrawnPattern, and assign a drawing method for the PictureBox control.

```
' Visual Basic
Public Sub New(ByVal pattern As BitmapPattern)
    MyBase.New()
    InitializeComponent()

    m_pattern = pattern
    m_bitmapFile = pattern.BitmapFile
    AddHandler Me.pictureBox1.Paint, AddressOf Me.Draw
End Sub
```

(continued)

```
// Visual C#
public BitmapPatternEditor(BitmapPattern pattern) {
    InitializeComponent();

    m_pattern = pattern;
    m_bitmapFile = pattern.BitmapFile;
    this.pictureBox1.Paint += new PaintEventHandler(this.Draw);
}
```

7   Add the *Draw* method.

```
' Visual Basic
Public Sub Draw(sender As Object, e As System.Windows.Forms.PaintEventArgs)
    e.Graphics.DrawImage(New Bitmap(m_bitmapFile), 0, 0)
End Sub
```

```
// Visual C#
public void Draw(object sender,
System.Windows.Forms.PaintEventArgs e) {
    e.Graphics.DrawImage(new
        System.Drawing.Bitmap(m_bitmapFile), 0, 0);
}
```

8   Create the event handler for the Browse button's Click event, and then add this code to display the open file dialog box.

```
' Visual Basic
Private Sub browse_Click(ByVal sender As System.Object, _
ByVal e As System.EventArgs) Handles browse.Click
    Me.openFileDialog1.ShowDialog()
    If (Me.openFileDialog1.FileName.Length <> 0) Then
        m_bitmapFile = Me.openFileDialog1.FileName
        Me.pictureBox1.Refresh()
    End If
End Sub
```

```
// Visual C#
private void browse_Click(object sender, System.EventArgs e) {
    this.openFileDialog1.ShowDialog();
    if (this.openFileDialog1.FileName.Length != 0) {
        m_bitmapFile = this.openFileDialog1.FileName;
        this.pictureBox1.Refresh();
    }
}
```

9   If you're using C#, add the following event declaration to the BitmapPatternEditor class:

```
// Visual C#
public override event SavedEventHandler Saved;
```

10 Create the Click event handler for the Save button and add this code to save the filename back to the BitmapPattern instance and raise the Saved event.

```
' Visual Basic
Private Sub save_Click(ByVal sender As System.Object, _
ByVal e As System.EventArgs) Handles save.Click
    m_pattern.BitmapFile = m_bitmapFile
    MyBase.RaiseSaved(Me, New System.EventArgs())
End Sub
```

```
// Visual C#
private void save_Click(object sender, System.EventArgs e) {
    m_pattern.BitmapFile = m_bitmapFile;
    if (Saved != null) {
        Saved(this, new System.EventArgs());
    }
}
```

11 Modify the class declaration to indicate that the class derives from the PatternEditor class instead of the UserControl class.

```
' Visual Basic
Public Class BitmapPatternEditor
    Inherits PatternEditor
End Class
```

```
// Visual C#
public class BitmapPatternEditor : PatternEditor {
}
```

The User Interface

As you have seen, the implementations of the drawn pattern and the bitmap pattern are very different. The user interface code, however, is fairly simple, and doesn't reveal the differences between the two types of patterns.

Create the user interface elements

The user interface contains panels for the template and edited patterns and an area for editing the patterns.

1 Open Form1 in the designer.

2 In the Properties window, change the Size property of Form1 to 344, 392 and the Text property to *Pattern Maker*.

3 Add the following controls and set their properties as shown in the table.

Control	Property	Value
Label	Text	*Templates*
	Location	*16, 24*
Label	Text	*Editor*
	Location	*120, 24*
Label	Text	*Patterns*
	Location	*16, 232*
Panel	Name	*templates*
	Location	*16, 48*
	Size	*90, 168*
	BorderStyle	*Fixed3D*
	AutoScroll	*True*
Panel	Name	*patterns*
	Location	*16, 256*
	Size	*304, 90*
	BorderStyle	*Fixed3D*
	AutoScroll	*True*
GroupBox	Name	*editor*
	Text	*(blank)*
	Location	*120, 40*
	Size	*200, 175*

The following graphic shows the user interface:

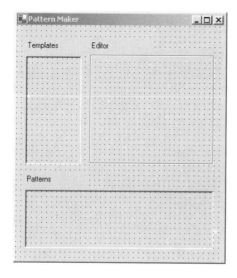

The Pattern class provides the *Draw* method needed to display each pattern, but the Pattern class does not contain any type of element that can be displayed on a form, such as a PictureBox, Button, or Panel control. The display of the pattern is left up to the user interface portion of the program.

4   Add the following small class, PatternButton, after the end of the Form1 class. This customized UserControl is used to display the patterns in the Templates and Patterns panels.

```vb
' Visual Basic
Public Class PatternButton
    Inherits UserControl

    Private m_pattern As Pattern
    Public Sub New(ByVal newPattern As Pattern)
        Me.Size = New Size(61, 61)
        m_pattern = newPattern
        AddHandler Me.Paint, AddressOf newPattern.Draw
    End Sub

    Public Property Pattern() As Pattern
        Get
            Return m_pattern
        End Get
        Set(ByVal Value As Pattern)
            m_pattern = Value
        End Set
    End Property
End Class
```

```csharp
// Visual C#
public class PatternButton : UserControl {
    private Pattern m_pattern;

    public PatternButton(Pattern newPattern) {
        this.Size = new Size(61, 61);
        m_pattern = newPattern;
        this.Paint += new PaintEventHandler(newPattern.Draw);
    }

    public Pattern Pattern {
        get { return m_pattern; }
        set { m_pattern = value; }
    }
}
```

Notice that you use the *Draw* method of the pattern as the *Paint* method of the control. In addition, you add the Pattern instance as a property of the control. That's a large improvement over what you did with the Card class in Chapter 4: when you used the Tag property of the Button control, you had to cast the Tag property if you wanted to use the *Card* instance associated with the button.

Create the template instances

The template patterns are instances of either the DrawnPattern class or the BitmapPattern class displayed in the PatternButton user control. The Pattern-Button instances are added to the Templates panel.

1   Double-click the form in the designer to create the Form_Load event handler in the code editor.

2   Add the following code to the *Form1_Load* event handler method to add template Pattern instances to the Templates panel. This is the only part of the user interface code that needs to know the actual types of the pattern classes. There's no reason to add more than one instance of BitmapPattern to the Templates panel. Adding multiple instances of DrawnPattern is an advantage because it can save the user from having to re-create common base drawings. If you extend the application to add more pattern types, this is the code you need to modify. The rest of the application will deal with the DrawnPattern and BitmapPattern instances using base class Pattern references. Replace ProjectFolder, shown in boldface, with your project path. The file bearpaw.bmp is located in the \Chapter10 folder on the companion CD.

```vb
' Visual Basic
Private Sub Form1_Load(ByVal sender As System.Object, _
ByVal e As System.EventArgs) Handles MyBase.Load
    Dim drawn1 As New DrawnPattern()
    drawn1.Points = New Point() {New Point(0, 30), New Point(60, 30), _
        New Point(60, 0), New Point(30, 0), New Point(30, 60)}

    Dim drawn2 As New DrawnPattern()
    drawn2.Points = New Point() {New Point(30, 0), New Point(60, 30), _
        New Point(30, 60), New Point(0, 30), New Point(30, 0), _
        New Point(0, 0)}

    Dim bitmap1 As New BitmapPattern()
    bitmap1.BitmapFile = "ProjectFolder\bearpaw.bmp"

    Dim patterns() As Pattern = {drawn1, bitmap1, drawn2}
    Dim pt As Integer
    For pt = 0 To patterns.Length - 1
        Dim button As New PatternButton(patterns(pt))
```

```
            button.Top = 70 * pt
            button.Left = 5
            AddHandler button.Click, AddressOf Me.TemplateClick
            Me.templates.Controls.Add(button)
    Next
End Sub

// Visual C#
private void Form1_Load(object sender, System.EventArgs e) {
    DrawnPattern drawn1 = new DrawnPattern();
    drawn1.Points = new Point[] { new Point(0,30), new Point(60,30),
        new Point(60,0), new Point(30,0), new Point(30,60) };

    DrawnPattern drawn2 = new DrawnPattern();
    drawn2.Points = new Point[] { new Point(30,0), new Point(60,30),
        new Point(30,60), new Point(0, 30), new Point(30,0),
        new Point(0,0)};

    BitmapPattern bitmap1 = new BitmapPattern();
    bitmap1.BitmapFile = "ProjectFolder\bearpaw.bmp";

    Pattern[] patterns = new Pattern[] { drawn1, bitmap1, drawn2 };
    for (int pt = 0; pt < patterns.Length; pt++) {
        PatternButton button = new PatternButton(patterns[pt]);
        button.Top = 70 * pt;
        button.Left = 5;
        button.Click += new EventHandler(this.TemplateClick);
        this.templates.Controls.Add(button);
    }
}
```

Edit and save the new patterns

As you enter the code in this section, notice that all manipulation of the
DrawnPattern and BitmapPattern instances is accomplished through Pattern reference variables. In the introduction to the chapter, I said that using polymorphism reduces the number of class names that the developer has to work with,
thereby simplifying the programming task. If you were to add other pattern
types to the application, none of this code would change, and you wouldn't have
to learn about more classes and work the details of each new class into the
application.

1   Add the following code to the Form1 class for the *TemplateClick* method,
      and then add a field to refer to the new Pattern instance. Notice that it
      doesn't matter which template was clicked or whether the type of that
      instance is DrawnPattern or BitmapPattern. Because PatternEditor derives

from UserControl, it doesn't matter whether the instance returns an instance of DrawnPatternEditor or BitmapPatternEditor. From the PatternEditor's inheritance path, it's also a UserControl and can be added to the Controls collection of the Editor group box.

```
' Visual Basic
Private m_newPattern As Pattern = Nothing
Private Sub TemplateClick(ByVal sender As Object, ByVal e As EventArgs)
    Dim button As PatternButton = CType(sender, PatternButton)
    m_newPattern = button.Pattern.Clone()
    Dim designer As PatternEditor = m_newPattern.GetEditor()
    designer.Location = New Point(10, 10)
    Me.editor.Controls.Add(designer)
    AddHandler designer.Saved, AddressOf Me.PatternSaved
End Sub
```

```
// Visual C#
private Pattern m_newPattern  = null;
private void TemplateClick(object sender, EventArgs e) {
    PatternButton button = (PatternButton) sender;
    m_newPattern = button.Pattern.Clone();
    PatternEditor designer = m_newPattern.GetEditor();
    designer.Location = new Point(10,10);
    this.editor.Controls.Add(designer);
    designer.Saved += new SavedEventHandler(this.PatternSaved);
}
```

2   Add the following code for the *PatternSaved* method. This adds the pattern to the Patterns panel. Once the pattern is saved, the PatternEditor control has no purpose. Dispose of it so that it doesn't hold on to any limited system resources. Because you control the code, you know that the sender parameter in the PatternSaved event is an instance of PatternEditor. Its sender parameter can therefore be cast to Control.

```
' Visual Basic
Private Sub PatternSaved(ByVal sender As Object, ByVal e As EventArgs)
    Me.Controls.Remove(CType(sender, Control))
    CType(sender, Control).Dispose()
    Dim pb As PatternButton = New PatternButton(m_newPattern)
    pb.Left = Me.patterns.Controls.Count * 70
    pb.Top = 5
    pb.Enabled = False
    Me.patterns.Controls.Add(pb)
End Sub
```

```
// Visual C#
private void PatternSaved(object sender, EventArgs e) {
    this.Controls.Remove((Control)sender);
    ((Control)sender).Dispose();
    PatternButton pb = new PatternButton(m_newPattern);
    pb.Left = this.patterns.Controls.Count * 70;
    pb.Top = 5;
    pb.Enabled = false;
    this.patterns.Controls.Add(pb);
}
```

That's all you need for the user interface code: one small class and three event handlers. Much of the work was pushed into the Pattern and PatternEditor classes and thus doesn't clutter up the user interface code.

Test the application

● Press F5 to run the application. The following graphic shows the results after adding new patterns:

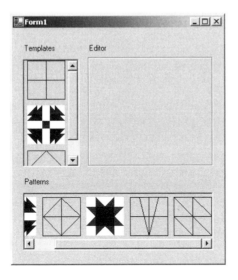

The obvious next addition to this application is support for saving the instances between invocations of the program. Saving the data of class instances will be covered in Chapter 13, "Saving Instance Data."

Quick Reference

To	Do this

Create an abstract base class	Add the *MustInherit* or *abstract* keyword to the class declaration.
	
	```vb' Visual BasicPublic MustInherit Class PatternEnd Class```
	
	```csharp// Visual C#public abstract class Pattern {}```

Create a derived class	Indicate the base class in the class declaration.
	
	```vb' Visual BasicPublic Class DrawnPattern Inherits PatternEnd Class```
	
	```csharp// Visual C#public class DrawnPattern : Pattern {}```

Assign an instance of a derived class to a reference variable of the base class	Use an assignment statement. No casting is necessary.
	```vb' Visual BasicDim aPattern As Pattern = New DrawnPattern()```
	
	```csharp// Visual C#Pattern aPattern = new DrawnPattern();```

Assign a base reference to the base class to a reference variable of the derived class	This is valid if the base reference refers to a derived instance. Use casting.
	```vb' Visual BasicPrivate Sub PatternSaved(ByVal sender As Object, _ByVal e As EventArgs) Dim aControl As Control = CType(sender, _ Control)End Sub```
	
	```csharp// Visual C#private void PatternSaved(object sender, EventArgs e) { Control aControl = (Control)sender;}```

11

Using Shared and Static Members

Shared and Static Members

**ESTIMATED
TIME
2 hr.**

In this chapter, you'll learn how to

✔ *Create and use shared and static fields and properties.*

✔ *Create and use shared and static constructors.*

✔ *Create and use shared and static methods.*

✔ *Embed a bitmap resource in the assembly and retrieve it at run time.*

✔ *Implement the Singleton pattern.*

In the preceding chapters, each class has defined a set of data fields and each instance maintains the state of its own data members. That is, each instance manipulates only its own data members. In some cases, however, you might want all the classes to have access to one piece of data. This chapter will demonstrate how to create shared and static data that can be shared by all the instances of a class. You'll also work with shared and static methods, which are also members of a class but don't require you to create an instance of a class before they can be called. You'll also see several examples of how the .NET Framework uses shared and static members.

Shared and Static Members

Each time an instance of a class is created, a section of memory is set aside to hold the fields for that new instance. This is commonly called the *instance data*, and the projects you've created so far have all used instance data. Another type of data, called *shared data* in Microsoft Visual Basic or *static data* in Microsoft Visual C#, is allocated for a class as a whole. In the case of this type of data, however, only one place in memory is reserved for the data, no matter how many instances of the class exist. Every instance of the class has access to this one copy of the data.

Properties, constructors, methods, and events can also be shared across class instances. These shared members, which don't require an instance of the class, provide services related to the class. An example is the .NET Framework's *Integer.Parse* method, which takes a string argument and returns an Integer value. It makes sense that the Integer class would know how to parse a string into an Integer, but obviously the Integer value doesn't exist until the string is parsed. It also wouldn't make sense to create an Integer value just so that you can call the *Parse* method to create a second instance of the Integer class. Static members are also used to manipulate the shared and static data of a class. For example, just as you've create properties to expose fields, you'll create shared properties to expose shared fields. Shared and static properties, constructors, and methods have a limitation in common: they can use only the shared or static fields of a class. These members have no access to any of the instance data. Offsetting this limitation is the ability to call these methods even if you haven't created an instance of the class.

> **note**
> Don't confuse shared fields in Visual Basic with static function variables in Visual Basic. (C# doesn't support static function variables.) You declare shared fields with the keyword *Shared*; you declare static function variables with the keyword *Static*. A static function variable retains its value between calls. If a class has a method with a static variable, a copy of that variable is created for every instance of the class. Thus static function variables are instance data.

A More Interesting Point

In Chapter 9, "Providing Services with Interfaces," you created a SortablePoint class that provided a sorting mechanism based on the distance from the origin. With the addition of a shared or static field and property, you can easily sort the points based on the distance from any point.

Creating the SortablePoint Class

The SortablePoint class will start with X and Y properties, a constructor, and an overridden *ToString* method as instance members, similar to the implementation in Chapter 9. You'll then add a shared or static member *Center* and modify the *CompareTo* function to use *Center* instead of the origin. Finally, you'll implement a shared or static *Parse* method that's able to read the same string format that the *ToString* method creates.

Create the class

1 Create a new Windows application project. Name it SortablePoint.

2 Add a new class to the project. Name it SortablePoint.

3 Modify the class to indicate that it will implement the IComparable interface.

```
' Visual Basic
Public Class SortablePoint
    Implements IComparable
End Class
```

```
// Visual C#
public class SortablePoint : IComparable {
}
```

4 Add the X and Y properties and fields. For this example, they'll be read-only.

```
' Visual Basic
Private m_x As Integer = 0
Public Readonly Property X() As Integer
    Get
        Return m_x
    End Get
End Property

Private m_y As Integer = 0
Public Readonly Property Y() As Integer
    Get
        Return m_y
    End Get
End Property

// Visual C#
private int m_x = 0;
public int X {
    get { return m_x; }
}
```

(continued)

```
private int m_y = 0;
public int Y {
    get { return m_y; }
}
```

5   Add the constructor to the SortablePoint class. In Visual C#, this replaces the parameterless constructor already in the class.

```
' Visual Basic
Public Sub New(ByVal x As Integer, ByVal y As Integer)
    m_x = x
    m_y = y
End Sub
```

```
// Visual C#
public SortablePoint(int x, int y) {
    m_x = x;
    m_y = y;
}
```

6   Override the *ToString* method inherited from *System.Object* by adding the following code:

```
' Visual Basic
Public Overrides Function ToString() As String
    Return String.Format("({0}, {1})", m_x, m_y)
End Function
```

```
// Visual C#
public override string ToString() {
    return string.Format("({0}, {1})", X, Y);
}
```

Add the shared or static field and property

Here you'll implement a shared or static SortablePoint field as the center of the points. Points will be compared based on their distance from this point, rather than from the origin. By creating the shared or static property, the client code only has to set one property to affect the distance calculation for all instances of SortablePoint. The field will be private to the class, and exposed in the interface as a shared or static property.

1   Add the shared or static field, *m_center*. You declare a class member shared or static by adding the *Shared* keyword in Visual Basic or the *static* keyword in Visual C#.

```
' Visual Basic
Private Shared m_center As New SortablePoint(0, 0)
```

```
// Visual C#
private static SortablePoint m_center = new SortablePoint(0, 0);
```

2 Add the shared or static *Center* property. Just as in other classes you've created, the property is used to control access to the field. As with the field declaration, you add the *Shared* or *static* keyword. When you set this property in the user interface, you'll see that using a shared or static property is a little different from using an instance property.

```
' Visual Basic
Public Shared Property Center() As SortablePoint
    Get
        Return m_center
    End Get
    Set(ByVal Value As SortablePoint)
        m_center = Value
    End Set
End Property
```

```
// Visual C#
public static SortablePoint Center {
    get { return m_center; }
    set { m_center = value; }
}
```

3 Implement the IComparable interface. In this implementation, the comparison is based on the distance from the SortablePoint instance *m_center*.

```
' Visual Basic
Public Function CompareTo(ByVal obj As Object) As Integer _
Implements System.IComparable.CompareTo
    Return Me.SquaredDistance() - CType(obj, _
        SortablePoint).SquaredDistance()
End Function

Private Function SquaredDistance() As Integer
    Dim xDistance As Integer = m_center.X - m_x
    Dim yDistance As Integer = m_center.Y - m_y
    Return (xDistance * xDistance) + (yDistance * yDistance)
End Function
```

```
// Visual C#
public int CompareTo(object obj) {
    return this.SquaredDistance() -
        ((SortablePoint)obj).SquaredDistance();
}
```

(continued)

```
private int SquaredDistance() {
    int xDistance = m_center.X - m_x;
    int yDistance = m_center.Y - m_y;
    return (xDistance * xDistance) + (yDistance * yDistance);
}
```

Add the shared or static *Parse* method

If you search the .NET Framework help documents, you'll see that many classes implement a shared or static *Parse* method. This method is the opposite of the *ToString* method: Instead of converting a class instance into a string, it converts a string into a class instance. For the SortablePoint class, you'll define a sort method that reads a string such as *(1, 2)* and returns a SortablePoint instance with X equal to 1 and Y equal to 2.

● Add this shared or static *Parse* method. Note that the shared or static method doesn't access any of the instance data of a class, although it does create an instance of the class and manipulate the instance data through the reference.

```vb
' Visual Basic
Public Shared Function Parse(ByVal pointString As String) As SortablePoint
    Try
        Dim values() As String = pointString.Split("( ,)".ToCharArray)
        Dim x As Integer = Integer.Parse(values(1))
        Dim y As Integer = Integer.Parse(values(3))
        Return New SortablePoint(x, y)
    Catch
        Throw New ArgumentException("Unable to parse " & pointString _
            & " into a SortablePoint instance.")
    End Try
End Function
```

```csharp
// Visual C#
public static SortablePoint Parse(string pointString) {
    try {
        string[] values = pointString.Split("( ,)".ToCharArray());
        int x = int.Parse(values[1]);
        int y = int.Parse(values[3]);
        return new SortablePoint(x, y);
    }
    catch {
        throw new ArgumentException("Unable to parse " + pointString
            + " into a SortablePoint instance.");
    }
}
```

We haven't used much exception handling in the book so far, but because this method isn't very flexible in its parsing and the function accepts any string, it's likely that incorrectly formatted strings will find their way into this function. As a general programming practice, you want to avoid returning any new instance of SortablePoint in the case of a failure of this type. The client code needs to respond to the error rather than continuing to use a SortablePoint that's not correct. Imagine a spreadsheet application that returned 0 for any numeric error. The user wouldn't have the opportunity to fix the problem and would likely not even be aware that there were any problems. As you'll see in the next section, the string for this method will be retrieved from the user through a TextBox control. Experience shows that the users often type the point in the wrong format, and adding the exception allows the client code to respond gracefully to typing errors.

Testing the Sortable Point Class

To test the SortablePoint class, you'll build an interface similar to the one in Chapter 9. In this case, you'll let the user change the center point at run time. The user will enter the new center as a string in the (x, y) format. The code then uses the *Parse* method to create an instance of SortablePoint and to change the *Center* property of the SortablePoint class.

Create a user interface

1. Open Form1 in the form designer.

2. Set the Height property of the form to 344.

3. Add controls and set their properties as shown in the following table.

Control	Property	Value
Button	Name	*addPoints*
	Text	*Add Points*
	Location	*136, 248*
	Size	*96, 23*
TextBox	Name	*newCenter*
	Text	(blank)
	Location	*16, 280*
Button	Name	*setNewCenter*
	Text	*Set New Center*
	Location	*136, 280*
	Size	*96, 23*

4   In the form designer, double-click the Set New Center button to create the Click event handler. Add the following code to set the shared or static *Center* property. To call a shared member in Visual Basic, you use the class name (SortablePoint) or an instance name. To call a static member in Visual C#, you use the class name (SortablePoint).

```
' Visual Basic
Private Sub setNewCenter_Click(ByVal sender As System.Object, _
ByVal e As System.EventArgs) Handles setNewCenter.Click
    Try
        Dim center As SortablePoint = SortablePoint.Parse(newCenter.Text)
        SortablePoint.Center = center
    Catch ex As Exception
        MessageBox.Show(ex.Message & ControlChars.CrLf & _
            "Setting center to the origin.")
        SortablePoint.Center = New SortablePoint(0, 0)
        newCenter.Text = SortablePoint.Center.ToString()
    End Try
    Me.Refresh()
End Sub

// Visual C#
private void setNewCenter_Click(object sender, System.EventArgs e) {
    try {
        SortablePoint center = SortablePoint.Parse(newCenter.Text);
        SortablePoint.Center = center;
    }
    catch (Exception ex) {
        MessageBox.Show(ex.Message + "\n" +
            "Setting center to the origin.");
        SortablePoint.Center = new SortablePoint(0, 0);
        newCenter.Text = SortablePoint.Center.ToString();
    }
    this.Refresh();
}
```

note

When you use Visual Basic, call static members by using the class name. Using an instance variable to call a static member can confuse other developers. For example, the expression *thisPoint.Center* could mislead other developers into thinking that the center can be set separately for each SortablePoint instance.

5   Double-click the Add Points button to create the event handler and add this code to draw points on the form. This is the same code you used in Chapter 9.

```vb
' Visual Basic
Private Sub addPoints_Click(ByVal sender As System.Object, _
ByVal e As System.EventArgs) Handles addPoints.Click
    Dim points As New ArrayList()
    Dim rgen As New System.Random()
    Dim pt As SortablePoint
    Dim count As Integer
    Dim graph As Graphics = Me.CreateGraphics()
    Dim aColor As Color

    For count = 0 To 249
        points.Add(New SortablePoint(rgen.Next(200), rgen.Next(200)))
    Next

    points.Sort()

    For count = 0 To 249
        pt = CType(points(count), SortablePoint)
        aColor = System.Drawing.Color.FromArgb(25, 25, count)
        Dim brush As New System.Drawing.SolidBrush(aColor)
        graph.FillEllipse(brush, pt.X, pt.Y, 10, 10)
        brush.Dispose()
     Next
End Sub

// Visual C#
private void addPoints_Click(object sender, System.EventArgs e) {
    ArrayList points = new ArrayList();
    System.Random rgen = new System.Random();
    SortablePoint pt;
    Graphics graph = this.CreateGraphics();

    for (int count = 0; count < 250; count++) {
        points.Add(new SortablePoint(rgen.Next(200), rgen.Next(200)));
    }

    points.Sort();

    for (int count = 0; count < 250; count++) {
        pt = (SortablePoint)(points[count]);
        Color color = System.Drawing.Color.FromArgb(25, 25, count);
        System.Drawing.SolidBrush brush =
        new System.Drawing.SolidBrush(color);
        graph.FillEllipse(brush, pt.X, pt.Y, 10,10);
        brush.Dispose();
    }
}
```

Shared and Static Members

11

Run the application

● Press F5 to run the application. An example of the output is shown here. You'll want to add some points, enter a new center point, click Set New Center, and finally add some more points. You'll see the light to dark pattern change to reflect the change in the center point. Note that the application doesn't limit the center to within the rectangle of dots. You can also enter a new center that's not correctly formatted—for example, *(12, abc)*, so that you can test the exception handling statement.

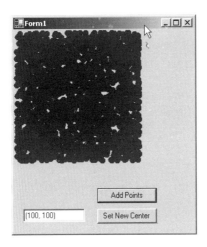

A More Efficient Card

Shared and static members don't have to be public. In Chapter 8, "Putting It All Together with Components," you created a Card class. Each instance of Card contained an ArrayList filled with Icon instances. If you had a thousand Card instances, you'd have a thousand identical instances of the Hearts icon. You can see that each instance doesn't need its own copy, because they are all the same. A shared or static ArrayList will allow the application to maintain only one copy of each icon. A shared or static constructor provides the means for adding the icons to the ArrayList.

Implementing the Card Class

The Card class in this example will have the same public members as the class you implemented in Chapter 8. You'll add a private shared or static SortedList field and a shared or static constructor. To fill the SortedList you'll use some of the shared or static methods of the .NET Framework.

Create the project

You'll create this project by adding the icon files and Card class source file from Chapter 8 to a basic Windows application project.

1   Create a new Windows application project. Name it BetterCard.

2   From the Project menu, click Add Existing Item. Type *.ico in the Filename box and locate and add the four icon files—Hearts.ico, Diamonds.ico, Spades.ico, and Clubs.ico—to the project. (The files are located in the Chapter08 folder of the companion CD.) In this exercise, an icon will be associated with a Suit enumeration based on the symbolic name of the enumeration value. That is, the Hearts.ico Icon object will be associated with the key *Suits.Heart* in a SortedList object. Please note that you'll also be using a .NET Framework method that's case sensitive. Therefore, if your Suit enumeration is *Clubs,* your icon file needs to be named *Clubs.ico.* You can rename the files before you add them to the project, or you can rename them now by using Solution Explorer.

3   In Solution Explorer, select the four icon files by holding down the Control key as you click each file.

4   In the Properties window, set the Build Action property for the icons to *Embedded Resource.*

You'll use classes in the *System.Reflection* namespace to retrieve the icons at run time. By using an embedded resource, you don't have to distribute the icon files separately and then find the paths to them at run time.

5   From the Project menu, select Add Existing Item. Browse to the Card.cs or Card.vb source file you created for Chapter 8, and add it to your project. You can also find this file on the companion CD in the GamesLibrary folder in either the \Chapter08\VisualBasic or \Chapter08\VisualCS folder. If you're using Visual C#, locate the namespace declaration in Card.cs and change it to *BetterCard.*

6   Double-click Card.vb or Card.cs in Solution Explorer to load the Card control into the form designer and the Toolbox.

Add the shared and static members

In this section, you'll make the SortedList field that holds the icons a shared or static data member instead of an instance member. You'll also use a shared or static constructor to add the icons to the SortedList member. This constructor will make a call to the shared or static method *GetExecutingAssembly* of the Assembly class. The Assembly instance returned by this call represents your application during run time.

The *GetManifestResourceStream* method of the Assembly class returns an instance of *System.IO.Stream* that lets you read the icon, as long as you know the name of the icon file in the assembly. The name of the file in the assembly takes the form *AssemblyName.IconFileName*. You can use the *GetName* method of the Assembly class to retrieve the assembly name at run time. Conveniently, the Icon class provides a constructor that takes a stream as a parameter. Just pass the Stream instance from the *GetManifestResourceStream* method to the Icon constructor, and you're done retrieving the icon from the assembly. That's a lot of classes and method calls to match up, so let's look at the code to see how it works out. The following code shows the basic process for retrieving the Hearts.ico icon:

```
' Visual Basic
Dim theAssembly As System.Reflection.Assembly
theAssembly = System.Reflection.Assembly.GetExecutingAssembly()
Dim assemblyName As String = theAssembly.GetName().Name
Dim resourceName As String = assemblyName & ".Hearts.ico"
Dim iconStream As System.IO.Stream = _
    theAssembly.GetManifestResourceStream(resourceName)
Dim theIcon As Icon = new Icon(iconStream)
```

```
// Visual C#
System.Reflection.Assembly assembly;
assembly = System.Reflection.Assembly.GetExecutingAssembly();
string assemblyName = assembly.GetName().Name;
string resourceName = assemblyName + ".Hearts.ico";
System.IO.Stream iconStream =
    theAssembly.GetManifestResourceStream(resourceName);
Icon theIcon = new Icon(iconStream);
```

1   In Solution Explorer, right-click Card.cs or Card.vb and click View Code on the shortcut menu.

2   Modify the Card class default constructor—the constructor that doesn't take arguments—to delete the calls to add icons to the *m_icons* SortedList. If you're using Visual Basic you'll find the constructor in the region labeled Windows Form Designer Generated Code. The constructor after modification is shown here:

```
' Visual Basic
Public Sub New()
    MyBase.New()
    'This call is required by the Windows Form Designer.
    InitializeComponent()
End Sub
```

```
// Visual C#
public Card()
{
    // This call is required by the Windows.Forms Form Designer.
    InitializeComponent();
}
```

3   If you're using Visual Basic, add an Imports statement at the top of the source file for the *System.ComponentModel* namespace. The Card class you defined in Chapter 8 was part of a Class Library project, and the *System. Component* namespace was a project-wide import. The namespace isn't imported by default in a Visual Basic Windows application and must be added. If you're using Visual C#, the *using* statement for *System.Component-Model* is already in the Card.cs file.

```
' Visual Basic
Imports System.ComponentModel
```

4   Modify the declaration of the SortedList field so that it's a shared or static data member.

```
' Visual Basic
Shared m_images As SortedList = New SortedList()
```

```
// Visual C#
static SortedList m_images = new SortedList();
```

5   Add the shared or static constructor to fill the *m_icons* SortedList with the embedded icons. Like shared and static methods, the shared or static constructor can use only shared or static data.

```
' Visual Basic
Shared Sub New()
    Dim theAssembly As System.Reflection.Assembly
    theAssembly = System.Reflection.Assembly.GetExecutingAssembly()
    Dim assemblyName As String = theAssembly.GetName().Name

    Dim iconStream As System.IO.Stream
    Dim resourceName As String
    Dim theIcon As Icon
    Dim theSuit As Object
    Dim aSuit As Integer
    Dim suitNames() As String =
        System.Enum.GetNames(System.Type.GetType("BetterCard.Suit"))
    For aSuit = 0 To suitNames.Length - 1
        resourceName = assemblyName & "." & suitNames(aSuit) & ".ico"
```

(continued)

```
            iconStream = theAssembly.GetManifestResourceStream(resourceName)
            theIcon = new Icon(iconStream)
            theSuit = System.Enum.Parse( _
                System.Type.GetType("BetterCard.Suit"), suitNames(aSuit))
            m_images.Add(theSuit, theIcon)
        Next
    End Sub

    // Visual C#
    static Card() {
        System.Reflection.Assembly assembly;
        assembly = System.Reflection.Assembly.GetExecutingAssembly();
        string assemblyName = assembly.GetName().Name;

        System.IO.Stream iconStream;
        string resourceName;
        Icon theIcon;
        object theSuit;
        string[] suitNames = Enum.GetNames(typeof(Suit));
        for (int aSuit = 0; aSuit < suitNames.Length; aSuit++) {
            resourceName = assemblyName + "." + suitNames[aSuit] + ".ico";
            iconStream = assembly.GetManifestResourceStream(resourceName);
            theIcon = new Icon(iconStream);
            theSuit = Enum.Parse(typeof(Suit),suitNames[aSuit],true);
            m_images.Add(theSuit, theIcon);
        }
    }
```

This constructor uses a generalized version of the code snippet shown on page 304 to collect the four icons. The constructor uses the shared or static *GetNames* and *Parse* methods of the *System.Enum* class. The Enum class provides several methods for manipulating enumerations. The *GetName* method returns an array of strings with the names of the enumeration members. You use this array to create the names of the icon files in the assembly. (Remember that you carefully named the icon files to match the enumeration names.) You then use the *Enum.Parse* method to return a Suit enumeration value to use as the key into the SortedList.

The shared or static constructor is called only once during an application's lifetime—some time after the application starts, but before the first instance of the class is created. Client code can't call the static constructor, meaning that the developer can't control when the constructor is called.

6   In the Paint event handler, *Card_Paint*, remove the *Me* or *this* scoping operator from the *m_images* reference. The *m_images* field is no longer instance data, and using the *this* operator isn't allowed, because the static *m_images* field isn't associated with a particular instance of Card. Visual Basic allows the reference to *Me.m_images*, but it's good practice and less confusing to someone readying the code to remove the *Me*. The code to remove is shown in bold.

```
' Visual Basic
g.DrawIcon(CType(Me.m_images(m_suit), Icon), 14, 40)
```

```
// Visual C#
g.DrawIcon((Icon)(this.m_images[m_suit]), 14, 40);
```

7   From the Build menu, select Build Solution.

Test the Card class

In testing the Card class, you'll create a form that has one card and two ListBox controls. At run time, the ListBox controls will contain Suit and FaceValue enumeration values. As you select a new value, the Card will reflect the new value. You'll use a shared or static member of the Enum class to retrieve the values of the Suit and FaceValue enumerations.

1   Open Form1 in the form designer.

2   Add controls and set their properties as shown in the following table. You'll find the Card control in the Toolbox. Arrange the controls however you like. The suitList control will contain a list of the Suit enumeration values and the faceValueList will contain a list of the FaceValue enumerations.

Control	Property	Value
Card	Name	*card1*
	FaceUp	*True*
ListBox	Name	*suitList*
ListBox	Name	*faceValueList*

3   Double-click on the form to create the Load event handler. Add the following code to fill the ListBox controls:

```
' Visual Basic
Private Sub Form1_Load(ByVal sender As System.Object, _
ByVal e As System.EventArgs) Handles MyBase.Load
    suitList.DataSource = _
        System.Enum.GetValues(System.Type.GetType("BetterCard.Suit"))
    faceValueList.DataSource = _
        System.Enum.GetValues(FaceValue.Queen.GetType())
End Sub
```

(continued)

```
// Visual C#
private void Form1_Load(object sender, System.EventArgs e) {
    suitList.DataSource = Enum.GetValues(typeof(Suit));
    faceValueList.DataSource = Enum.GetValues(typeof(FaceValue));
}
```

The *Enum.GetValues* method takes a Type parameter representing the enumeration and returns the values of the enumeration in an Array instance. Each member of the Array instance is an enumeration value. The Type class is a .NET Framework class that represents classes defined in an application. Before you can call the *Enum.GetValues* method, you need to get a Type instance representing the enumeration. The *typeof* operator of Visual C# returns the Type instance representing a defined type. To retrieve the Type instance in Visual Basic, you can use the *GetType* method on a particular enumeration value, or the shared *Type.GetType* method. An example of each is used in the code.

4   In the form designer, double-click the *suitList* list box to create the SelectedIndexChanged event handler. The SelectedItem property of the ListBox control returns a *System.Object* instance that must be cast back to Suit to be used as the Suit property of the *card1* object.

```
' Visual Basic
Private Sub suitList_SelectedIndexChanged(ByVal sender As System.Object, _
ByVal e As System.EventArgs) Handles suitList.SelectedIndexChanged
    Me.card1.Suit = CType(Me.suitList.SelectedItem, Suit)
End Sub
```

```
// Visual C#
private void suitList_SelectedIndexChanged(object sender,
System.EventArgs e) {
    this.card1.Suit = (Suit) this.suitList.SelectedItem;
}
```

5   In the form designer, double-click the *faceValueList* list box to create the SelectedIndexChanged event handler.

```
' Visual Basic
Private Sub faceValueList_SelectedIndexChanged( _
ByVal sender As System.Object, ByVal e As System.EventArgs) _
Handles faceValueList.SelectedIndexChanged
    Me.card1.FaceValue = _
        CType(Me.faceValueList.SelectedItem, FaceValue)
End Sub
```

```
// Visual C#
private void faceValueList_SelectedIndexChanged(object sender,
System.EventArgs e) {
    this.card1.FaceValue = (FaceValue) this.faceValueList.SelectedItem;
}
```

6 Press F5 to run the program. Example output is shown below. As you select different Suit and FaceValues values in the ListBox controls, the appearance of the card changes.

The Singleton Pattern

One of the most well-known uses of shared and static members is to implement the Singleton design pattern. A *design pattern* is a solution to a common problem. The description of a pattern generally includes the pattern name, a description of the problem, a description of the solution, and an analysis of the consequences of using the pattern. The classic reference on design patterns is *Design Patterns* by Erich Gamma, Richard Helm, Ralph Johnson, and John Vlissides (Addison-Wesley, 1995). I'll talk about design patterns again in Chapter 14, "Reducing Complexity by Design."

Your application might have a constraint that only one instance of the class can be created. This is a common limitation when the class is an abstraction of a hardware or operating system component, such as a file manager or a print spooler. In this case, you want to implement the Singleton pattern, a well-known object-oriented design pattern.

Implement the Singleton pattern

The implementation of the Singleton pattern has these characteristics:

- The constructor is private so that no client code can create an instance. This allows the class to create and control access to the one instance.

- The single instance is available only through the shared or static method.

The essential implementation of the Singleton pattern is short and simple and is shown in the following steps.

1   Create a new Windows application. Name it Singleton.

2   From the Project menu, select Add New Item, and then select Code File from the list of templates. Name the new code file Singleton.

3   Add the following code to the code file to define the basic Singleton class. This implementation uses lazy initialization, meaning the instance isn't created until the first time it's retrieved.

```vb
' Visual Basic
Class Singleton
    Shared m_instance As Singleton
    Public Shared Function GetInstance() As Singleton
        If (m_instance Is Nothing) Then
            m_instance = New Singleton()
        End If
        Return m_instance
    End Function

    Private Sub New()
    End Sub
End Class
```

```csharp
// Visual C#
namespace Singleton {
    class Singleton {
        static Singleton m_instance;
        public static Singleton GetInstance() {
            if (m_instance == null) {
                m_instance = new Singleton();
            }
            return m_instance;
        }
        private Singleton() {}
    }
}
```

4 Add two member functions and a field to the class to store and return a collection of strings. You'll use these methods to demonstrate that only one instance of the Singleton class is created. Note that *m_list* is instance data, not shared or static data.

```vb
' Visual Basic
Dim m_list As System.Collections.ArrayList = _
    New System.Collections.ArrayList()
Public Sub AddString(ByVal newString As String)
    m_list.Add(newString)
End Sub

Public Function GetStrings() As String()
    Return CType(m_list.ToArray(System.Type.GetType("System.String")), _
        String())
End Function
```

```csharp
// Visual C#
System.Collections.ArrayList m_list =
    new System.Collections.ArrayList();
public void AddString(string newString) {
    m_list.Add(newString);
}

public string[] GetStrings() {
    return (string[])m_list.ToArray(typeof(string));
}
```

Test the Singleton class

To demonstrate that there is only one instance of the Singleton class, you'll use the array returned by the *GetStrings* method as the data source to two ListBox controls. When you add strings to one of the references, you'll see the change propagated to both ListBox controls.

1 Open Form1 in the form designer and add controls and set their properties as shown in the following table. Arrange the controls as you like.

Control	Property	Value
ListBox	Name	*listOne*
ListBox	Name	*listTwo*
TextBox	Name	*newString*
	Text	(blank)
Button	Name	*addString*
	Text	*Add String*

2 Double-click Form1 to create the form's Load event. Add code to create the Singleton instance. Also add two fields for the Singleton references.

```
' Visual Basic
Dim singletonOne As Singleton
Dim singletonTwo As Singleton

Private Sub Form1_Load(ByVal sender As System.Object, _
ByVal e As System.EventArgs) Handles MyBase.Load
    ' The following line won't compile because there's no
    ' public constructor.
    ' singletonOne = New Singleton()
    singletonOne = Singleton.GetInstance()
    singletonTwo = Singleton.GetInstance()
End Sub
```

```
// Visual C#
Singleton singletonOne;
Singleton singletonTwo;

private void Form1_Load(object sender, System.EventArgs e) {
    // The following line won't compile because there's no
    // public constructor.
    // Singleton aSingleton = new Singleton();
    singletonOne = Singleton.GetInstance();
    singletonTwo = Singleton.GetInstance();
}
```

3 Create a Click event handler for the Add String button and add this code to demonstrate that both Singleton references, *singletonOne* and *singletonTwo*, refer to the same instance of Singleton.

```
' Visual Basic
Private Sub addString_Click(ByVal sender As System.Object, _
ByVal e As System.EventArgs) Handles addString.Click
    singletonOne.AddString(newString.Text)

    listOne.DataSource = Nothing
    listOne.Items.Clear()
    listOne.DataSource = singletonOne.GetStrings()

    listTwo.DataSource = Nothing
    listTwo.Items.Clear()
    listTwo.DataSource = singletonTwo.GetStrings()
End Sub
```

```
// Visual C#
private void addString_Click(object sender, System.EventArgs e) {
    singletonOne.AddString(newString.Text);

    listOne.DataSource = null;
    listOne.Items.Clear();
    listOne.DataSource = singletonOne.GetStrings();

    listTwo.DataSource = null;
    listTwo.Items.Clear();
    listTwo.DataSource = singletonTwo.GetStrings();
}
```

You could also add a test to the button that simply tests whether the references are the same:

```
' Visual Basic
If (singletonOne Is singletonTwo) And (Not IsNothing(singletonOne)) Then
    MessageBox.Show("They are the same.")
End If
```

```
// Visual C#
if ((singletonOne == singletonTwo) && (singletonOne != null)) {
    MessageBox.Show("They are the same.");
}
```

4   Press F5 to run the program. Add several strings and note that both list boxes have the same list of items, even though the code is only adding strings to the *singletonOne* reference. Example output is shown here:

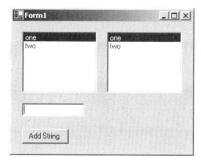

Design Considerations

Shared and static members solve many programming tasks, but like any programming construct, they need to be used wisely. What follows are some tips and warnings about using shared and static members.

- **Too many static members**   Since static members often track information about groups of instances, you might be tempted to add members that represent a group abstraction to the class. Rather than provide static properties *TotalCars* and *AverageWeight* for the Car class, you're better off creating a ParkingLot class to maintain the data. In general, don't complicate the design with unnecessary classes, but do make sure that each class represents one abstraction.

- **When static properties become global data**   Using global data is, in general, a poor programming practice. When you make data global, you lose control of it. Global data can be passed to any method and then changed in unexpected ways. Public static data is available to any method in which the class is in scope. Used without planning, static data can easily become global data. Look closely at your design if you have a significant amount of public static data.

- **Multithreaded applications**   If you're working with a multithreaded application, you have to take synchronization into account. Suppose you have a class with a shared or static array of integers. You might have two instances of the class, on different threads, modifying the array. One instance might be able to complete only part of its modifications before the second instance starts modifying the data, leading to unexpected results. For information on synchronizing access to static variables, see the *lock* keyword in Visual C# and the *SyncLock* keyword in Visual Basic. The .NET Framework documentation provides threading information on many classes.

Quick Reference

To	Do this
Create a shared or static field	Add the *Shared* or *static* keyword to the declaration.

```
' Visual Basic
Shared m_number As Integer
```

```
// Visual C#
static int m_number;
```

To	Do this
Create a shared or static property	Add the *Shared* or *static* keyword to the declaration.

```
' Visual Basic
Public Shared Property Number() As Integer
    Get
        Return m_number
    End Get
    Set(ByVal Value As Integer)
        m_center = Value
    End Set
End Property

// Visual C#
public static int Number {
    get { return m_number; }
    set { m_number = value; }
}
```

| Create a shared or static method | Add the *Shared* or *static* keyword to the declaration. |

```
' Visual Basic
Public Shared Sub SomeMethod()
End Sub

// Visual C#
public static void SomeMethod() {
}
```

| Create a shared or static constructor | Add the *Shared* or *static* keyword to the declaration. |

```
' Visual Basic
Shared Sub New()
End Sub

// Visual C#
static Card() {
}
```

| Call a shared or static member | In Visual Basic, use the class name or an instance name. In Visual C#, use the class name. |

```
' Visual Basic
SomeClass.Number = 5
SomeClass.SomeMethod()

// Visual C#
SomeClass.Number = 5;
SomeClass.SomeMethod();
```

12

Overloading Operators with Visual C#

In this chapter, you'll learn how to

✔ *Overload the arithmetic +, −, and * operators.*

✔ *Overload the == and != relational operators.*

✔ *Use delegates to control program behavior at run time.*

ESTIMATED TIME
1 hr. 30 min.

In Chapter 4, you saw how overloading methods allowed you to implement several different but related behaviors under one method name. In Chapter 5, you saw how the same method name could implement different but related behaviors in derived classes. With operator overloading, you'll see how a C# operator can behave differently depending on the context in which it appears. For example, if you use the + operator with two integer operands, as in 1 + 1, the result is another integer, 2. In this chapter, you'll overload the + operator to add two vectors, so that the sum of two vectors, vector A + vector B, returns a third vector, vector C.

Visual Basic .NET doesn't support operator overloading. Depending on the problem you're solving, operator overloading might be a deciding factor in whether you implement the application in Visual Basic or Visual C#. Even if you aren't using Visual C#, you might want to read through the implementation of the user interface to see how delegates are used. The method works equally well in Visual Basic, as you'll see in Chapter 13, "Saving Instance Data."

A Short Lesson on Vectors

In this chapter, you'll use the vector as the basis for an exercise in overloading operators. A vector is a line segment with direction and magnitude. You can specify both the direction and magnitude of the vector by specifying a coordinate pair (x, y). Using this notation, the three vectors in the following diagram are $(2, 4)$, $(3, 0)$, and $(-4, -4)$.

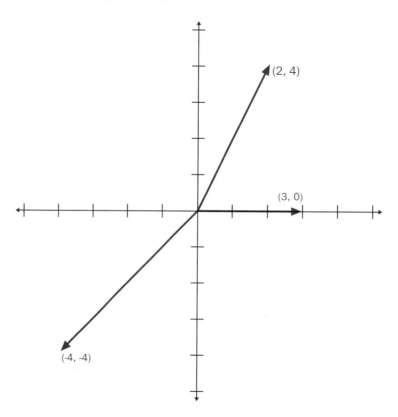

Addition, subtraction, multiplication, and equality are defined on vectors, making the vector a good candidate for operator overloading. Vector addition is defined by placing two vectors end to end, with the first vector placed at the origin. The sum is the vector from the origin to the end of the second vector. The x value of the vector sum is the sum of the x components of the two vectors. Similarly, the y value is the sum of the y components of the two vectors. The sum of $(1, 3)$ and $(3, 1)$ is $(4, 4)$, and is shown in the following diagram.

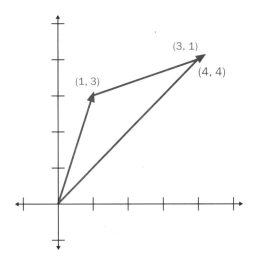

You can also multiply a vector by a scalar. A vector is multiplied by a scalar (a nonvector value) by multiplying both the x and y components by the scalar. For example, $2 * (1, 3) = (2, 6)$. Note that you can also multiply a vector times a vector, but you won't go that far in this chapter. Vectors can also be subtracted. To subtract a vector B from a vector A multiply vector B by -1 and add it to vector A. The difference $(1, 3) - (3, 1) = (-2, 2)$ is shown in the following diagram.

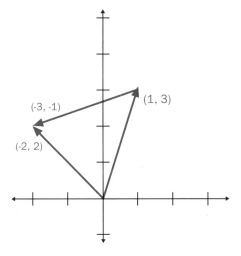

Vector Algebra Application

Your task in this chapter is to create an application that will add, subtract, and multiply vectors. The user can vary the *x* and *y* components of Vectors A and B independently. Vector B can be multiplied by a scalar. Finally, the user can choose whether to add or subtract the two vectors. The following graphic shows the application you'll develop:

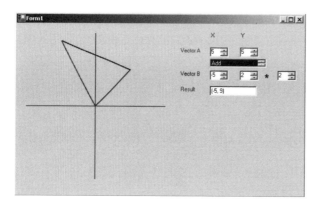

Operator overloading allows you to specify the behavior of an operator in the context of a class you've defined. Not all operators can be overloaded. The operators that can be overloaded are shown in the following table, divided among unary and binary operators. Unary operators, such as ++ and --, take only one operand—for example, *i*++. Binary operators, such as * and ==, take two operands—for example, *a* * *b*.

Operator Type	Operators That Can Be Overloaded
Unary	+ - ! ~ ++ -- *true* *false*
Binary	+ - * / % & | ^ << >> == != > < >= <=

Probably the most glaring omissions from the table are the assignment operators, including =, +=, -=, and *=, which can't be overloaded. At run time, the assignment operator is replaced by its expanded form, so that *a* += 2 is evaluated as *a* = *a* + 2. By not allowing the assignment operators to be overloaded, the language designers have guaranteed consistency in the meaning of operator pairs such as + and +=.

In this exercise, you'll overload the ==, !=, +, -, and * operators. You'll also see functions from the base *System.Object* class that by convention are overloaded when some operators are overloaded.

Implementing the Vector Class

The Vector class consists of two properties, X and Y, several overloaded operators, ==, !=, +, −, and *, and a few general purpose methods: *ToString*, *Parse*, and *GetHashCode*. The Vector class won't contain any methods for drawing Vectors—that will be left to the user interface component of the application.

Create the project and class

The Vector Algebra project consists of just a form and the Vector class.

1 Create a new Visual C# Windows application project. Name it VectorAlgebra.

2 Add a new class named Vector to the project.

3 Add the following fields and properties for X and Y.

```
private int m_x;
public int X {
    get { return m_x; }
    set { m_x = value; }
}

private int m_y;
public int Y {
    get { return m_y; }
    set { m_y = value; }
}
```

4 Modify the constructor as shown here:

```
public Vector(int x, int y) {
    m_x = x;
    m_y = y;
}
```

Overload == and !=

The == operator, if not overloaded, returns a Boolean value that indicates whether two references point to the same instance of a class. With a class such as Vector, you might not care if two references point to the same instance. What you're interested in is whether two vectors have the same direction and magnitude. In other words, do the two references have the same *x* and *y* components? Overloading the == operator allows you to change the meaning of equality for the Vector class.

There are rules and conventions for overloading the == operator. When you overload the == operator, you must also overload the != operator. By convention, if you overload the == operator, you should also (but are not required to) override the *Equals* and *GetHashCode* methods. Also, by convention, the == operator shouldn't throw an exception, but should instead return *false*.

1   Add the following code to overload the == operator.

```
public static bool operator ==(Vector aVector, Vector bVector) {
    return (aVector.X == bVector.X) && (aVector.Y == bVector.Y);
}
```

The syntax for overloading an operator is to declare a public static method with the return types and parameter types you want to define. For binary operators, you must specify two parameters. As you'll see with the * operator, the parameters do not need to be the same type, though they usually are.

The == operator is a comparison operator and thus returns a Boolean value. When the operator is used, the call will look something like *vectorA == vectorB*.

2   Add the following code to overload the != operator. Note that inequality is defined as the opposite of equality. You don't have to define inequality separately.

```
public static bool operator !=(Vector aVector, Vector bVector) {
    return !(aVector == bVector);
}
```

Override *Equals* and *GetHashCode*

Both the *Equals* method and the == operator of the *System.Object* class (the base class of Vector) return *true* if two references point to the same instance. When you overloaded the == and != operators, you defined == to mean that the two vectors had the same direction and magnitude. By overloading the *Equals* method, you give the *Equals* method the same meaning as the == operator.

The *GetHashCode* method is called if the Vector class is used as the key for a key-value pair in a hash table. A hash table is a data structure, implemented in the HashTable class, for storing key-value pairs. The *GetHashCode* method must return the same value for an instance every time it's called on the instance. Because of this rule, the *GetHashCode* method usually returns a calculation based on fields that don't change. The method doesn't have to return a unique value for every instance; two instances can return the same hash code.

1   Add the following code to override the *Equals* method. The *Equals* method
    is defined by calling the == operator. Because the *Equals* method takes an
    object as a parameter, you must also test that the object is the correct type,
    and you must cast the object to Vector before you can use the == operator.

```
public override bool Equals(object o) {
    return (o is Vector) && (this == (Vector)o);
}
```

2   Add the following code to override the *GetHashCode* method.

```
public override int GetHashCode() {
    return this.X;
}
```

Overload the unary – operator

●   Add the following code to overload the unary – operator. You'll use the
    unary – operator in the next section to define subtraction of vectors.

```
public static Vector operator -(Vector vector) {
    return new Vector(-vector.X, -vector.Y);
}
```

Overload the binary + and – operators

The addition or subtraction of two vectors produces a third, new vector. Consider a statement such as *vectorSum = vectorA + vectorB*. You can see that you
wouldn't expect *vectorA* or *vectorB* to be changed by adding them together. You
need a third, new Vector instance to assign to *vectorSum*.

1   Add the following code to overload the + operator.

```
public static Vector operator +(Vector aVector, Vector bVector) {
    return new Vector(aVector.X + bVector.X, aVector.Y + bVector.Y);
}
```

2   Add the following code to overload the – binary operator. Notice that you
    can define subtraction by using addition and the unary – operator. By reus-
    ing the operators this way, the operators behave consistently.

```
public static Vector operator -(Vector aVector, Vector bVector) {
    return aVector + (-bVector);
}
```

Overloading Operators

12

Overload the * operator for scalar multiplication

The operators you've defined so far have used only Vector operands. You can also define operators that take different types of operands by changing the parameters to the overload method.

● Add the following code to define the * operator. When you use the * operator, you'll use it in an expression such as *2 * vectorA*. If you want to reverse the operators, as in *vectorA * 2*, you have to define a second operator overload for * with the parameters reversed so that the integer parameter is second.

```
public static Vector operator *(int scalar, Vector vector) {
    return new Vector(scalar * vector.X, scalar * vector.Y);
}
```

Define the *ToString* and *Parse* methods

● Add the following code to define the *ToString* and *Parse* methods. These methods are similar to the ones you defined for the SortablePoint class in Chapter 9.

```
public static Vector Parse(string vectorString) {
    try {
        string[] values = vectorString.Split("( ,)".ToCharArray());
        int x = int.Parse(values[1]);
        int y = int.Parse(values[3]);
        return new Vector(x, y);
    }
    catch {
        throw new ArgumentException("Unable to parse '" + vectorString
            + "' into a Vector instance.");
    }
}

public override string ToString() {
    return string.Format("({0}, {1})", m_x, m_y);
}
```

Implementing the Vector Algebra Application

The user interface will allow the user to specify two vectors and the operation to perform on them—addition, subtraction, or equality. The second vector is multiplied by a scalar specified by the user.

The following interface shows the sum of the vectors (3, 3) and (−5, 3).

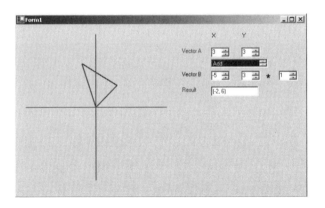

Add the user interface elements

1   To allow the user to specify the A vector, add controls and set their properties as shown in the following table. Use the preceding graphic as a guide.

Control	Property	Value
Label	Text	*X*
Label	Text	*Y*
Label	Text	*Vector A*
	ForeColor	*Red*
NumericUpDown	Name	*XVectorA*
NumericUpDown	Name	*YVectorA*

2   Add a ListBox that will be used to specify the operation to perform with the
vectors. Set the Name property to *functions*.

3   Add controls to specify the B vector, including the scalar multiplier.

Control	Property	Value
Label	Text	*Vector B*
	ForeColor	*Blue*
NumericUpDown	Name	*XVectorB*
NumericUpDown	Name	*YVectorB*
Label	Text	*
NumericUpDown	Name	*scalar*
	Minimum	−3
	Maximum	3
	Value	1
	Increment	1
	DecimalPlaces	0

12

Overloading Operators

3   Add controls to display the results of the vector calculation.

Control	Property	Value
Label	Text	*Result*
	ForeColor	*Green*
TextBox	Name	*result*
	ForeColor	*Green*
	Text	(blank)

4   Select the four NumericUpDown controls for the vector components by drawing a box around them with the mouse. With all four selected, set the properties as shown in the following table. If you accidentally select the NumericUpDown for the scalar, too, the default behavior of your application will be to multiply the B vector by zero, and you won't see any interesting results.

Property	Value
Minimum	*−5*
Maximum	*5*
Value	*0*
Increment	*1*
DecimalPlaces	*0*

Add the drawing methods

Now add the methods for drawing vectors on the form. The graph will represent the *x* and *y* axes from −10 to 10. The graph will be drawn on the form between pixels 20 and 170. Therefore, each unit of the vector graph is 15 pixels on the form. The entire graph is offset 20 pixels from the top and left of the form.

1   Create the event handler for the form's *Paint* method by clicking the Events toolbar button in the Properties pane for the form and double-click Paint. Add the following code to draw the axes of the graph:

```
private void Form1_Paint(object sender,
System.Windows.Forms.PaintEventArgs e) {
    e.Graphics.DrawLine(Pens.Black, 20, 170, 320, 170);
    e.Graphics.DrawLine(Pens.Black, 170, 20, 170, 320);
}
```

2   Add the following function to the form class.

This function translates a location relative to the graph (−10 to 10) to a location on the form (20 to 170).

```
private Point VectorToPoint(Vector vector) {
    return new Point(vector.X*15 + 170, -vector.Y*15 + 170);
}
```

3 Add the following overloaded methods to draw a vector on the form.

The first overload draws the vector from the origin. The second overload draws the vector from the end of another vector and is used to draw the vectors in addition.

```
private void DrawVector(Vector vector, Color color) {
    Point origin = VectorToPoint(new Vector(0, 0));
    Point end = VectorToPoint(vector);
    this.CreateGraphics().DrawLine(
        new Pen(new SolidBrush(color), 2), origin, end);
}

private void DrawVector(Vector aVector, Vector bVector, Color color) {
    Point origin = VectorToPoint(bVector);
    Point end = VectorToPoint(aVector + bVector);
    this.CreateGraphics().DrawLine(
        new Pen(new SolidBrush(color), 2), origin, end);
}
```

Add the logic

In this exercise, you'll use delegates to call the addition and subtraction operators.

1 Add the following delegate declaration and SortedList to the form class. In the third step, you'll create methods for addition, subtraction, and equality that comply with the signature of the VectorMath delegate.

```
private delegate void VectorMath(Vector a, Vector b);
System.Collections.SortedList m_maths =
    new System.Collections.SortedList();
```

2 Add private properties to convert the values of the NumericUpDown controls into Vector instances.

```
private Vector VectorA {
    get {
        return new Vector((int)this.XVectorA.Value,
            (int)this.YVectorA.Value);
    }
}

private Vector VectorB {
    get {
        return new Vector((int)this.XVectorB.Value,
            (int)this.YVectorB.Value);
    }
}
```

3   Add the following functions to add and subtract the vectors or test for equality. In these methods, you're using the overloaded +, –, and == operators.

```
private void AddVectors(Vector a, Vector b) {
    DrawVector(a, Color.Red);
    DrawVector(b, a, Color.Blue);
    Vector sum = a + b;
    DrawVector(sum, Color.Green);
    this.result.Text = sum.ToString();
}

private void SubtractVectors(Vector a, Vector b) {
    DrawVector(a, Color.Red);
    DrawVector(-b, a, Color.Blue);
    Vector difference = a - b;
    DrawVector(difference, Color.Green);
    this.result.Text = difference.ToString();
}

private void AreEqual(Vector a, Vector b) {
    bool equal = (a == b);
    this.result.Text = equal.ToString();
}
```

4   Create the event handler for the form's Load event and add this code to add delegates to *m_maths* and items to the function's ListBox control. A delegate is a type, and as such, you can create an instance of it. You can then add that instance to any collection, such as the SortedList instance used here. In the next section, you'll use the instances to call the *AddVectors* and *SubtractVectors* methods. (Create the Load event handler by double-clicking the form in the form designer.)

```
private void Form1_Load(object sender, System.EventArgs e) {
    m_maths.Add("Add", new VectorMath(AddVectors));
    m_maths.Add("Subtract", new VectorMath(SubtractVectors));
    m_maths.Add("Are equal", new VectorMath(AreEqual));
    functions.DataSource = m_maths.Keys;
}
```

Add the user interface event methods

The vectors on the graph will change as the user changes the values in the NumericUpDown controls and the ListBox control. Each of these controls uses the same *System.EventHandler* delegate for the value-changing event. That means that the event handler signatures for *NumericUpDown.ValueChanged* and *ListBox.SelectedIndexChanged* are the same. You can take advantage of this similarity to assign one method as the event handler for all the change events.

1 Add the following method to the form class to respond to changes in the form controls.

```
private void VectorChanged(object sender, System.EventArgs e) {
    this.Refresh();
    VectorMath theMath = (VectorMath)m_maths[functions.Text];
    theMath(this.VectorA, (int)scalar.Value * this.VectorB);
}
```

The strings "Add", "Subtract", and "Are equal" were used as keys for the VectorMath delegate instances you added to the *m_maths* SortedList instance. When the delegates are retrieved from the SortedList, they are returned as *System.Object* types and must be cast to the VectorMath type. Once the delegates are cast, you can call the method with the Vector values. Using delegates allows you to call the appropriate method without having to create a switch statement and test on the string "Add", "Subtract", or "Are equal". This means that you could add other calculations easily.

2 Open the form in the form designer and click the Event toolbar button in the Properties window.

3 Select the *XVectorA* control.

4 Click the Event toolbar button in the Properties window. (It has a lightning bolt on it.) The Properties window now displays the events of the XVectorA control.

5 Locate and click the ValueChanged event in the list.

6 If you click the ValueChanged drop-down arrow, a list of all the methods defined in the class that have signatures that match the event will appear. In this case, the *VectorChanged* method is in the list. Click it.

7 Repeat steps 3 through 6 for the other NumericUpDown controls.

8 Select the *VectorChanged* method as the event handler for the SelectedIndexChanged event of the *functions* ListBox control.

Test the application

Use the NumericUpDown controls to test the operators. Here are some interesting tests:

- Add a vector to itself. You get a new vector twice the length in the same direction.
- Subtract a vector from itself. The result is the (0, 0) vector.
- Compare A − B to A + (−1 * B). The results are the same.

Quick Reference

To	Do this
Overload a unary operator	Create a static method to indicate the parameter and the return type. ```\npublic static Vector operator -(Vector vector) {\n return new Vector(-vector.X, -vector.Y);\n}\n```
Overload a binary operator	Create a static method to indicate the parameter and the return type. ```\npublic static bool operator ==(Vector aVector,\n Vector bVector) {\n return (aVector.X == bVector.X) &&\n (aVector.Y == bVector.Y);\n}\n```

Assign one method to events of multiple controls	Create a method in the class with the correct signature.
	```\nprivate void ButtonClick(object sender, System.EventArgs e)\n{\n}\n```
	Use the designer to assign the method to the control's event, or, use the += statement to assign the event to multiple controls.
	```\nbutton1.Click += new System.EventHandler(ButtonClick);\nbutton2.Click += new System.EventHandler(ButtonClick);\n```

Call a method by storing and retrieving a delegate	Create the delegate. ```\nprivate delegate void VectorMath(Vector a, Vector b);\n```
Create the method to match the delegate	```\nprivate void AreEqual(Vector a, Vector b) {\n bool equal = (a == b);\n this.result.Text = equal.ToString();\n}\n```
Add the delegate to a data structure	```\nm_maths.Add("Are equal", new VectorMath(AreEqual));\n```
Retrieve, cast, and call the delegate	```\nVectorMath theMath = (VectorMath)m_maths["Are equal"];\ntheMath(this.VectorA, (int)scalar.Value * this.VectorB);\n```

13

Saving Instance Data

In this chapter, you'll learn how to

✔ *Store and retrieve instance data by using XML serialization.*

✔ *Store and retrieve instance data by using binary serialization.*

✔ *Use a typed DataSet to retrieve data from a database.*

ESTIMATED
TIME
3 hr. 30 min.

Almost too conveniently, the class instances you've created so far have been instantiated either in code or through some user input. In this chapter, you'll take a look at some of the classes provided by the .NET Framework for storing instance data. This will be a brief overview, because a single chapter can't even begin to explain the options available. Instead, this chapter will provide a short introduction to two common mechanisms—serialization and the ADO.NET DataSet class. We'll look at these mechanisms and the object-oriented concepts that they support and demonstrate.

Serialization

Serialization is the process of laying down the instance data one field after the other, often—but not always—in a file. If you're serializing several instances, the data for each instance is laid down in order. For example, if you're serializing the X and Y properties of two Point instances, A and B, the serialized file contains the values of *A.X*, *A.Y*, *B.X*, and *B.Y*, in that order.

Deserialization is the process of reading that data back into a class instance. The actual bytes written and read are defined by an industry standard, by an application standard, or by you. Two well-known industry standards are bitmap files and Extensible Markup Language (XML) files. The sequence of bytes in a

Microsoft Word file is an example of an application standard. You might define your own serialization format, perhaps by listing two numbers in a line of a text file to represent one (x, y) point.

You use serialization for more than just saving instance data from one running of an application to the next. You'll also use serialization when you need to move data from one application to another. For example, you use serialization to move data from an application to the Clipboard.

The .NET Framework provides several classes for serialization tasks. In the first exercise in this chapter, you'll use the BinaryFormatter and the XMLSerializer classes. Each class has its advantages and limitations, as the test application will demonstrate.

The user interface of the application you'll create is shown in the following graphic:

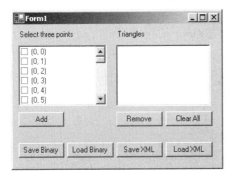

The user creates a list of triangles by defining each vertex of the triangle as a point (x, y). The user can then save the list of triangles in binary form or in XML form. Once the list is saved, the user can retrieve the data at a later time to restore the list of triangles. The design includes three classes: XYPoint, Triangle, and TriangleCollection. The Triangle class contains three XYPoint instances, and the TriangleCollection contains zero or more Triangle instances. The nesting of these classes lets you examine how serialization works and investigate the rules and conventions that apply to implementing serialization with the .NET Framework.

Implementing Binary Serialization

Binary serialization preserves the state of a class instance as a stream of bytes. This stream of bytes can be saved to a file, stored in memory, or moved across a network. By default, the byte stream contains the entire state of the object, including all the public and private fields of the instance. You can control which data is saved and restored by implementing the ISerializable interface. You might want to do this if there is information in the class that you don't want to make publicly available. The serialized data isn't readable as plain text, but it's not encrypted, either.

Create the data classes

The data model of this application includes the three classes: XYPoint, Triangle, and TriangleCollection. The user interface contains methods to create, delete, save, and load the instances created.

1 Create a new Windows application. Name it Serialize.

2 Add a new class named XYPoint to the project.

3 Add the integer X and Y properties to the class:

```vb
' Visual Basic
Private m_x As Integer
Private m_y As Integer
Public Property X() As Integer
    Get
        Return m_x
    End Get
    Set(ByVal Value As Integer)
        m_x = value
    End Set
End Property

Public Property Y() As Integer
    Get
        Return m_y
    End Get
    Set(ByVal Value As Integer)
        m_y = value
    End Set
End Property
```

```csharp
// Visual C#
private int m_x, m_y;
public int Y {
    get { return m_y; }
    set { m_y = value; }
}

public int X {
    get { return m_x; }
    set { m_x = value; }
}
```

4   Add constructors and override the *ToString* method. The *ToString* method is used to display the XYPoint instances at run time.

```vbnet
' Visual Basic
Public Sub New()
End Sub

Public Sub New(ByVal x As Integer, ByVal y As Integer)
    m_x = x
    m_y = y
End Sub

Public Overrides Function ToString() As String
    Return String.Format("({0}, {1})", Me.X, Me.Y)
End Function
```

```csharp
// Visual C#
public XYPoint() {
}

public XYPoint(int x, int y) {
    m_x = x;
    m_y = y;
}

public override string ToString(){
    return string.Format("({0}, {1})", this.X, this.Y);
}
```

5   Add a class named Triangle to the project.

6   Add the Points property for the three vertices of the triangle:

```vbnet
' Visual Basic
Private m_points() As XYPoint = _
    {New XYPoint(), New XYPoint(), New XYPoint()}

Public Property Points() As XYPoint()
    Get
        Return m_points
    End Get
    Set(ByVal Value As XYPoint())
        If (Value.Length = 3) Then
            m_points = Value
        End If
    End Set
End Property
```

```csharp
// Visual C#
private XYPoint[] m_points = new XYPoint[3];
public XYPoint[] Points {
```

```
    get {
        return m_points;
    }
    set {
        if (value.Length == 3) {
            m_points = value;
        }
    }
}
```

7 Add a constructor and override the *ToString* method:

```
' Visual Basic
Public Sub New(ByVal a As XYPoint, ByVal b As XYPoint, ByVal c As XYPoint)
    m_points = New XYPoint() {a, b, c}
End Sub

Public Overrides Function ToString() As String
    Dim triangleString As String
    Dim point As Integer
    For point = 0 To m_points.Length - 1
        triangleString += m_points(point).ToString() + " "
    Next
    Return triangleString
End Function

// Visual C#
public Triangle(XYPoint a, XYPoint b, XYPoint c) {
    m_points = new XYPoint[] { a, b, c };
}
public override string ToString() {
    string triangle = "";
    for (int point = 0; point < m_points.Length; point++) {
        triangle += m_points[point].ToString() + " ";
    }
    return triangle;
}
```

8 Add a class named TriangleCollection to the project. This class will be a strongly typed collection based on the CollectionBase class.

9 Modify the class declaration to indicate the base class:

```
' Visual Basic
public class TriangleCollection
    Inherits System.Collections.CollectionBase
end class
```

(continued)

13

Saving Instance Data

```
// Visual C#
public class TriangleCollection : System.Collections.CollectionBase {
}
```

10   Add the *Add* and *Remove* methods:

```
' Visual Basic
Public Sub Add(ByVal tri As Triangle)
    Me.InnerList.Add(tri)
End Sub

Public Sub Remove(ByVal tri As Triangle)
    Me.InnerList.Remove(tri)
End Sub

// Visual C#
public void Add(Triangle tri) {
    this.InnerList.Add(tri);
}

public void Remove(Triangle tri) {
    this.InnerList.Remove(tri);
}
```

11   Override the *ToString* method, and then add a *ToArray* method to facilitate displaying the triangles in a ListBox control:

```
' Visual Basic
Public Overrides Function ToString() As String
    Dim triangles As String
    Dim tri As Triangle
    For Each tri In Me.InnerList
        triangles += tri.ToString() & ControlChars.CrLf
    Next
    Return triangles
End Function

Public Function ToArray() As Object()
    Dim triangles(Me.Count - 1) As Object
    Dim tri As Integer
    For tri = 0 To Me.Count - 1
        triangles(tri) = innerlist(tri)
    Next
    Return triangles
End Function

// Visual C#
public override string ToString() {
```

```
        string triangles = "";
        foreach(Triangle tri in this.InnerList) {
            triangles += tri.ToString() + "\n";
        }
        return triangles;
    }

    public object[] ToArray() {
        object[] triangles = new object[this.Count];
        this.InnerList.CopyTo(triangles, 0);
        return triangles;
    }
```

Next you'll add a user interface to create, save, and load the instance data.

Create the user interface

1   Open Form1 in the form designer and add the controls listed in the following table, setting the properties as shown. Size and arrange the controls as shown in the illustration on page 332.

Control	Property	Value
CheckedListBox	Name	*selectedPoints*
Label	Text	*Select three points*
ListBox	Name	*triangleList*
Label	Text	*Triangles*
Button	Name	*addTriangle*
	Text	*Add*
Button	Name	*removeTriangle*
	Text	*Remove*
Button	Name	*clearAll*
	Text	*Clear All*
Button	Name	*saveBinary*
	Text	*Save Binary*
Button	Name	*loadBinary*
	Text	*Load Binary*
Button	Name	*saveXML*
	Text	*Save XML*
Button	Name	*loadXML*
	Text	*Load XML*

2   Double-click the form to create the Load event handler. Add the following
code to fill the CheckedListBox control with points:

```
' Visual Basic
Private Sub Form1_Load(ByVal sender As System.Object, _
ByVal e As System.EventArgs) Handles MyBase.Load
    Dim x As Integer
    Dim y As Integer
    For x = 0 To 6
        For y = 0 To 6
            Me.selectedPoints.Items.Add(New XYPoint(x, y))
        Next
    Next
End Sub
```

```
// Visual C#
private void Form1_Load(object sender, System.EventArgs e) {
    for (int x = 0; x < 6; x++) {
        for (int y = 0; y < 6; y++) {
            this.selectedPoints.Items.Add(new XYPoint(x, y));
        }
    }
}
```

3   Create the Click event handler for the Add button by double-clicking the
button in the form. Add a field for the TriangleCollection to the Form1 class
and add code to the event handler to add a new Triangle instance to the
m_triangles TriangleCollection object. The CheckedItemCollection property
of CheckedListBox is a collection of all the items that have been checked.
These objects are returned as *System.Object* instances, so you must cast
them back to XYPoint to instantiate a new Triangle object with them.

```
' Visual Basic
Private m_triangles As New TriangleCollection()
Private Sub addTriangle_Click(ByVal sender As System.Object, _
ByVal e As System.EventArgs) Handles addTriangle.Click
    Dim checkedPoints As CheckedListBox.CheckedItemCollection = _
        Me.selectedPoints.CheckedItems
    If checkedPoints.Count = 3 Then
        m_triangles.Add(New Triangle( _
            CType(checkedPoints(0), XYPoint), _
            CType(checkedPoints(1), XYPoint), _
            CType(checkedPoints(2), XYPoint)))
        triangleList.Items.Clear()
        triangleList.Items.AddRange(m_triangles.ToArray())
        Dim item As Integer
        For Each item In selectedPoints.CheckedIndices
            selectedPoints.SetItemChecked(item, False)
        Next
```

```
        Else
            MessageBox.Show("You must select exactly three points.")
        End If
End Sub
```

```
// Visual C#
private TriangleCollection m_triangles = new TriangleCollection();
private void addTriangle_Click(object sender, System.EventArgs e) {
    CheckedListBox.CheckedItemCollection checkedPoints =
        this.selectedPoints.CheckedItems;
    if (checkedPoints.Count == 3) {
        m_triangles.Add(new Triangle((XYPoint)checkedPoints[0],
            (XYPoint)checkedPoints[1], (XYPoint)checkedPoints[2]));
        this.triangleList.Items.Clear();
        this.triangleList.Items.AddRange(m_triangles.ToArray());
        foreach (int item in selectedPoints.CheckedIndices) {
            selectedPoints.SetItemChecked(item, false);
        }
    }
    else {
        MessageBox.Show("You must select exactly three points.");
    }
}
```

4   Create the Click event handler for the Remove button. Add the following
code to remove the selected triangle from *m_triangles*. As with the
CheckedItemCollection property of the CheckedListBox, the SelectedItem
property of the ListBox returns a *System.Object* reference. You need to cast
this to a Triangle before you can call the *Remove* method of the
TriangleCollection instance, *m_triangles*.

```
' Visual Basic
Private Sub removeTriangle_Click(ByVal sender As System.Object, _
ByVal e As System.EventArgs) Handles removeTriangle.Click
    If triangleList.SelectedIndex <> -1 Then
        m_triangles.Remove(CType(triangleList.SelectedItem, Triangle))
        triangleList.Items.Clear()
        triangleList.Items.AddRange(m_triangles.ToArray())
    End If
End Sub
```

```
// Visual C#
private void removeTriangle_Click(object sender, System.EventArgs e) {
    if (triangleList.SelectedIndex != -1) {
        m_triangles.Remove((Triangle)triangleList.SelectedItem);
        triangleList.Items.Clear();
        triangleList.Items.AddRange(m_triangles.ToArray());
    }
}
```

5   Create the Click event handler for the Clear All button. Add the following
code to remove all the Triangle instances from *m_triangles*.

```
' Visual Basic
Private Sub clearAll_Click(ByVal sender As System.Object, _
ByVal e As System.EventArgs) Handles clearAll.Click
    m_triangles.Clear()
    triangleList.Items.Clear()
End Sub
```

```
// Visual C#
private void clearAll_Click(object sender, System.EventArgs e) {
    m_triangles.Clear();
    triangleList.Items.Clear();
}
```

With all the classes defined and methods for creating and deleting instances
of them, you can now define the serialization and deserialization methods.
This will require additions to both the user interface and to the classes
themselves.

Define the serialization

In this exercise, you'll serialize the TriangleCollection instance, *m_triangles*, which
in turn contains Triangle instances, which in turn contain XYPoint instances. This
dependence of classes is known as the object graph of a class. The .NET runtime
is able to traverse the object graph during serialization and serialize all the contained instances. Your job is to ensure that all the classes are defined correctly to
support serialization.

To use binary serialization, you need to add the Serializable attribute to each
class you want to serialize. Additionally, if you want to define which fields are
serialized and how they are serialized, you can implement the ISerializable interface. The object graph of TriangleCollection contains the Triangle and XYPoint
classes. Triangle and TriangleCollection will use the default serialization provided by adding the Serializable attribute. The XYPoint class will define its own
serialization by implementing the .NET Framework ISerializable interface and
adding the Serializable attribute.

1   Add the Serializable attribute and the ISerializable interface to the XYPoint
class declaration:

```
' Visual Basic
<Serializable()> Public Class XYPoint
    Implements System.Runtime.Serialization.ISerializable
    ⋮
End Class
```

```csharp
// Visual C#
[Serializable()]
public class XYPoint : System.Runtime.Serialization.ISerializable {
    ⋮
}
```

2 Add code to define the *GetObjectData* method, the ISerializable interface's only member. This first parameter, *info*, of type SerializationInfo, is a collection of name/value pairs that is passed to the serialization process. Only the information you add to the SerializationInfo instance is serialized. In this way, you can control what is serialized, and in what form it's serialized. In this case, you will add the values of *m_x* and *m_y* to the collection:

```vbnet
' Visual Basic
Public Sub GetObjectData(ByVal info As _
System.Runtime.Serialization.SerializationInfo, _
ByVal context As System.Runtime.Serialization.StreamingContext) _
Implements System.Runtime.Serialization.ISerializable.GetObjectData
    info.AddValue("X", m_x)
    info.AddValue("Y", m_y)
End Sub
```

```csharp
// Visual C#
public void GetObjectData(System.Runtime.Serialization.SerializationInfo
info, System.Runtime.Serialization.StreamingContext context) {
    info.AddValue("X", m_x);
    info.AddValue("Y", m_y);
}
```

3 Provide a constructor that takes the *SerializationInfo* and *StreamingContext* parameters. This method is required for serialization but isn't enforced by the interface definition, because interfaces can't define constructors. This constructor is called when the object is deserialized and is necessary when you're implementing the ISerializable interface. The constructor needs to read the data back in exactly as that data was written out.

```vbnet
' Visual Basic
Public Sub New(ByVal info As _
System.Runtime.Serialization.SerializationInfo, _
ByVal context As System.Runtime.Serialization.StreamingContext)
    m_x = info.GetInt32("X")
    m_y = info.GetInt32("Y")
End Sub
```

```csharp
// Visual C#
public XYPoint(System.Runtime.Serialization.SerializationInfo info,
System.Runtime.Serialization.StreamingContext context) {
    m_x = info.GetInt32("X");
    m_y = info.GetInt32("Y");
}
```

4   Add the Serialization attribute to the Triangle and TriangleCollection classes. No other changes are needed if you want to use the default serialization.

```
' Visual Basic
<Serializable()> Public Class Triangle
    ⋮
End Class

<Serializable()> Public Class TriangleCollection
    ⋮
End Class

// Visual C#
[Serializable()]
public class Triangle {
    ⋮
}
[Serializable()]
public class TriangleCollection : System.Collections.CollectionBase {
    ⋮
}
```

Serialize and deserialize the data

With the serialization defined for the classes, you have only to create BinaryFormatter and FileStream instances to serialize the *m_triangles* instance data to a file on disk.

1   Add an *Imports* or *using* statement to the Form1 source file. This will let you use the unqualified name of the BinaryFormatter class.

```
' Visual Basic
Imports System.Runtime.Serialization.Formatters.Binary

// Visual C#
using System.Runtime.Serialization.Formatters.Binary;
```

2   Create a field in the Form1 class to hold the name of the file. The data file will reside in the bin or bin\debug folder of the project folder.

```
' Visual Basic
Private m_binaryFile as string = _
    Application.StartupPath + "\triangles.dat"

// Visual C#
private string m_binaryFile = Application.StartupPath + "\\triangles.dat";
```

3   Create the Click event handler for the Save Binary Button and add code to to serialize the *m_triangles* field. The steps in serialization are simple: just create a stream (in this case a file stream) and a BinaryFormatter object. The *Serialize* method takes as parameters the serialization stream and the object you're going to serialize.

```vb
' Visual Basic
Private Sub saveBinary_Click(ByVal sender As System.Object, _
ByVal e As System.EventArgs) Handles saveBinary.Click
    Dim stream As _
        New System.IO.FileStream(m_binaryFile, System.IO.FileMode.Create)
    Dim binary As New BinaryFormatter()
    binary.Serialize(stream, m_triangles)
    stream.close()
End Sub
```

```csharp
// Visual C#
private void saveBinary_Click(object sender, System.EventArgs e) {
    System.IO.Stream stream = new System.IO.FileStream(m_binaryFile,
        System.IO.FileMode.Create);
    BinaryFormatter binary = new BinaryFormatter();
    binary.Serialize(stream, m_triangles);
    stream.Close();
}
```

4 Create the Click event handler for the Load Binary Button and add code to deserialize the *m_triangles* field. After loading the data, fill the *triangleList* ListBox control with the new data.

```vb
' Visual Basic
Private Sub loadBinary_Click(ByVal sender As System.Object, _
ByVal e As System.EventArgs) Handles loadBinary.Click
    Dim stream As New System.IO.FileStream(m_binaryFile, _
        System.IO.FileMode.Open)
    Dim binary As New BinaryFormatter()
    m_triangles = CType(binary.Deserialize(stream), TriangleCollection)
    stream.Close()
    triangleList.Items.Clear()
    triangleList.Items.AddRange(m_triangles.ToArray())
End Sub
```

```csharp
// Visual C#
private void loadBinary_Click(object sender, System.EventArgs e) {
    System.IO.Stream stream = new System.IO.FileStream(m_binaryFile,
        System.IO.FileMode.Open);
    BinaryFormatter binary = new BinaryFormatter();
    m_triangles = (TriangleCollection) binary.Deserialize(stream);
    stream.Close();
    triangleList.Items.Clear();
    triangleList.Items.AddRange(m_triangles.ToArray());
}
```

You used the BinaryFormatter class to both serialize, in step 3, and now deserialize the *m_triangles* field. The *Deserialize* method takes a stream instance and returns a *System.Object* instance. You cast that object back to the type you serialized to the stream.

Run and test the application

You can now run and test the application. Note that you'll need to add and save some data before you attempt to load the data because the data file won't exist until you create it. Try the following steps:

1   Start the application. The Triangles list box is empty.

2   Select three points and click the Add button. You have one Triangle instance in the ListBox.

3   Add another Triangle instance.

4   Click the Save Binary button. You've saved two Triangle instances to the file.

5   Click the Clear All button. This deletes all the Triangle instances in memory.

6   Click the Load Binary button. The two instances you saved appear in the list box.

A portion of the binary data file is shown in Notepad in the following graphic. Little is readable here; the stream is designed to be compact.

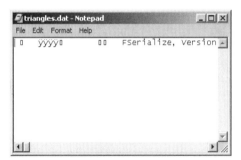

If you scroll through the file, you'll find mention of the three classes and the x and y values. In the next section, you'll see another serialization with readable output.

Implementing XML Serialization

XML is a text markup language similar to HTML, except that XML allows the developer to define the tags. While HTML contains a predefined set of tags, such as Title and Style, developers can create whatever tags they need to define their data, such as XYPoint, Triangle, and TriangleCollection. XML serialization differs from binary serialization in several ways:

■   Only the public fields and properties are serialized. If the instance data can't be reached from public fields or properties, it won't be initialized when the object is deserialized.

■   XML serialization requires a public constructor with no parameters. The instance is recreated by constructing the instance and setting the public data fields and properties. There are special conventions for implementing collection classes such as the TriangleCollection so that the data can be serialized and deserialized.

■ The output of the serialization is readable, plain text.

Serialize and deserialize the data

To support XML serialization, you'll add the public members needed to instantiate an instance, and set its properties.

1   Add parameterless constructors to the Triangle, and TriangleCollection Visual Basic classes. The XYPoint class already has one. The Visual C# classes already have parameterless constructors.

```
' Visual Basic
' Add to the Triangle and TriangleCollection classes
Public Sub New()
End Sub
```

2   To serialize a class that implements ICollection, as the TriangleCollection class does through its base class CollectionBase, you must implement the following members:

■ An *Add* method that takes one parameter. That parameter must be the same type as the object returned by the Current property of the *GetEnumerator* method. An acceptable *Add* method was created when you defined the TriangleCollection class.

■ A Count property that returns an integer. The base class, CollectionBase, provides the Count property.

■ An indexed *Item* method in Visual Basic or an indexer in Visual C#. The return value of this method must have the same type as the parameter of the *Add* method.

Taken together, these members allow the serialization process to access all the collection objects through the *Item* method or the indexer and to deserialize the object through the *Add* method.

Add the Item property or indexer to the TriangleCollection class as shown here:

```
' Visual Basic
Default Public Property Item(ByVal index As Integer) As Triangle
    Get
        Return CType(Me.InnerList.Item(index), Triangle)
    End Get
    Set(ByVal Value As Triangle)
        Me.InnerList.Item(index) = Value
    End Set
End Property
```

(continued)

```csharp
// Visual C#
public Triangle this[int index] {
    get {
        return (Triangle)(this.List[index]);
    }
    set {
        this.List[index] = value;
    }
}
```

That completes the changes you need to make to the classes.

3   In the Form1 class source file, add an *Imports* or *using* statement for the *XML.Serialization* namespace:

```vb
' Visual Basic
Imports System.Xml.Serialization
```

```csharp
// Visual C#
using System.Xml.Serialization;
```

4   In the Form1 class, define the string for the XML filename.

```vb
' Visual Basic
Private m_xmlFile As String = Application.StartupPath & "\triangles.xml"
```

```csharp
// Visual C#
private string m_xmlFile = Application.StartupPath + "\\triangles.xml";
```

5   Create the Click event handler for the Save XML Button and add code to serialize *m_triangles*. The methods for XML serialization and deserialization are similar to the binary methods. The XMLSerializer needs to know the type of instance being serialized.

```vb
' Visual Basic
Private Sub saveXML_Click(ByVal sender As System.Object, _
ByVal e As System.EventArgs) Handles saveXML.Click
    Dim writer As New System.IO.StreamWriter(m_xmlFile)
    Dim xmlSerial As New XmlSerializer(m_triangles.GetType())
    xmlSerial.Serialize(writer, m_triangles)
    writer.Close()
End Sub
```

```csharp
// Visual C#
private void saveXML_Click(object sender, System.EventArgs e) {
    System.IO.TextWriter writer = new System.IO.StreamWriter(m_xmlFile);
    XmlSerializer xmlSerial =
        new XmlSerializer(typeof(TriangleCollection));
    xmlSerial.Serialize(writer, m_triangles);
    writer.Close();
}
```

6   Create the Click event handler for the Load XML Button and add code to deserialize *m_triangles*.

```
' Visual Basic
Private Sub loadXML_Click(ByVal sender As System.Object, _
ByVal e As System.EventArgs) Handles loadXML.Click
    Dim reader As New System.IO.StreamReader(m_xmlfile)
    Dim xmlSerial As New XmlSerializer(System.Type.GetType( _
        "Serialize.TriangleCollection"))
    m_triangles = CType(xmlserial.Deserialize(reader), TriangleCollection)
    reader.close()
    triangleList.Items.Clear()
    triangleList.Items.AddRange(m_triangles.ToArray())
End Sub
```

```
// Visual C#
private void loadXML_Click(object sender, System.EventArgs e) {
    System.IO.TextReader reader = new System.IO.StreamReader(m_xmlFile);
    XmlSerializer xmlSerial =
        new XmlSerializer(typeof(TriangleCollection));
    m_triangles = (TriangleCollection) xmlSerial.Deserialize(reader);
    reader.Close();
    triangleList.Items.Clear();
    triangleList.Items.AddRange(m_triangles.ToArray());
}
```

7   Run and test the program.

Load and save the data

Now you can load and save the data in the XML format as well as the binary format. Try these steps:

1   Start the application.

2   Click the Load Binary button to load the data you saved the last time you ran the application.

3   Click the Save XML button. Now the binary file and the XML file contain the same data.

4   Click the Clear All button.

5   Click the Load XML button. You see the same data you retrieved from the binary file in the first step.

A portion of the XML data file is shown in Notepad in the graphic at the top of the next page. XML uses opening and closing tags to define data elements. Even if you have no knowledge of XML, it's fairly obvious what's being stored in this file.

DataSets

ADO.NET is the .NET Framework's model for data access. Data is stored in DataSet objects that are disconnected from the database. Other data access objects in the model move the data between the database and the datasets. XML support is built into the model, as DataSet objects can easily be serialized into and deserialized from XML. No doubt bookstores will soon have shelves of thick books about ADO.NET. In this section, you'll see a small selection of the many options available in ADO.NET. For more comprehensive coverage, try *Microsoft ADO.NET Step by Step* (Microsoft Press, 2002).

In this second exercise, you'll fill a DataGrid control with data stored in a DataSet instance. In the first portion of the exercise, you'll define the structure of the DataSet at run time, creating what's known as an untyped DataSet. In the second portion, you'll let the Microsoft Visual Studio development environment create the DataSet structure at design time, using what's known as a typed DataSet. The user interface is shown in the following graphic.

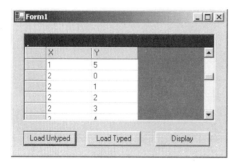

The objects you'll create in this application include the following:

- **DataSet**   The DataSet object is a container object that holds DataTable objects and information about the relationships between DataTable objects. DataSets can be either untyped or typed. The typed DataSet is created by inheriting from the DataSet class, which is untyped, and adding strongly typed access properties to the class.

- **DataTable**   The DataTable holds the data of interest, organized in rows and columns. Through *Item* methods and indexers, you can access the data in a table almost as though it were a two-dimensional matrix.

- **DataAdapter and DataConnection**   These two objects provide the process for moving data between a DataSet and a database or other data source.

Implementing an Untyped DataSet

In this first section of the application, you'll create and fill a DataSet in code at run time. Created this way, the DataSet is untyped.

Create the user interface

1   Create a new Windows application project. Name it DataSetExercise.

2   Add the controls in the following table to the form and set their properties as shown. Arrange the controls as shown in the previous graphic.

Control	Property	Value
DataGrid	Name	*xyPoints*
Button	Name	*loadUntyped*
	Text	*Load Untyped*
	Width	*88*
Button	Name	*loadTyped*
	Text	*Load Typed*
	Width	*88*
Button	Name	*display*
	Text	*Display*

Create the DataSet

1 Create the Load event handler for the form. Add the following code to create the DataSet:

```vbnet
' Visual Basic
Private m_pointsSet As New DataSet()
Private Sub Form1_Load(ByVal sender As System.Object, _
ByVal e As System.EventArgs) Handles MyBase.Load
    Dim pointsTable As New DataTable("XYPoints")
    m_pointsSet.Tables.Add(pointsTable)
    Dim xColumn As New DataColumn("X", System.Type.GetType("System.Int32"))
    Dim yColumn As New DataColumn("Y", System.Type.GetType("System.Int32"))
    pointsTable.Columns.Add(xColumn)
    pointsTable.Columns.Add(yColumn)
    Dim x As Integer
    Dim y As Integer
    For x = 0 To 5
        For y = 0 To 5
            Dim newRow As DataRow = pointsTable.NewRow()
            newRow("X") = x
            newRow("Y") = y
            pointsTable.Rows.Add(newRow)
        Next
    Next
End Sub
```

```csharp
// Visual C#
private DataSet m_pointsSet = new DataSet();
private void Form1_Load(object sender, System.EventArgs e) {
    DataTable pointsTable = new DataTable("XYPoints");
    m_pointsSet.Tables.Add(pointsTable);
    DataColumn xColumn = new DataColumn("X", typeof(int));
    DataColumn yColumn = new DataColumn("Y", typeof(int));
    pointsTable.Columns.Add(xColumn);
    pointsTable.Columns.Add(yColumn);
    for(int x = 0; x < 6; x++) {
        for (int y = 0; y < 6; y++) {
            DataRow newRow = pointsTable.NewRow();
            newRow["X"] = x;
            newRow["Y"] = y;
            pointsTable.Rows.Add(newRow);
        }
    }
}
```

You create the DataSet by using the following objects:

- **DataSet**   The DataSet contains the DataTable objects.

■ **DataTable**   You define the DataTable by adding DataColumn objects and Row objects. The DataColumn object defines the data contained in the table, and the Row object contains the data. In this example, the DataSet contains only one table, XYPoints.

■ **DataColumn**   You instantiate the DataColumn with a name and a data type. The name of the column is used later in the application to retrieve the data from a row. In this example, the DataTable includes two integer columns named X and Y. You can use the column name to find a particular piece of data in a DataRow.

■ **DataRow**   The DataRow object contains the data. With an untyped DataSet, you are on your own to make sure the data you add matches the types defined in the columns. In this example the data is added to the row by using the default *Item* method or indexer, using the column name as the index.

2   Create the Click event handler for the Load Untyped button and add the following code:

```
' Visual Basic
Private Sub loadUntyped_Click(ByVal sender As System.Object, _
ByVal e As System.EventArgs) Handles loadUntyped.Click
    xyPoints.DataSource = m_pointsSet
    xyPoints.DataMember = "XYPoints"
End Sub
```

```
// Visual C#
private void loadUntyped_Click(object sender, System.EventArgs e) {
    this.xyPoints.DataSource = m_pointsSet;
    this.xyPoints.DataMember = "XYPoints";
}
```

The DataSet object implements all the requirements to be used as a data source in the DataGrid. Because a DataSet can contain more than one DataTable, you also select the table to display in the grid by using the DataMember property.

3   Run the application and note the contents of the grid. The grid is editable, and changes you make to the data in the grid are persisted back to the DataSet.

Implementing a Typed DataSet

In this section of the exercise, you'll fill the grid with the data from a typed DataSet. Although you can create a typed DataSet by using the designer tools in Visual Studio, in this example you'll use some of the Visual Studio wizards to create a DataSet that matches a table in a Microsoft Access database.

Create the typed DataSet class

If your needs are simple, wizards can accomplish most of the work of filling a DataSet from a database. In this exercise, you need only to add two lines of code to the wizards' work to display a database table in a DataGrid.

1   Open Form1 in the form designer.

2   From the Data area of the Toolbox, drag the OleDbDataAdapter component onto the form. The Data Adapter Configuration Wizard appears.

3   Click Next, and then click the New Connection button. The Data Link Properties dialog appears.

4   On the Provider tab, click the Microsoft Jet provider. Click Next.

5   On the Connection Tab, browse to the database. The companion CD contains an Access database named SomeData.mdb in the \Chapter13 folder. Use admin as the user name and click OK. In the wizard, click Next.

6   Click Next to use SQL statements to define the dataset.

7   Type *select * from points* in the box. Click Next, and then click Finish. An OleDbConnection and OleDbDataAdapter are added to the component tray.

8   Click Generate Dataset on the Data menu. The Generate Dataset dialog box appears. Click OK to accept the defaults. A DataSet instance named dataSet11 is added to the component tray. A new file named DataSet1.xsd is added to the project.

Fill and display the DataSet

The data adapter component you created has data commands associated with it that can fill the DataSet with data from the database. Thus, filling the database is a method of the data adapter object, not a method of the DataSet object.

1   Double-click the Load Typed button to create the Click event handler. Add the following code to load the data from the database into the DataGrid control:

```
' Visual Basic
Private Sub loadTyped_Click(ByVal sender As System.Object, _
ByVal e As System.EventArgs) Handles loadTyped.Click
    OleDbDataAdapter1.Fill(DataSet11)
    xyPoints.DataSource = dataSet11.Points
End Sub

// Visual C#
private void loadTyped_Click(object sender, System.EventArgs e) {
    oleDbDataAdapter1.Fill(dataSet11);
    xyPoints.DataSource = dataSet11.Points;
}
```

2   Create the Click event for the Display button and add the following code to
    display the contents of the current row. Because the DataGrid can contain
    two different types of data, you will first use the DataMember property to
    determine which DataSet is displayed in the DataGrid. The data from the
    selected row is displayed in a message box.

```
' Visual Basic
Private Sub display_Click(ByVal sender As System.Object, _
ByVal e As System.EventArgs) Handles display.Click
    Dim row As Int16 = xyPoints.CurrentCell.RowNumber
    Dim point As String
    Dim x, y As Integer

    If (xyPoints.DataMember = "XYPoints") Then
        x = CType(m_pointsSet.Tables("XYPoints").Rows(row)("X"), _
            Integer)
        y = CType(m_pointsSet.Tables("XYPoints").Rows(row)("Y"), _
            Integer)
    Else
        x = DataSet11.Points(row).X
        y = DataSet11.Points(row).Y
    End If
    point = String.Format("({0}, {1})", x, y)
    MessageBox.Show(point)
End Sub
```

```
// Visual C#
private void display_Click(object sender, System.EventArgs e) {
    int row = this.xyPoints.CurrentCell.RowNumber;
    string point;
    int x, y;
    if (xyPoints.DataMember == "XYPoints") {
        x = (int) m_pointsSet.Tables["XYPoints"].Rows[row]["X"];
        y = (int) m_pointsSet.Tables["XYPoints"].Rows[row]["Y"];
    }
    else {
        x = dataSet11.Points[row].X;
        y = dataSet11.Points[row].Y;
    }
    point = string.Format("({0}, {1})", x, y);
    MessageBox.Show(point);
}
```

There are some interesting differences between the two DataSets. Although
you can easily access the data in the untyped DataSet, you need to use the
names of the columns and the table. You could also use the integer index of
the column, but that would be even more cryptic. In the typed DataSet, the
table and column names are properties of the DataSet class. Another difference is in the types returned from the DataRow. In the untyped DataSet, a

System.Object instance is returned from any column of the DataRow. To use the *System.Object* instance, you must cast it to the correct type. In the typed DataSet, the property is defined to be of the correct type. Clearly, the typed DataSet is designed to simplify your programming task and prevent type-casting errors.

3   Run the application.

You can now switch between the untyped DataSet created in code and the typed DataSet from the Access database. You haven't added the code necessary to propagate changes in the DataGrid back to the database. Any changes you make in the grid won't be stored between the times you run the application. Additionally, you are filling the DataSet from the database each time the Load Typed button is clicked, so any changes you make are lost if you click the Load Untyped button.

Examine the typed DataSet

When you generated the DataSet from the data adapter, a file named DataSet1.xsd was added to the project. This file, which defines the DataSet1 class, can be displayed in a designer to give you a graphical description of the DataSet.

1   In Solution Explorer, double-click the file DataSet.xsd. The graphical representation of the DataSet appears as shown in the following graphic. You can click the XML tab to view the XML used to generate the diagram.

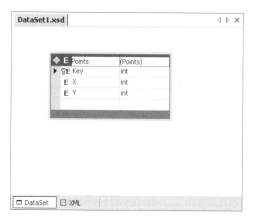

2   The XML definition is used to create a class that derives from the DataSet class. To view that class source file, click the Show All Files button in Solution Explorer. Expand the DataSet1.xsd node to find the DataSet1.vb or DataSet1.cs file. Double-click this file to display it in the code editor.

3   Locate the class declaration for the DataSet1 class. It derives from the DataSet class. Therefore, you could have used the typed DataSet just as you used the untyped DataSet.

```
' Visual Basic
Public Class DataSet1
    Inherits DataSet
    ⋮
End Class

// Visual C#
public class DataSet1 : System.Data.DataSet {
    ⋮
}
```

4   The Points property of DataSet1 is equivalent to *Tables["Points"]* in the
        untyped DataSet. The Points property is of type PointsDataTable, which is a
        class that inherits from DataTable. If you look in the source file, you'll find
        the pieces of code that wrap the table into a typed property.

```
' Visual Basic
Private tablePoints As PointsDataTable
Public ReadOnly Property Points As PointsDataTable
    Get
        Return Me.tablePoints
    End Get
End Property

Public Class PointsDataTable
    Inherits DataTable

    Friend Sub New()
        MyBase.New("Points")
        Me.InitClass
    End Sub
End Class

// Visual C#
private PointsDataTable tablePoints;
public PointsDataTable Points {
    get {
        return this.tablePoints;
    }
}

public class PointsDataTable : DataTable, System.Collections.IEnumerable {
    internal PointsDataTable() : base("Points") {
        this.InitClass();
    }
}
```

You'll find the same sort of wrapping of the untyped columns to create
typed columns, by using a typed row class. The following code demonstrates how the PointDataTable creates a column just as the untyped

DataSet does, but the PointsRow class does the casting to prevent the developer from entering the wrong type for the X column.

```vb
' Visual Basic
Public Class PointsRow
    Inherits DataRow

    Public Property X As Integer
        Get
            Try
                Return CType(Me(Me.tablePoints.XColumn),Integer)
            Catch e As InvalidCastException
                Throw New StrongTypingException( _
                    "Cannot get value because it is DBNull.", e)
            End Try
        End Get
        Set
            Me(Me.tablePoints.XColumn) = value
        End Set
    End Property
End Class
```

```csharp
// Visual C#
public class PointsRow : DataRow {
    public int X {
        get {
            try {
                return ((int)(this[this.tablePoints.XColumn]));
            }
            catch (InvalidCastException e) {
                throw new StrongTypingException(
                    "Cannot get value because it is DBNull.", e);
            }
        }
        set {
            this[this.tablePoints.XColumn] = value;
        }
    }
}
```

You can see similar constructs throughout the DataSet1 class source file. Creating a typed DataSet makes the compiler do some of the work of the developer by checking data types at compile time, to prevent exceptions being thrown at run time.

Quick Reference

To	Do this

Support binary serialization of a class	Add the Serializable attribute to the declaration of the class.
	```' Visual Basic```
	```<Serializable()> Public Class XYPoint```
	```end class```
	
	```// Visual C#```
	```[Serializable()]```
	```public class XYPoint {```
	```}```

Implement binary serialization	Create a BinaryFormatter instance and a Stream instance and call the *Serialize* and *Deserialize* methods.

Define custom binary serialization	Implement the ISerializable interface.
	```<Serializable()> Public Class XYPoint```
	``` Implements System.Runtime.Serialization.ISerializable```
	```End Class```
	
	```// Visual C#```
	```[Serializable()]```
	```public class XYPoint :```
	``` System.Runtime.Serialization.ISerializable {```
	```}```

Support XML serialization	Add the public properties and fields needed to recreate the class.
Implement XML serialization	Create a XMLSerializer instance and a Stream instance and call the *Serialize* and *Deserialize* methods.
Create a DataSet at runtime	Create a DataSet instance. Add DataColumn instances and DataRow instances.
Create a DataSet from a database	Use the OleDbDataConnection, OleDbDataAdapter, and OleDbDataCommand objects. Visual Studio provides several wizards for configuring these items.

14

Reducing Complexity by Design

ESTIMATED TIME
1 hr. 30 min.

In this chapter, you'll learn how to

✔ *Apply some of the .NET Design Guidelines.*
✔ *Perform a "Pull Up Field" refactoring.*
✔ *Recognize the Observer design pattern.*

Complexity

The chapters you've read so far have concentrated on the mechanics of object-oriented programming. You've learned about properties, methods, inheritance, interfaces, events, constructors, and exceptions. You've learned about the common uses of these elements, the general recommendations for using these constructs, and some conventions for developing with the .NET Framework. But your programs get larger and more complex, knowing the mechanics isn't enough. You need a good design to reduce the complexity of your task. You've seen how encapsulating the methods and data into a class can reduce the complexity visible to client code. Design doesn't stop at the class level, though. There are lots of object-oriented design methodologies in the literature. In this chapter you'll look at two methodologies: design patterns and refactoring. You'll also look at the .NET Design Guidelines, which can reduce the complexity of your designs by encouraging the use of consistency and predictability. Use this chapter as a jumping-off point for further studies in object-oriented design.

The .NET Design Guidelines

An easy way to reduce complexity in your application is by following the guidelines for .NET development. When you follow the guidelines, your code behaves in a predictable and familiar way, thereby reducing the amount of effort required by a developer, even yourself, to read and maintain the code. If you're creating a class library for others to use, following the guidelines becomes even more important, even though these developers don't have access to the code. Other developers depend on your library meeting the guidelines, and deviations from the guidelines can make your library frustrating to work with, if not altogether broken. You can find the .NET Framework Design Guidelines online by going to *http://msdn.microsoft.com* and searching for .NET Framework Design Guidelines.

The guidelines listed in the following sections are not exhaustive; you can find the complete guidelines online. The information listed here is particularly relevant to the classes created in this book.

Naming Objects

Consistent naming can go a long way in making your code more readable and therefore easier to maintain. Name choices provide clues about the scope of an object and the object's role in the application. The .NET Framework itself provides an excellent resource for examples of member names.

Pascal Casing and camel Casing

In .NET applications, you'll find two styles of capitalization: *Pascal Casing* and *camel Casing*. When you use Pascal Casing, you capitalize each word in an identifier (the name of something), just as both Pascal and Casing are capitalized. Examples include FirstName and LastName. Using camel Casing, you capitalize every word except the first word of the identifier. Examples include firstName and lastName. The capitalized letter in the middle of the identifier might remind you of a camel's hump.

Private fields, function parameters, and variables declared inside functions use camel Casing. Everything else uses Pascal Casing. An easy way to determine the casing is to remember that any identifier (class, property, method, interface name) visible outside the class has its first letter capitalized. Look closely at IntelliSense when you use the code editor. Almost without exception, everything uses Pascal Casing.

The following short class demonstrates the rules of casing. The field, parameter, and variable names—name, volume, time, and speed—are camel-Cased. The other identifiers—Dog, Name, Bark, and RunAway—are Pascal-Cased. (Note that the parameter, Value, passed to the Set of the Name property is Camel Cased in Visual Basic. The Set code is generated by Visual Studio. You can rename this parameter to follow the guideline.)

```vb
' Visual Basic
Public Class Dog
    Dim dogName As String

    Public Property Name() As String
        Get
            Return dogName
        End Get
        Set(ByVal Value As String)
            dogName = Value
        End Set
    End Property

    Public Sub Bark(ByVal volume As Integer)
        ' Add code to make dog bark here.
    End Sub

    Public Function RunAway(ByVal time As Integer) As Integer
        Dim speed As Integer = 25
        Return speed * time
    End Function
End Class
```

```csharp
// Visual C#
public class Dog {
    string dogName;

    public string Name {
        get { return dogName; }
        set { dogName = value; }
    }

    public void Bark(int volume) {
        // Add code to make dog bark here.
    }

    public int RunAway(int time) {
        int speed = 25;
        return speed * time;
    }
}
```

Case Insensitive Identifiers

Not all languages are case sensitive. Microsoft Visual Basic is a notable example. Visual Basic doesn't distinguish between *Dog.RunAway* and *Dog.runaway*, for example. Therefore, to ensure that your library is usable across different languages, your identifiers must be case insensitive. This rule applies to several objects, as shown in the following table. In the Correct Identifiers column, the two items don't depend on capitalization to distinguish them. In the Incorrect Identifiers column, the two items are indistinguishable in Visual Basic because they differ only by case.

Element	Correct Identifiers	Incorrect Identifiers
	The two items don't depend on capitalization to distinguish them.	The two items depend on capitalization to distinguish them.
Namespace	*RuffRuff.Kennel* *RuffRuff.Reservation*	*RuffRuff.Kennel* *RuffRuff.kennel*
Properties	*Dog.LastName* *Dog.FirstName*	*Dog.Name* *Dog.name*
Methods	*Dog.Bark* *Dog.Whisper*	*Dog.Bark* *Dog.bark*
Method parameters	Visual Basic *Sub Bark(ByVal sound As String, ByVal length As Integer)* Visual C# *void Bark(string sound, int length)*	Visual Basic (Note: This won't compile.) *Sub Bark(ByVal Sound As String, ByVal sound As Integer)* Visual C# *void Bark(string Sound, int sound)*
Types	*RuffRuff.Kennel.Run* *RuffRuff.Kennel.Suite*	*RuffRuff.Kennel.Run* *RuffRuff.Kennel.run*

No Hungarian Prefixes

Prefixes, known as Hungarian prefixes, that indicate field types have been standard in Windows programming environments for years. Visual Basic documentation even included lists of standard prefixes for controls: *btn* for the CommandButton control, *txt* for the TextBox, and so on. There were also systems for indicating whether a variable was a string, integer, Boolean, or double. The .NET Framework guidelines call for the elimination of these prefixes. In the Microsoft Visual Studio .NET environment, the type information about a field or variable is readily available by moving the mouse over the field name in the code editor. In addition, the type prefixes limit the developer's ability to change the type of the variable when necessary. Or worse yet, the developer changes the type of the variable, doesn't rename the variable, and creates misleading code.

Also eliminated are prefixes indicating the scope of fields. It's been common to see *m_* for member fields, *s_* for shared or static fields, and *g_* for global variables. You must be wondering why the *m_* prefix is used throughout this book. My experience with teaching object-oriented programming is that the concept of instance data versus method variables is one of the major shifts in thinking in the move from structural programming (method-based) to object-oriented programming (class-based). The *m_* prefix is useful in emphasizing this difference. Another deciding factor in using the *m_* prefix is that the fields in the examples have been nearly always private. Therefore, the *m_* prefix is not exposed in any of the public interfaces of the classes created.

Designing Class Members

The following guidelines apply to the behavior and implementation of the members of a class. The guidelines include conventions about naming and behavior, as well as performance tips.

Class Guidelines

- Use Pascal Casing because class names have public scope. Examples include Button, ListBox, and ArrayList.
- Use complete words, avoiding abbreviations. For example, ButtonGrid is longer but more readable than BtnGrd.
- Use nouns, in general. Classes generally represent objects, and objects usually have noun names.
- Do not use the prefix C or underscores. Though this usage is common in previous versions of Visual Basic and in other languages, it has been dropped in the .NET Framework. You won't find any .NET Framework classes with C prefixes.

Interface Guidelines

- Append the prefix I to the interface name.
- Interface names tend to be descriptive and adjective-based, because they are often used to add abilities to a class. Examples of adjective-based names include IComparable and IFormattable.

■ Consider providing a class that is a default implementation of an interface. Developers can use this default implementation through inheritance or composition. Name the class by dropping the I prefix. For example, the default implementation of IComponent is Component.

Method Guidelines

■ Use Pascal Casing.

■ Method names are typically verbs. Methods implement the behavior of an object. Methods *do* something. Examples include *Read*, *Write*, *Start*, and *Stop*.

■ When overloading methods, be consistent in the order and naming of parameters. The following example shows three overloads of *Dog.Bark*. The new parameters are added at the end of the parameter list so that the order of parameters is the same in all the methods.

```
' Visual Basic
Public Class Dog
    Public Sub Bark(ByVal volume As Integer)
        ' Add code to make dog bark here.
    End Sub

    Public Sub Bark(ByVal volume As Integer, ByVal howLong As Integer)
        ' Add code to make dog bark here.
    End Sub

    Public Sub Bark(ByVal volume As Integer, _
    ByVal howLong As Integer, ByVal addExtraHowl As Boolean)
        ' Add code to make dog bark here.
    End Sub
End Class

// Visual C#
public class Dog {
    public void Bark(int volume) {
        // Add code to make dog bark here.
    }

    public void Bark(int volume, int howLong) {
        // Add code to make dog bark here.
    }

    public void Bark(int volume, int howLong, bool addExtraHowl) {
        // Add code to make dog bark here.
    }
}
```

Property Guidelines

▦ Use Pascal Casing.

▦ Property names are typically nouns. Examples include Text, SelectedIndex, and Width.

▦ Avoid using a property name that is also a type name. If you're determined to use a property name that is a type name, the property should be of the type of the same name. In the following example, if you use the second declaration, the *System.Drawing.Color* class is hidden. Any reference to Color would return the *Color* property, which is an integer. If you're also determined to use a type name as a property name and use a different type for the property, you can still use the *System.Drawing.Color* class by using the fully qualified name.

```
' Visual Basic
Public Class BookCover
    Private coverColor As Color

    Public ReadOnly Property Color() As Color
        Get
            Return coverColor
        End Get
    End Property

    ' Not recommended. This declaration hides the
    ' System.Drawing.Color class.
    ' Private coverColor As Integer
    ' Public ReadOnly Property Color() As Integer
    '     Get
    '         Return coverColor
    '     End Get
    ' End Property
End Class

// Visual C#
public class BookCover {
    private Color coverColor;
    public Color Color {
        get { return coverColor; }
    }

    // Not recommended. This declaration hides the
    // System.Drawing.Color class.
    // private int coverColor;
    //     public int Color {
    //     get { return coverColor; }
    // }
}
```

14

Reducing Complexity

■ Preserve the value of a property if an attempt to set the property throws an exception. The class is responsible for maintaining a usable state and this leaves the instance in a consistent usable state.

■ Provide a PropertyChanged event if it would be useful for the client of your class. Examples in the .NET Framework include *Control.TextChanged* and *Control.VisibleChanged*.

■ Allow the client code to set the properties in any order. If *Dog.LastName* must be set before *Dog.FirstName*, create a method for changing the properties that has parameters for *LastName* and *FirstName*. Within the method, set *LastName* first. This way, the developer doesn't have to remember obscure property dependencies.

■ Performing the get should not have an observable side effect. If retrieving the value has a side effect, using a method is preferable.

■ Avoid using properties that return arrays. These properties are potentially inefficient, because of multiple accesses to the underlying field array and the likelihood that the array will be copied before returning it. Use a method to return the array instead of a property.

Event Guidelines

■ Use Pascal Casing.

■ Event names are typically verbs. Examples include Click, Load, and Paint.

■ Event delegates have two parameters, *sender* of type *System.Object* and *e* of *System.EventArgs* or a class derived from *System.EventArgs*. An example from the .NET Framework is the MouseEventHandler delegate, shown below.

```
' Visual Basic
Public Delegate Sub MouseEventHandler(ByVal sender As Object, _
    ByVal e As MouseEventArgs)

// Visual C#
public delegate void MouseEventHandler(object sender, MouseEventArgs e);
```

■ Events should be *Subs* in Visual Basic and *void* methods in C#.

■ Use past and present verb forms for events that carry the concept of time relative to the event. In contrast to previous versions, do not use the Before and After prefixes for event naming. Examples include *Form.Closed* and *Form.Closing*.

- The event delegate name ends in EventHandler. Examples include *MouseEventHandler* and *System.EventHandler*.

- The name of the class that derives from *System.EventArgs* ends in EventArgs. This is the type of the second parameter to the event handler method. Examples include *MouseEventArgs*, *DragEventArgs*, and *ScrollEventArgs*.

- Program defensively because control returns to the method that raised the event after the event handler is executed, and the client code might change the object in the event handler method. The following code highlights the location of code that would execute after the event handler call. Consider wrapping the event call in a *Try* or *try* structure.

```vb
' Visual Basic
Public Class DogBone
    Public Event Eaten As System.EventHandler
    Private weight As Integer

    Public Sub Eat(ByVal howMuch As Integer)
        weight -= howMuch
        If (weight <= 0) Then
            RaiseEvent Eaten(Me, New System.EventArgs())
            ' State of the instance could be changed in the event
            ' handler in the client code.
        End If
    End Sub
End Class
```

```csharp
// Visual C#
public class DogBone {
    public event System.EventHandler Eaten;
    private int weight;

    public void Eat(int howMuch) {
        weight -= howMuch;
        if (weight <= 0) {
            if (Eaten != null) {
                this.Eaten(this, new System.EventArgs());
                // State of the instance could be changed in the event
                // handler in the client code.
            }
        }
    }
}
```

Refactoring

Each chapter in this book has presented a problem statement, followed by a design and an implementation. That's neat and tidy, but not necessarily how things work during development and maintenance. Often when you implement something more than a trivial application, you'll look at it at the end and decide the code is messy. Perhaps you've had to add method parameters with obscure effects to handle special cases. Maybe your classes are loaded with state fields that keep track of things you didn't plan for when you designed the application. Or maybe your classes are carrying references to each other and you're losing track of the communication lines between classes. Even if you're content with the completed application, sooner or later you'll need to make modifications. After a few modifications, your design starts to break down. Finally, you decide that you can't make one more change without rewriting the code. That process of rewriting the code is called *refactoring*.

During the design phase of each exercise, you factor the classes out of the problem specification. You decide what the base classes were and which classes derive from them. You decide which methods to include in the base class and override in the derived classes, and which methods appear only in the derived classes.

When you refactor, you can change your mind regarding all these choices. You can add derived classes, move fields between base classes and derived classes, and implement other reorganizations. *Refactoring: Improving the Design of Existing Code* by Martin Fowler et al (Addison-Wesley, 1999) is a thorough catalog of the techniques you can employ in refactoring your code.

This section describes how you might apply the "Pull Up Field" refactoring to the Pattern Maker application from Chapter 10. Before applying the "Pull Up Field" refactoring, two derived classes contain the same field. The goal is to move the common field into the base class. As you recall from Chapter 10, the base class PatternEditor contains an event, Saved, shown here:

```
' Visual Basic
Public Event Saved(ByVal sender As Object, ByVal e As EventArgs)
```

```
// Visual C#
public virtual event SavedEventHandler Saved;
```

The Saved event was raised by a Save button added to both derived classes, DrawnPatternEditor and BitmapPatternEditor. Remember that user controls are classes, and the controls they contain are simply fields of the user control class. The Save Button fields in the base classes can be pulled up into the base class as the Save button. The two editor controls are shown here as they appear at design time. Each has a Save Button control.

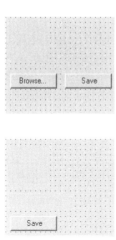

The controls work just fine, but it would be easier for the user if the Save button was placed in the same place in both controls? You can enforce that placement by moving the Button control into the base class. This simplifies development as well, because you don't have to create the Button control twice.

Implementing the "Pull Up Field" Refactoring

In this exercise, you'll move the Save button into the base class, PatternEditor.

Pull the Save button up into the PatternEditor class

1   Open the PatternMaker project from Chapter 10.

2   Double-click PatternEditor.vb or PatternEditor.cs in the Solution Explorer to open the control in the designer.

3   Set the Size property to 175, 150, to match the derived controls.

4   Drag a Button control onto the control. Set the Location to *88, 112*, the Text property to *Save*, and the Name property to *save*.

The new base control, PatternEditor, is shown here:

Now that the Save button is in the base class, you don't have a way to raise the Saved event even though you still need to have the derived class handle saving the pattern information back to the Pattern instance. Solve this problem by adding an overridable method, *SavePattern*, to the base class.

5   Double-click the Save button to create the Click event handler and call the *SavePattern* method. You'll define the *SavePattern* method in the next step.

```
' Visual Basic
Private Sub save_Click(ByVal sender As System.Object, _
ByVal e As System.EventArgs) Handles save.Click
    SavePattern()
    RaiseEvent Saved(Me, New System.EventArgs())
End Sub
```

```
// Visual C#
private void save_Click(object sender, System.EventArgs e) {
    SavePattern();
    if (Saved != null) {
        Saved(this, new System.EventArgs());
    }
}
```

6   Add the *SavePattern* method to the PatternEditor class.

```
' Visual Basic
Public Overridable Sub SavePattern()
End Sub
```

```
// Visual C#
public virtual void SavePattern() {
}
```

The *SavePattern* method is overridden in the derived classes to save the pattern data.

7   If you're using Visual Basic, delete the *RaiseSaved* event method in PatternEditor.vb. Don't delete the Saved event. You still need to raise the event to the user interface.

Now that the Saved button is in the base class, you no longer need it in the derived classes.

Move the Save button out of the BitmapPatternEditor class

To finish the refactoring, you need to delete the Save buttons and override the *SavePattern* method.

1   Right-click on BitmapPatternEditor.vb or BitmapPatternEditor.cs in the Solution Explorer and click View Code on the shortcut menu.

2 Add the *SavePattern* method to the BitmapPatternEditor class, and move the code from the *save_Click* method into the *SavePattern* method. If you're using Visual Basic, you no longer need to call the *RaiseSaved* method. If you're using Visual C#, you no longer need to raise the Saved event. The event is raised in the base class when the Save button is clicked.

```
' Visual Basic
Public Overrides Sub SavePattern()
    m_pattern.BitmapFile = m_bitmapFile
End Sub
```

```
// Visual C#
public override void SavePattern() {
    m_pattern.BitmapFile = m_bitmapFile;
}
```

3 Delete the *save_Click* method in the BitmapPatternEditor class.

4 If you're using Visual C#, delete the overridden Saved event.

```
// Visual C#
// Delete this override
public override event SavedEventHandler Saved;
```

5 Double-click BitmapPatternEditor.vb or BitmapPatternEditor.cs in the Solution Explorer to open the control in the designer.

6 Delete the Save button from the control.

7 Set the location of the Browse button to *8, 112*. When the application is compiled in the next section, the control appears as shown below with the inherited button marked with a special icon.

Move the Save button out of the DrawnPatternEditor class

The changes are similar to those you made for the BitmapPatternEditor class. The steps are outlined here.

1 Right-click DrawnPatternEditor.vb or DrawnPatternEditor.cs in the Solution Explorer and click View Code on the shortcut menu.

2   Add the *SavePattern* method to the DrawnPatternEditor class, and move the code from the *save_Click* method into the *SavePattern* method. If you're using Visual Basic, you no longer need to call the *RaiseSaved* method.

```
' Visual Basic
Public Overrides Sub SavePattern()
    m_pattern.Points = m_Points
End Sub
```

```
// Visual C#
public override void SavePattern() {
    m_pattern.Points = m_points;
}
```

3   Delete the *save_Click* method in the DrawnPatternEditor class.

4   Double-click DrawnPatternEditor.vb or DrawnPatternEditor.cs in the Solution Explorer to open the control in the designer.

5   Delete the Save button from the control. Click Build Solution on the Build menu. The inherited Save button appears on the control.

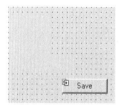

6   Press F5 to run the application. You can create new bitmap patterns and drawn patterns. The functionality is identical to the first version you created, but the Save button doesn't move around.

Refactoring a project might involve several changes such as the one you just saw. You'll want to take a controlled approach to refactoring, unless you're willing to take your application out of production and redo all your testing from scratch. With a more controlled approach, you can test your application, make a change, and then retest the application to ensure you haven't introduced bugs into the system.

Design Patterns

A design pattern describes a common problem found in an object-oriented system and provides a solution to that problem. The classic text *Design Patterns* (Addison-Wesley, 1995), by Erich Gamma, Richard Helm, Ralph Johnson, and John Vlissides, catalogs 23 of the most common and important patterns.

A complete design pattern description includes the following elements:

- **Pattern name**   Each pattern has a one- or two-word name that captures the abstraction of the pattern.

- **Problem**   This describes the problem to be solved and defines when the pattern is applicable.

- **Solution**   The solution describes the classes, their responsibilities, and the collaborations among them. The solution is described in an abstract way that can be applied in many contexts.

- **Consequences**   Every design is a balance of advantages and disadvantages. For example, a solution might be fast, but consume a large amount of memory. Or the design might be optimized for a particular set of data, but unable to handle changes to the data structure.

While pattern descriptions often give concrete examples of known uses in software, the problem statement is unlikely to be an exact description of the problem you're trying to solve. After reading and using some patterns, you'll become familiar with the patterns and you'll recognize how your problem falls into the same pattern.

Observer

The exercises in this book and the .NET Framework objects you've used have employed several patterns. By having some insight into the design, you'll better understand how to use the object and make predictions about how well the objects are going to work in your applications. In Chapter 11, you implemented the Singleton pattern. Now take a look at another pattern, the Observer.

- **Problem**   The Observer pattern is concerned with how objects in an application behave. If you were writing a kennel reservation system, you might have three forms in your application: one to take reservations, one to present a diagram showing empty and full kennels, and one to list the number of reservations each night. As reservations are made and canceled, the forms with kennels and reservation totals must change also. How do you keep the forms synchronized, making sure that the two other forms are notified each time there is a change in the reservations? Can you do this so that you can add more dependent forms without rewriting the reservation form?

- **Solution**   The solution is to identify the subject and the observers in the system. In this example, the reservation form is the subject. The other forms are considered *observers*; they watch for changes in the subject. The subject class maintains a list of the observers through two methods it provides, *Attach* and *Detach*. For its part, the observer class provides an *Update* method that is called by the subject whenever the subject changes. When the subject changes, the *Notify* method calls the *Update* method for each observer in its list of observers. The subject also provides a *GetState* method that allows the observer to extract the information needed from the subject. The design is shown in the following UML diagram:

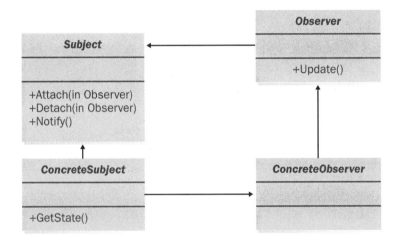

This pattern is also known as *publish-subscribe*. The subject publishes notifications when it changes. The observers subscribe to receive notifications.

Event-Handling and the Observer Pattern

The event-handling protocol of Visual Basic .NET and Visual C# displays the hallmarks of the Observer pattern. Consider the Button class as the subject. The Button publishes a Click event. Observers, usually forms, subscribe to the Click event of the Button. The *Attach* method is implemented as *AddHandler* in Visual Basic and += in C#. The *Detach* method is implemented as *RemoveHandler* in Visual Basic and −= in C#. The *Update* method is implemented as a method in the form class, something like *Button1_Click(object sender, System.EventArgs e)*. When the Click event is raised, each method assigned through *AddHandler* or += is called. Information about the Button is found in the sender argument of the event handler. Note that we don't actually know or care how event handling is implemented in the .NET Framework. Still, the Observer pattern provides an understanding of event handling that can make it easier to use and explain event-handling behavior.

Quick Reference

To	Do this
Name a public member of a class or interface	Use Pascal Casing. Example: *Client.LastName*
Name a private field of a class or a method parameter	Use camel Casing. Example:

```
' Visual Basic
Private coverColor As Color

Public Sub Bark(ByVal volume As Integer, _
    ByVal howLong As Integer)
    ⋮
End Sub

// Visual C#
private Color coverColor;

public void Bark(int volume, int howLong){
    ⋮
}
```

To	Do this
Apply the "Pull Up Field" refactoring	Move a field that exists in all the derived classes into the base class. Remove the field from the derived classes.

Additional Resources

The following sources provide more information about object-oriented development.

Books

- Booch, Grady, Ivar Jacobson, and James Rumbaugh. *The Unified Modeling Language User Guide*. Boston: Addison-Wesley. 1998.
  This book, by the original designers of the Unified Modeling Language, covers every detail of UML diagrams.

- Fowler, Martin. *Refactoring: Improving the Design of Existing Code*. Boston: Addison-Wesley. 1999.
  This book provides practical, concrete techniques for improving existing code and for writing new code.

- Fowler, Martin with Kendall Scott. *UML Distilled Second Edition: A Brief Guide to the Standard Object Modeling Language*. Boston: Addison-Wesley. 1999.
  This short, readable book covers the basics of the Unified Modeling Language. There is enough information in this book to cover most basic designs.

- Gamma, Erich, Richard Helm, Ralph Johnson, and John Vlissides. *Design Patterns*. Boston: Addison-Wesley. 1995.
  This classic book of object-oriented designs is a great read that you can come back to again and again. It's also a rich source for programming practice.

- Meyer, Bertrand. *Object-Oriented Software Construction, Second Edition*. Upper Saddle River: Prentice Hall PTR. 2000.
  This book is an update of a classic and definitive work on object-oriented software construction.

Riel, Arthur J. *Object-Oriented Design Heuristics*. Boston: Addison-Wesley. 1996.

This book provides practical advice for designing object-oriented applications.

Weisfeld, Matt, and Bill McCarty. *The Object-Oriented Thought Process*. Indianapolis: Sams Publishing. 2000.

This short, readable book covers the basic of object-oriented design, including class design, interfaces, inheritance, and composition.

Organizations

Association for Computing Machinery

The ACM is a professional and educational organization that includes special interest groups for programming languages (SIGPLAN) and software engineering (SIGSOFT). For more information, see *www.acm.org*.

The ACM sponsors the annual OOPSLA conference, which is designed for both developers and researchers. OOPSLA stands for object-oriented programming, systems, languages, and applications. For more information, see *http://oopsla.acm.org/*.

IEEE Computer Society

The Computer Society of the Institute of Electrical and Electronics Engineers (IEEE) supports conferences, publications, committees, and technical standards groups related to computer technology. For more information, see *www.computer.org*.

Index

Send feedback about this index to
mspindex@microsoft.com

Symbols and Numbers

A

R

S

Robin A. Reynolds-Haertle

Robin's interest in computing began when she taught herself to program in C to fulfill a programming language requirement for her master's degree in bio-mathematics at the University of Washington. Fascinated by the subject, Robin attended as many computer science classes as her schedule would permit, and took a position as a programmer with the University of Washington after graduation. Robin spent several years in the biotechnology industry, writing data applications in various database management systems, C, and Microsoft Visual Basic. Not content to just read computer science and software engineering books, she then pursued and completed a master's degree in software engineering at Seattle University. During these years, Robin presented training sessions on software engineering topics to her peers. After so many years in the classroom, Robin wanted to try teaching, and jumped at the opportunity to teach object-oriented programming with Visual Basic for the University of Washington Outreach program. Here she discovered she loved writing instructional materials and sample projects for her students. This led Robin to her current position as a programmer/writer at Microsoft, writing conceptual documentation for Visual Basic and Microsoft Visual C#.

When not at the computer, Robin is trying to make peace with her abandoned husband and sons. After she completes this book, they look forward to Mom's attention to Cub Scouts, Boy Scouts, hiking, and watching BattleBots. After catching up with the family, Robin hopes to sew a few quilts.

Height Gage

The **height gage**—the experienced craftsman's friend—is a rugged and reliable tool that gives precise and dependable measurements over long ranges. It's used in tool rooms and inspection departments in layout, jig, and fixture work to measure or mark off vertical distances accurately and to locate center distances in accuracies of up to a thousandth of an inch.

At Microsoft Press, we use tools to illustrate our books for software developers and IT professionals. Tools are an elegant symbol of human inventiveness and a powerful metaphor for how people can extend their capabilities, precision, and reach. From basic calipers and pliers to digital micrometers and lasers, our stylized illustrations of tools give each book a visual identity and each book series a personality. With tools and knowledge, there are no limits to creativity and innovation. Our tag line says it all: The tools you need to put technology to work.

Get a **Free**
*e-mail newsletter, updates,
special offers, links to related books,
and more when you*

register on line!

Register your Microsoft Press® title on our Web site and you'll get a FREE subscription to our e-mail newsletter, *Microsoft Press Book Connections.* You'll find out about newly released and upcoming books and learning tools, online events, software downloads, special offers and coupons for Microsoft Press customers, and information about major Microsoft® product releases. You can also read useful additional information about all the titles we publish, such as detailed book descriptions, tables of contents and indexes, sample chapters, links to related books and book series, author biographies, and reviews by other customers.

Registration is easy. Just visit this Web page and fill in your information:

http://www.microsoft.com/mspress/register

Microsoft®

Proof of Purchase

OOP with Microsoft® Visual Basic® .NET and Microsoft Visual C#™ Step by Step
0-7356-1568-3

CUSTOMER NAME

Microsoft Press, PO Box 97017, Redmond, WA 98073-9830

MICROSOFT LICENSE AGREEMENT

Book Companion CD

IMPORTANT—READ CAREFULLY: This Microsoft End-User License Agreement ("EULA") is a legal agreement between you (either an individual or an entity) and Microsoft Corporation for the Microsoft product identified above, which includes computer software and may include associated media, printed materials, and "online" or electronic documentation ("SOFTWARE PRODUCT"). Any component included within the SOFTWARE PRODUCT that is accompanied by a separate End-User License Agreement shall be governed by such agreement and not the terms set forth below. By installing, copying, or otherwise using the SOFTWARE PRODUCT, you agree to be bound by the terms of this EULA. If you do not agree to the terms of this EULA, you are not authorized to install, copy, or otherwise use the SOFTWARE PRODUCT; you may, however, return the SOFTWARE PRODUCT, along with all printed materials and other items that form a part of the Microsoft product that includes the SOFTWARE PRODUCT, to the place you obtained them for a full refund.

SOFTWARE PRODUCT LICENSE

The SOFTWARE PRODUCT is protected by United States copyright laws and international copyright treaties, as well as other intellectual property laws and treaties. The SOFTWARE PRODUCT is licensed, not sold.

1. **GRANT OF LICENSE.** This EULA grants you the following rights:

   a. **Software Product.** You may install and use one copy of the SOFTWARE PRODUCT on a single computer. The primary user of the computer on which the SOFTWARE PRODUCT is installed may make a second copy for his or her exclusive use on a portable computer.

   b. **Storage/Network Use.** You may also store or install a copy of the SOFTWARE PRODUCT on a storage device, such as a network server, used only to install or run the SOFTWARE PRODUCT on your other computers over an internal network; however, you must acquire and dedicate a license for each separate computer on which the SOFTWARE PRODUCT is installed or run from the storage device. A license for the SOFTWARE PRODUCT may not be shared or used concurrently on different computers.

   c. **License Pak.** If you have acquired this EULA in a Microsoft License Pak, you may make the number of additional copies of the computer software portion of the SOFTWARE PRODUCT authorized on the printed copy of this EULA, and you may use each copy in the manner specified above. You are also entitled to make a corresponding number of secondary copies for portable computer use as specified above.

   d. **Sample Code.** Solely with respect to portions, if any, of the SOFTWARE PRODUCT that are identified within the SOFTWARE PRODUCT as sample code (the "SAMPLE CODE"):

      i. **Use and Modification.** Microsoft grants you the right to use and modify the source code version of the SAMPLE CODE, *provided* you comply with subsection (d)(iii) below. You may not distribute the SAMPLE CODE, or any modified version of the SAMPLE CODE, in source code form.

      ii. **Redistributable Files.** Provided you comply with subsection (d)(iii) below, Microsoft grants you a nonexclusive, royalty-free right to reproduce and distribute the object code version of the SAMPLE CODE and of any modified SAMPLE CODE, other than SAMPLE CODE, or any modified version thereof, designated as not redistributable in the Readme file that forms a part of the SOFTWARE PRODUCT (the "Non-Redistributable Sample Code"). All SAMPLE CODE other than the Non-Redistributable Sample Code is collectively referred to as the "REDISTRIBUTABLES."

      iii. **Redistribution Requirements.** If you redistribute the REDISTRIBUTABLES, you agree to: (i) distribute the REDISTRIBUTABLES in object code form only in conjunction with and as a part of your software application product; (ii) not use Microsoft's name, logo, or trademarks to market your software application product; (iii) include a valid copyright notice on your software application product; (iv) indemnify, hold harmless, and defend Microsoft from and against any claims or lawsuits, including attorney's fees, that arise or result from the use or distribution of your software application product; and (v) not permit further distribution of the REDISTRIBUTABLES by your end user. Contact Microsoft for the applicable royalties due and other licensing terms for all other uses and/or distribution of the REDISTRIBUTABLES.

2. **DESCRIPTION OF OTHER RIGHTS AND LIMITATIONS.**

   - **Limitations on Reverse Engineering, Decompilation, and Disassembly.** You may not reverse engineer, decompile, or disassemble the SOFTWARE PRODUCT, except and only to the extent that such activity is expressly permitted by applicable law notwithstanding this limitation.

   - **Separation of Components.** The SOFTWARE PRODUCT is licensed as a single product. Its component parts may not be separated for use on more than one computer.

   - **Rental.** You may not rent, lease, or lend the SOFTWARE PRODUCT.

   - **Support Services.** Microsoft may, but is not obligated to, provide you with support services related to the SOFTWARE PRODUCT ("Support Services"). Use of Support Services is governed by the Microsoft policies and programs described in the user manual, in "online" documentation, and/or in other Microsoft-provided materials. Any supplemental software code provided to you as part of the Support Services shall be considered part of the SOFTWARE PRODUCT and subject to the terms and conditions of this EULA. With respect to technical information you provide to Microsoft as part of the Support Services, Microsoft may use such information for its business purposes, including for product support and development. Microsoft will not utilize such technical information in a form that personally identifies you.

- **Software Transfer.** You may permanently transfer all of your rights under this EULA, provided you retain no copies, you transfer all of the SOFTWARE PRODUCT (including all component parts, the media and printed materials, any upgrades, this EULA, and, if applicable, the Certificate of Authenticity), **and** the recipient agrees to the terms of this EULA.

- **Termination.** Without prejudice to any other rights, Microsoft may terminate this EULA if you fail to comply with the terms and conditions of this EULA. In such event, you must destroy all copies of the SOFTWARE PRODUCT and all of its component parts.

3. **COPYRIGHT.** All title and copyrights in and to the SOFTWARE PRODUCT (including but not limited to any images, photographs, animations, video, audio, music, text, SAMPLE CODE, REDISTRIBUTABLES, and "applets" incorporated into the SOFTWARE PRODUCT) and any copies of the SOFTWARE PRODUCT are owned by Microsoft or its suppliers. The SOFTWARE PRODUCT is protected by copyright laws and international treaty provisions. Therefore, you must treat the SOFTWARE PRODUCT like any other copyrighted material **except** that you may install the SOFTWARE PRODUCT on a single computer provided you keep the original solely for backup or archival purposes. You may not copy the printed materials accompanying the SOFTWARE PRODUCT.

4. **U.S. GOVERNMENT RESTRICTED RIGHTS.** The SOFTWARE PRODUCT and documentation are provided with RESTRICTED RIGHTS. Use, duplication, or disclosure by the Government is subject to restrictions as set forth in subparagraph (c)(1)(ii) of the Rights in Technical Data and Computer Software clause at DFARS 252.227-7013 or subparagraphs (c)(1) and (2) of the Commercial Computer Software—Restricted Rights at 48 CFR 52.227-19, as applicable. Manufacturer is Microsoft Corporation/One Microsoft Way/Redmond, WA 98052-6399.

5. **EXPORT RESTRICTIONS.** You agree that you will not export or re-export the SOFTWARE PRODUCT, any part thereof, or any process or service that is the direct product of the SOFTWARE PRODUCT (the foregoing collectively referred to as the "Restricted Components"), to any country, person, entity, or end user subject to U.S. export restrictions. You specifically agree not to export or re-export any of the Restricted Components (i) to any country to which the U.S. has embargoed or restricted the export of goods or services, which currently include, but are not necessarily limited to, Cuba, Iran, Iraq, Libya, North Korea, Sudan, and Syria, or to any national of any such country, wherever located, who intends to transmit or transport the Restricted Components back to such country; (ii) to any end user who you know or have reason to know will utilize the Restricted Components in the design, development, or production of nuclear, chemical, or biological weapons; or (iii) to any end user who has been prohibited from participating in U.S. export transactions by any federal agency of the U.S. government. You warrant and represent that neither the BXA nor any other U.S. federal agency has suspended, revoked, or denied your export privileges.

DISCLAIMER OF WARRANTY

NO WARRANTIES OR CONDITIONS. MICROSOFT EXPRESSLY DISCLAIMS ANY WARRANTY OR CONDITION FOR THE SOFTWARE PRODUCT. THE SOFTWARE PRODUCT AND ANY RELATED DOCUMENTATION ARE PROVIDED "AS IS" WITHOUT WARRANTY OR CONDITION OF ANY KIND, EITHER EXPRESS OR IMPLIED, INCLUDING, WITHOUT LIMITATION, THE IMPLIED WARRANTIES OF MERCHANTABILITY, FITNESS FOR A PARTICULAR PURPOSE, OR NONINFRINGEMENT. THE ENTIRE RISK ARISING OUT OF USE OR PERFORMANCE OF THE SOFTWARE PRODUCT REMAINS WITH YOU.

LIMITATION OF LIABILITY. TO THE MAXIMUM EXTENT PERMITTED BY APPLICABLE LAW, IN NO EVENT SHALL MICROSOFT OR ITS SUPPLIERS BE LIABLE FOR ANY SPECIAL, INCIDENTAL, INDIRECT, OR CONSEQUENTIAL DAMAGES WHATSOEVER (INCLUDING, WITHOUT LIMITATION, DAMAGES FOR LOSS OF BUSINESS PROFITS, BUSINESS INTERRUPTION, LOSS OF BUSINESS INFORMATION, OR ANY OTHER PECUNIARY LOSS) ARISING OUT OF THE USE OF OR INABILITY TO USE THE SOFTWARE PRODUCT OR THE PROVISION OF OR FAILURE TO PROVIDE SUPPORT SERVICES, EVEN IF MICROSOFT HAS BEEN ADVISED OF THE POSSIBILITY OF SUCH DAMAGES. IN ANY CASE, MICROSOFT'S ENTIRE LIABILITY UNDER ANY PROVISION OF THIS EULA SHALL BE LIMITED TO THE GREATER OF THE AMOUNT ACTUALLY PAID BY YOU FOR THE SOFTWARE PRODUCT OR US$5.00; PROVIDED, HOWEVER, IF YOU HAVE ENTERED INTO A MICROSOFT SUPPORT SERVICES AGREEMENT, MICROSOFT'S ENTIRE LIABILITY REGARDING SUPPORT SERVICES SHALL BE GOVERNED BY THE TERMS OF THAT AGREEMENT. BECAUSE SOME STATES AND JURISDICTIONS DO NOT ALLOW THE EXCLUSION OR LIMITATION OF LIABILITY, THE ABOVE LIMITATION MAY NOT APPLY TO YOU.

MISCELLANEOUS

This EULA is governed by the laws of the State of Washington USA, except and only to the extent that applicable law mandates governing law of a different jurisdiction.

Should you have any questions concerning this EULA, or if you desire to contact Microsoft for any reason, please contact the Microsoft subsidiary serving your country, or write: Microsoft Sales Information Center/One Microsoft Way/Redmond, WA 98052-6399.

PN 097-0002296